The Cinematic Voyage of
The Pirate

THE CINEMATIC VOYAGE OF

The Pirate

Kelly, Garland, and Minnelli at Work

EARL J. HESS

PRATIBHA A. DABHOLKAR

UNIVERSITY OF MISSOURI PRESS
Columbia

Cataloging-in-Publication data available from the Library of Congress
ISBN 978-0-8262-2022-6

∞ This paper meets the requirements of the
American National Standard for Permanence of Paper
for Printed Library Materials, Z39.48, 1984.

Cover design: Jennifer Cropp
Interior design and composition: Richard Farkas
Typefaces: Palatino Linotype, Mistral

To Julie and all our Angels
With eternal love

Contents

Illustrations

Preface

Among the many products of the Arthur Freed Unit at M-G-M, *The Pirate* has garnered a great deal of attention from viewers and critics alike as one of the most interesting film musicals of all time. Although not as universally acclaimed as *Singin' in the Rain*, *The Pirate* is an important film musical to study for a number of reasons. It represents the start of Gene Kelly's glory period as actor, choreographer, and dancer. It is a highlight of Vincente Minnelli's directorial career, especially in the use of color, camera angles, and vivid depictions of sets and people. It shows Judy Garland at her best in a unique role that showcases her comedic talents. It is a superb case study of the difficult process of creating a film from a stage play and also a wonderful case study of the complexities involved in making a film under difficult circumstances. It was the first film musical to show a white man dancing with black men as equals and to show ethnically mixed crowd scenes in a natural way.

In addition, there are secondary reasons to pick *The Pirate* over other popular musicals as a subject deserving careful study. It is not merely a musical with an appealing story and songs such as Minnelli and Garland's *Meet Me in St. Louis* or many of Garland's other films, but it also has vibrant and superbly executed dances. Moreover, whereas other film musicals with good stories and vibrant dances, such as Kelly's *On the Town*, have several weak segments that repeat viewers tend to skip in order to focus on the better parts, there is no weak segment in *The Pirate*—the entire film is delightfully watchable.

It is not that scholars have ignored *The Pirate*. It was a controversial film in several ways and has attracted considerable commentary, negative as well as positive, over the years. Arguments about its plot, acting, sets, and dances, as well as the place it holds in the creative work of director Vincente Minnelli, and stars Gene Kelly and Judy Garland, have raged since its initial release in 1948. Those arguments continue today, more than sixty-five years later, with some scholars calling the film a classic failure despite much merit and others extolling it as one of M-G-M's brightest accomplishments. Nevertheless, we believe *The Pirate* has not received the acclaim it deserves in scholarly literature. The remarkable ways in which the film helped the careers of Kelly, Minnelli, and Garland, its pioneering depiction of race relations in musicals, and the mastery displayed in the staging, filming, and choreography of Kelly's dances lead us to conclude that *The Pirate* is an underappreciated masterpiece.

It is often said that *The Pirate* became a cult classic soon after its release, rather than a general favorite among fans of film musicals, but that is only partially true. *The Pirate* did appeal to gay audiences soon after its release but it was appreciated by mainstream audiences as well. The film has been a hit with many college students since the 1970s, and a decade later, it began to be a popular topic of analysis for scholars who deal with gay theory and the cinema. At the same time, the film has won high praise from many viewers, critics, and scholars who savor the particular aesthetics of dance on film, with appreciation for the movie growing over the years. In fact, many fans of the film musical rank it as their favorite. In addition, devotees of the more than 300 films that have been made about pirates have often included the Kelly-Minnelli-Garland product among the top ten.

The Pirate is consistently ranked as among the best products of the Freed Unit, but there has not been an extensive study of the film to date. This book, *The Cinematic Voyage of The Pirate: Kelly, Garland, and Minnelli at Work*, provides a rich and detailed history of this highly acclaimed motion picture. It is a follow-up to our book entitled *Singin' in the Rain: The Making of an American Masterpiece*, which is a comprehensive history of the most famous film musical of all time. Following the model for that book, we based our study of *The Pirate* on definitive research, including extant interviews conducted with participants and archival material held in repositories across the United States. Moreover, similar to our approach for *Singin' in the Rain*, this study offers a comprehensive look at *The Pirate* by discussing all aspects of the film's history: from the development of the initial idea for the movie through preproduction, filming, initial release, and marketing to its legacy in the writings of film scholars and critics well into the twenty-first century.

Although many viewers enjoyed *The Pirate* when it was first released, it was not universally appreciated by audiences at that time. Actually, musicals made shortly after World War II that emphasized fantasy and spectacle had a chance of doing very well. A likely reason *The Pirate* did not live up to its merit, despite its emphasis on fantasy and spectacle, is that audiences of the day simply did not get Minnelli and Kelly's tongue-in-cheek humor underlying Kelly's role as Serafin.

In contrast, critical reviews on the film's initial release were mostly positive. Contrary to much commentary in books on the film musical, our extensive research in primary materials shows that *The Pirate* was *not* panned by critics when released in 1948. In fact, most critics went into raptures about the film, while others wrote negatively about only some aspects of it. Some reviewers since 1948, such as David Vaughan and Douglas McVay, have gone so far as to proclaim *The Pirate* the best film musical of all time. Nor was it a financial loss for M-G-M, as scholars have claimed. The movie actually made a profit, although not as great as it might have been.

The majority of commentators and critics between 1948 and 2010 have, at least, ranked it as a pivotal project in the careers of Minnelli (in terms of his use of color, boom camera work, and stylized setting) and Kelly (in terms of the development of his athletic dance choreography and the creation of "star" qualities). It also was the project where Minnelli and Kelly began their successful collaboration on films, and in which Garland began to experience the full impact of years of drug addiction and troubled relationships with her husband and mother. This book highlights the film's role in the careers of Kelly, Minnelli, and Garland.

Kelly probably gained more than any single individual from his experience in working on *The Pirate*. Not only was the film the true beginning of his postwar fame as a dancer on the big screen, but he worked more intimately on choreography in this movie than on any previous film, and he played an important part in character development. His acting in an unusual role received much praise despite some criticism from those who missed or disliked the tongue-in-cheek quality of his portrayal. Kelly also learned a good deal about camera work and direction from Minnelli that he later employed very successfully in his own career as a director, starting with *On the Town* (1949) and proceeding all the way to *Hello, Dolly!* (1969).

For Minnelli, *The Pirate* was a landmark film. It exemplified his fascination with colorful locale, exotic costumes, and strongly defined characters, especially women. The director used his trademark boom camera work to full effect as cinematographer Harry Stradling shot a beautiful film. Minnelli also worked extensively to revise the final screenplay, imprinting his own vision on it. He worked closely with the Technicolor Corporation to create a richer product than the company had tended to produce. *The Pirate* is one of Minnelli's most effective creations, displaying verve, irony, and a sardonic gusto that is unique among his films. It is Minnelli at his best.

Garland's career hit a watershed with *The Pirate*. Her personal problems with drugs and her troubled relationship with her husband, Minnelli, came to a head during the filming of this movie. She missed many days of production, costing M-G-M a good deal of money and wasted time, but she turned in a stellar performance in a role that was unusual for her. Our history of *The Pirate* discusses Garland's contributions as well as her problems.

The Pirate became, among other things, a gay cult movie, and Garland's presence in the film helped to start that process. Gay audiences also appreciated Minnelli's aesthetics and Kelly's virile dancing. The book explains how *The Pirate* grew into an icon of gay studies scholarship.

In offering readers many opportunities to examine important aspects of filmmaking, this book starts with the development of the plot and script. *The Pirate* was based on a successful Broadway comedy of the same name that ran for 177 performances beginning in November 1942. It was written by Samuel N. Behrman and starred the famous Broadway actors Alfred Lunt and Lynn Fontanne. That production in turn was based on the 1911 play by German author Ludwig Fulda. After M-G-M purchased the rights to the Behrman play, the studio had some difficulty turning it into a film. Eight writers worked on the screenplay from 1943 to 1946 before Frances Goodrich and Albert Hackett were assigned to it and came up with a suitable script, with help from Minnelli and Freed. But even this was not the final version of the screenplay. Minnelli and Freed, with the help of three assistants, heavily revised the screenplay during preproduction, making a total of thirteen writers, not counting the director and producer. This complex genealogy of the movie offers many opportunities to understand how film scripts evolved from previous works during M-G-M's golden era and who among the many people working for the studio played a role in shaping the scripts.

The topic of plot and character development becomes even more complex when discussing a dance film, because the numbers are the highlights of the screen experience and their development takes place in the studio or in the mind of the choreographer, rather than on paper. The dance numbers may appear in places other than where the screenplay indicates, and the way the dances develop characters or plot can significantly modify the script. Although scholars tend to think of *The Pirate* as Minnelli's project, Kelly played a huge role in planning and executing the film. As mentioned earlier, this was the start of their wonderful collaboration, and in his memoirs, Minnelli gave full credit to Kelly for his contributions. *The Pirate* was anything but an example of the auteur in action; it was a highly collaborative project, not only for Minnelli and Kelly but stretching from Ludwig Fulda to the most obscure technician on the sound stage of M-G-M.

Another contribution of this study to film history involves a detailed analysis of the movie's "film ballet," an extended dance number with balletic aspects. *The Pirate* contains one of the most elaborate and impressive examples of film ballet in the genre. The purpose of this ballet was to represent important emotions and character developments portrayed thus far in the film. Dance director Robert Alton initially proposed a pedantic, literal scheme for the ballet in an extensive scenario that we found in the Vincente Minnelli Collection. But Minnelli and Kelly preferred a psychologically charged, surrealistic framework for the ballet that worked much better than Alton's idea in extending the storyline and the characterizations. Ballets had become all the rage in dance films by the later 1940s, and both Minnelli and Kelly worked hard on this one. It involved impressive pyrotechnic displays and feats of dancing by Kelly that are noted by even those who do not particularly like the overall film. In subsequent movies, Kelly elaborated on the ballet concept, building on his work in *The Pirate* to produce classic examples of this type of dance in *On the Town* (1949), *An American in Paris* (1951), and *Singin' in the Rain* (1952).

The creation of the songs in this musical and Cole Porter's contributions are also discussed in detail. However, Porter took little interest in the film itself and did not work to shape the movie. Arthur Freed, however, did play a prominent role as producer, not just in casting but in authorizing complex sets and costumes as well as in working with Minnelli to guide script revision and editing.

Our book also discusses the role of *The Pirate* in depicting race relations on film. Minnelli staged crowd scenes that were ethnically and racially mixed in ways that were unusual for the time. Kelly insisted on dancing with the Nicholas Brothers, a black dancing team, in a spectacular number. This is something no other film musical had done to date. Dances in films were segregated by race, and many musicals of that era even showed white dancers in blackface. Kelly's dancing with the Nicholas Brothers as equals was a daring challenge to the segregated world of America in the late 1940s. Theater managers in many southern cities refused to show the film or requested the deletion of "Be a Clown," the brothers' dance number with Kelly, from the release prints. The Lunt-Fontanne stage version of *The Pirate* also included racial mixing, but it had no dancing in it, and the play was booked only in northern cities.

As a study in filmmaking, this book deals with the many goofs and gaffes to be seen in the release print of *The Pirate*, which the movie's fans tend to find endearing rather than targets for criticism. We also discuss the censorship issues involving the script and lyrics in *The Pirate*, explaining why they arose and how they were resolved. Thematic, stylistic, and other types of links between this film and others are highlighted, so the reader can appreciate such connections.

As in *Singin' in the Rain: The Making of an American Masterpiece*, we draw on a wide range of primary and secondary research sources. Archival and published primary materials are at the heart of our study. Reactions to *The Pirate* in the secondary literature are used to offer insights about the film's long-range reception. We recognize that many online sources might not be fully reliable. Therefore, we use information from online sites in a sparing and critical way, and if no other source is available. For example, factual information from the Internet Movie Data Base (IMDB) is used in compiling the list of technical crew members who worked on the film. For that matter, we have critically evaluated the reliability of *all* material used in the preparation of this study, including archival and scholarly sources. Having studied the film and its history in great detail, we include our own analysis and scholarly opinions wherever relevant.

Although movie audiences were less enthusiastic than film critics when *The Pirate* was first released, enthusiasm for the film certainly grew with the passage of time. Freed may well have been right when he said this motion picture was at least twenty years ahead of its time when it was released in 1948. Our book includes a full discussion of critical and scholarly commentary over the years (including commentary by gay studies scholars) to help readers appreciate diverse views about the film as well as how perspectives changed over time.

British commentator John Cutts called *The Pirate* "a masterpiece of extravagant entertainment, a boisterous rococo romp" that continued to grow in stature as "a rich and rare musical experiment." "There is no denying that this is a weird movie," Victoria Large wrote nearly sixty years after its release, "one that comes by its status as a cult classic honestly. It's loopy, knowingly camp, brightly colored, ambitious, and absolutely unique." Adherents of the cult built around the film had all along proclaimed it a masterpiece, but the appeal of *The Pirate* extends beyond cult boundaries. David Vaughan thought the movie had come "very near to achieving one's ideal of a dance film—that is, a film which dances *all* the time, and not merely in its spectacular set-pieces." As Douglas McVay put it, bringing all the elements together accounted for Minnelli's success in *The Pirate*. "If one is going to try to blend words, music, movement, dance sets, costumes, props, color photography and camera fluency into a total, effortless harmony, then this, surely, is the way to do it." And yet, as film historians John Russell Taylor and Arthur Jackson have bemoaned, *The Pirate* "has never really had its due."

Our book sets out to correct this situation and give this classic film its full credit. In addition to discussing all the issues mentioned in this preface, Appendix A includes our synopses and analyses of all the discarded screenplays so that interested readers can follow the twists and turns in creating the perfect screenplay for *The Pirate*. Appendix B catalogs something that scholars have missed in consistently praising the Goodrich-Hackett script over Behrman's—namely, the huge number of lines from Behrman's stage play that appear in the Goodrich-Hackett screenplay. Finally, we include short biographies of the major players wherever relevant in the book and also include Appendix C, which contains mini-biographies of everyone involved in the making of *The Pirate*—in order to give some credit to all the people who were part of this underappreciated masterpiece.

Acknowledgments

Finding all the wonderful sources that serve as the foundation of this history of *The Pirate* was made easier by the hearty cooperation of the staff at all the libraries and archives we visited. We especially wish to thank Ned Comstock at the University of Southern California, Ryan Hendrickson at Boston University, and the staff at the Margaret Herrick Library of the Academy of Motion Picture Arts and Sciences. Without their sharing rich archival material with us, this book would not have been possible. We also thank Michelle Brannen for her excellent technical assistance.

We are grateful to have found such a knowledgeable and enthusiastic acquisitions editor as Gary Kass, who played a significant role in the publication of this book. The two anonymous reviewers of our manuscript offered not only high praise but important suggestions for making it better. It has been a meaningful experience to work with Gary and the reviewers in this mutually beneficial way. Our thanks go to Kristi Henson for her enthusiastic help and cooperation, and to the rest of the staff at the University of Missouri Press for their support. We also thank David Rosenbaum, director of the press, for his invaluable assistance and support.

CHAPTER ONE

The Pirate on Stage

The plot, themes, and characters of M-G-M's classic film musical *The Pirate* originated in the mind of a German playwright and social critic thirty-seven years before the movie was released in 1948. Ludwig Fulda conceived *The Pirate* as a sardonic commentary on deception, love, and the unreliability of human nature. His play, *Der Seerauber*, was written for the German stage, and it had only a brief run in the United States as *The Pirate* in 1917. But one of the actors in it, a young and still unknown Alfred Lunt, liked the play well enough to encourage Samuel N. Behrman to write a new version which starred himself and his wife Lynn Fontanne in 1942. This production was a resounding commercial success, with mostly positive reviews from critics. The popularity of this version of *The Pirate* on Broadway led to Hollywood interest, resulting in M-G-M's purchase of the rights to the play before the end of its run in 1943. Neither Fulda's nor Behrman's play was a musical, and the studio initially intended to make a non-musical comedy as well. In fact, they employed several writers who worked on varied versions of the screenplay until Lemuel Ayers, an art director at M-G-M, had the bright idea to turn this property into a full-blown musical for the screen. Louis B. Mayer, head of M-G-M, agreed; it was then turned over to the studio's best producer, Arthur Freed, and his star director, Vincente Minnelli.

Before diving into the complex stage background that formed the basis for M-G-M's classic film, it may help readers who have not seen the movie to read a synopsis of the film. Even those who have seen the film long ago may be better able to imagine the plots of the stage versions with the film plot in mind.

A Brief Synopsis of M-G-M's *The Pirate* (1948)

The story is set in the fictitious town of Calvados, supposedly in the Caribbean and possibly in the early 1800s. (Minnelli purposely left the time period and the exact location vague to create the aura of fantasy.) A naïve young woman named Manuela (played by Judy Garland) dreams that the notorious pirate Black Macoco will show up and snatch her away from her boring village to a life of excitement and adventure on the high seas.

Unknown to her, the pirate (played by Walter Slezak) has "retired" from his criminal career and is now known as Pedro Vargas, the dull, staid mayor of her little town. Manuela's Aunt Inez (played by Gladys Cooper) has arranged a marriage between Manuela and Pedro to secure the family's material comfort. Manuela is dismayed to hear of this arrangement but accepts her fate stoically.

A strolling player, Serafin (played by Gene Kelly), comes to nearby Port Sebastian with his troupe and encounters Manuela. She has come there with her aunt to pick up her trousseau shipped from Paris. Her real motivation is to see the Caribbean Sea, which holds the last promise of romance for her. Serafin falls in love with Manuela and hypnotizes her during his performance that evening, thus learning of her fascination with the pirate Macoco. He pursues Manuela to her village, arriving just before her wedding to Pedro, and tries to persuade her to leave with him but to no avail.

When Don Pedro appears, Serafin recognizes him as Macoco from a past encounter and privately threatens to expose him. But then, realizing that Manuela will be only too happy to marry the man of her dreams, Serafin pretends to be the pirate himself in return for keeping Don Pedro's secret and for a chance to give a performance in the town of Calvados.

Pedro agrees to the scheme, but later it dawns on him that he can have Serafin arrested and hanged as Macoco. So he rushes off to fetch the militia to arrest Serafin. Meanwhile, Manuela finds out that Serafin is not really Macoco, and after throwing a fit at being tricked, she inadvertently hurts Serafin during her tantrum. On seeing him prone and motionless, she realizes that she loves him after all. She manages to wake Serafin and tell him so, just before the Viceroy (played by George Zucco) arrives and arrests the actor.

Right before his planned execution, Serafin begs the Viceroy to allow him to give a last performance, secretly hoping to hypnotize Pedro into revealing his true identity as Macoco. Although the Viceroy agrees to the performance, Serafin's plan to hypnotize Don Pedro backfires. But Manuela saves the day. She pretends to be hypnotized and shows her adoration for Serafin (as Macoco), goading Pedro to reveal, in a fit of jealousy, that *he* is the pirate. All's well as the militia captures the real Macoco and leads him away, and Manuela joins Serafin as his partner in life and as part of his strolling band of players.

The basic elements of the story that M-G-M brought to the screen in 1948 lay within Ludwig Fulda's initial stage play of 1911. But Minnelli's motion picture contained a plot that was far more simple and streamlined than Fulda's. It also was more streamlined than all subsequent versions of Fulda's concept, including Behrman's stage play and the various attempts by M-G-M screenwriters who worked on the project before Minnelli put his stamp on it. The making of *The Pirate* for the cinema was a long and complex task stretching across two continents and thirty-seven years.

LUDWIG FULDA

Ludwig Fulda was born Ludwig Anton Salomon on July 15, 1862, in Frankfurt-am-Main. He studied at the University of Berlin and in universities at Leipzig and Heidelberg, earning his doctoral degree in 1883. After changing his name to Fulda, the writer moved to Munich in 1884 and to Berlin four years later, making the German capital his home for the rest of his long life. Behrman described Fulda as "a passionate liberal and democrat" who in many ways was uncomfortable in the world of the Second Reich. Kaiser Wilhelm II refused to approve the award of the Schiller Prize to Fulda because of *Der Talisman,* a play inspired by Hans Christian Andersen's fairytale "The Emperor's New Clothes." In Fulda's version, a mysterious man promises to make a suit of clothes for the emperor that he claims only the wise can see. The emperor struts down the street in his underwear, believing he is wearing the promised magical robes, until a child exclaims, "His robes? His majesty has nothing on!" The political message was not lost on Emperor Wilhelm.[1] But by withholding the Schiller Prize, he made it obvious that he identified with the emperor in the play, and Wilhelm's decision brought more fame to Fulda.

Fulda initially visited the United States in 1906 and returned for a second visit in 1913. According to Behrman, Fulda lectured in thirty cities and at sixteen universities. Between the two visits, he finished *Der Seerauber,* or *The Pirate,* in 1911. The American movie industry was attracted to Fulda's many works because of the clever twists and turns in their plots as well as the basic ideas underlying his critical view of traditions and social constructs. At least nine films were made from his plays in the United States and in Germany, including *The Lost Paradise* (1914); *Das Verlorene Paradies* (1917); *Der Dummkopf* (1921); *Carlos and Elisabeth* (1924); *Her Sister from Paris* (1925); *Die Durchgangerin* (1928), which was known as *The Runaway Girl* in the United States and the United Kingdom; *Fraulein Frau* (1934), known as *Miss Madam* in the United States; *Two-Faced Woman* (1941); and *The Pirate* (1948). Behrman had co-authored the screenplay for *Two-Faced Woman*, which George Cukor had directed. Ostracized by the Nazis, and distraught about the way they ran Germany, Fulda committed suicide in Berlin on April 8, 1939.[2]

Five months later, Europe was engulfed in World War II. Having been born a few years before the creation of a modern, united Germany, Fulda had been spared the experience of witnessing its final descent into madness.

Fulda's Play

A synopsis of Fulda's play is provided here so readers will have a clear idea of the original concept that *The Pirate* was based on and understand how later versions built on this or varied from it.

Fulda's version of *The Pirate* is set in Andalusia, a province of Spain, in the seventeenth century.[3] A notorious pirate known as Estornudo has retired to Andalusia under the name Don Pedro Vargas. No one knows of his past, and he marries a local woman named Manuela, whose parents are Inez and Capacho. The family has many interactions with Mercedes and Hurtado, two gabby neighbors. Pedro boasts of his virtues to everyone who will hear him, but Manuela sees her husband as a fat and lazy clod. She is bored and frustrated, finding solace in novels of passion that allow her to fantasize about a life she can never enjoy. Her friend, a loose widow named Isabel Galvez, loans her these books and encourages her to have an affair. Pedro and Isabel hate each other.

Manuela's world is turned upside down by the introduction of Serafin, a poor, wandering minstrel who visits Manuela's town with his troupe of players. While the troupe is preparing for a performance, a beggar named Torribio recognizes Pedro as the pirate Estornudo, whom he had encountered years before. The former pirate reveals that all other witnesses to his past deeds have been drowned and that he has taken the identity of a businessman named Pedro Vargas whom he killed. He then hires the beggar as the overseer of his estate to keep him quiet.

The troupe gives its first performance but the town shows little interest. To increase attendance for the second performance, Serafin spreads a rumor that he is Estornudo. Serafin's ruse works as hordes come to see the notorious pirate, and the troupe raises the ticket price to rake in money. Serafin has a fling with Isabel and his aide-de-camp Trillo romances Lisarda, Manuela's maid. Manuela hears of the pirate's presence in town, becomes excited, and goes to the performance.

Meanwhile, Serafin has learned that Manuela is the richest woman in town, which excites the player's ambition. When they meet, Manuela believes that Serafin truly is Estornudo and becomes fascinated by him and his exploits. Serafin flatters her, interested mostly in her money. They plan a rendezvous when Pedro will be away at his estate. Isabel overhears the two plotting their meeting and is jealous. She brings the Alcade (or mayor) to Manuela's house to arrest "the pirate."

Manuela promises to run away with Serafin and bring her money along, but the mayor and his guards show up, so she quickly hides Serafin in her bed. Pedro returns unexpectedly and is frightened when he sees the Alcade, but recovers when he realizes that Serafin is the target of the search. He orders the guards to leave, not realizing that Serafin is hidden in the house. When the coast is clear, Manuela urges Serafin to escape, promising to join him, to which he replies, "Don't forget the money." He then walks across a clothesline tied between Pedro's home and the next house but gets stuck because the neighbor's window is closed.

While Serafin vainly tries to extricate himself from his predicament, Manuela ties money and jewels in a handkerchief and abruptly tells Pedro that she has met the pirate Estornudo and is in love with him. Pedro looks out the window, sees Serafin, and threatens to cut the clothesline. The strolling player quickly walks back and explains he is only a juggler. But Pedro starts to choke him and Manuela enjoys watching them fight. Serafin manages to get away and escapes through the front door, with Manuela hot on his heels. Pedro screams for help, saying that Manuela has been abducted. Several neighbors arrive, followed by Manuela's parents. Everyone assumes that the pirate has kidnapped Manuela, but Pedro insists the man is not a pirate, without explaining how he knows this. People start to wonder if Pedro has gone mad.

Serafin tells Trillo to steal two fast horses from Don Pedro's estate so the actor and Manuela can escape quickly. Trillo steals the horses but rides away with Lisarda instead. Serafin and Manuela are prevented from making a speedy getaway and are easily captured by the cavalry sent after them by the Corregidor (or chief magistrate).

But Manuela refuses to allow Serafin to be charged with abduction, insisting that she had willingly gone with him. Pedro becomes furious. Screaming, "If you only knew," he reveals that *he* is the pirate. Now everyone is convinced that Pedro is crazy, but he provides complex proof, backed by the beggar's testimony, and Serafin explains why he pretended to be the pirate. Manuela is stunned.

The Corregidor believes Pedro deserves the gallows, but because a war is raging, he decides to use the ex-pirate to fight sea battles instead. He pronounces Pedro's marriage to Manuela to be void because it had taken place under false pretenses. Manuela's mother, Inez, wails on hearing this, but her father, Capacho, insists that Serafin marry Manuela. Serafin is delighted because Manuela is so wealthy. The play ends as Manuela warns Serafin that if he gets fat and lazy like Pedro, she will find someone else.

As readers can see, many aspects of Fulda's play found their way into the film, but many other aspects were changed drastically. The basic premise remained as the core attraction for all who were interested in the property, but the cast of characters, the way in which they interact with each other, and the thrust of the comedic elements were altered quite a bit. Deception, crass materialism conducted with a worldly flair, and a willingness to break down the boundaries encompassing social morals characterized Fulda's original conception, and much of those elements were retained in one way or another through the many permutations into the final screen product.

BEHRMAN, LUNT, AND FONTANNE

The one brief showing of Fulda's *The Pirate* in the United States was a one-week production by the Pabst Theater stock company in Milwaukee, Wisconsin, beginning August 20, 1917. Alfred Lunt, then about twenty-five, played Serafin, and Cathleen Nesbitt performed as Manuela. Although popular, the production was not satisfying to Lunt, who later blamed the translation of the original German play by an Englishman named Louis N. Parker. Lunt never detailed what he thought was wrong with the translation, but Parker was an experienced writer and musician who had been involved in about ninety stage works in England from 1890 to 1913. The play gave Lunt an opportunity to eat a raw onion on stage, which he recalled as a personal highlight of his career, and which dismayed poor Nesbitt, who had to play opposite him while he ate it. The production also led to Lunt's first offer to perform on Broadway in October 1917, in *Romance and Arabella*.[4]

Many years later, after he had gained stature as a stage actor, Lunt recalled the translated Fulda property as "'no great shakes as a play, but it did have a vastly amusing idea.'" Lunt explained the plot to his friend, writer and actor Noel Coward, in an effort to revive the play. He also discussed it with playwright Robert E. Sherwood and composer George Gershwin. In fact, Gershwin was reportedly working on a musical comedy based on Fulda's play when he passed away in 1937. Two years later, Behrman became involved in the project. Lunt wanted some songs, and he also longed for a production in which he could do something unusual, like perform tricks of magic and walk a tightrope across the stage before a live audience. The Theatre Guild of New York committed to staging the production.[5]

By the time they became interested in *The Pirate*, Lunt and Fontanne were among the leading actors of the American stage, specializing in light comedy. Alfred Lunt was born in Milwaukee in 1892 and began to act at an early age. His mother moved the family to a farm near Genesee Depot, twenty-seven miles west of the city, in 1906. Lunt attended college and entered acting as a profession, gaining his first big break with the leading role in *Clarence* in 1919, the same year he met Lynn Fontanne. *Clarence* was also Helen Hayes's big break in show business.[6]

Lillie Louise Fontanne, who later called herself Lynn, was born in Essex, ten miles northeast of London, in 1887. She also took to acting at an early age and came to the United States in 1916 upon the invitation of the well-known actress Laurette Taylor. The turning point in Fontanne's career occurred with *Dulcy* in 1921, two years after meeting Lunt, and the pair were married in 1922. They developed into one of the great acting teams in the American theater through dozens of productions for many decades. Biographers of the couple have strongly implied that both were bisexual, linked by mutual friendship and passion for their craft. Lunt and Fontanne had no children and spent much time in three-sided friendships with gay or bisexual males like Noel Coward.[7]

Lunt and Fontanne performed in many of the works of Samuel Nathaniel Behrman, whose parents were Jewish immigrants from

Russian Lithuania. While the record of his birth date was lost, Behrman estimated it to be June 9, 1893. He was the third son of the family, born in Worcester, Massachusetts, where his father ran a grocery store. As a boy, Behrman heard a speech by socialist Eugene V. Debs, and it influenced him to sympathize with the oppressed and regard capitalism with suspicion. He also heard Sigmund Freud speak at Clark College, Cambridge University, when Behrman was a student there. After two years at Clark, Behrman attended Harvard University to finish his bachelor's degree. He then earned a master's degree at Columbia University in 1918 and worked for the *New York Times* for two years before trying to make a living as a playwright. He struggled for some time before gradually making a mark by the mid-1920s. Behrman went to Hollywood in 1935 to write screenplays but maintained his connection with the New York stage. Over the years, the Theatre Guild produced a number of his best plays.[8]

Behrman worked up five outlines for *The Pirate* in July and August 1939 before completing the first draft of Act 1 on September 9. The project hung fire for three years after that. Even though it had been his own idea, Alfred Lunt could not commit himself and his wife to a firm date for opening the play. Behrman and composer Kurt Weill were eager to move forward with the project but were frustrated by the Lunts' lack of commitment. Weill, in particular, was excited about the prospects. He praised Behrman's work, telling him, "Your writing is so rich and poetic that it allows for music at any moment so that play and music will form a real unity." Weill had already started to work on the music for the play in late September, even though only one act had been drafted. He had waited for an opportunity all his life, he told Behrman, "to work out this combination of drama and music."[9]

If Weill had had his way, *The Pirate* would have been transformed from a stage comedy with some music into a full-blown stage musical. Weill was at the height of his newfound popularity in America as a composer of stage works that mixed serious music with popular appeal.

Born in Germany in 1900, the son of a cantor, Weill began composing and privately staging his own works at age twelve. His first opera was performed in 1926, and his collaboration with the writer Bertolt Brecht resulted in challenging stage productions in Germany that pushed the envelope of aesthetics, style, and subject matter, earning Weill the enmity of the Nazis. He fled Germany in 1933 and came to the United States two years later. Weill quickly established himself on Broadway with ambitious, sophisticated works that nevertheless caught the imagination of many mainstream theatergoers.[10]

Weill was a thorough professional who sought to integrate words and music into an opera-like production without losing the basic elements that appealed to audiences. What Weill could have done with *The Pirate* if he had been given the reins is interesting to contemplate.

The composer was very eager to take on the job and even urged Behrman to drop Lunt and Fontanne if they could not commit to a production date, suggesting Maurice Chevalier take on the play instead. Behrman could not turn his back on his friends that way and wanted to give them more time. Weill had tried for two years to collaborate on some stage production with Lunt and Fontanne with no luck, and he found it difficult to understand why they did not see the potential he saw in *The Pirate*. He considered a musical play "with actors instead of singers as my special field." By late November 1939, with Lunt and Fontanne still not able to "make up their precious minds" about a production date, Weill suggested to Behrman that Walter Huston and Ina Clair take over the roles of Serafin and Manuela. Huston could play the part as a ham actor who is getting old and wants to settle down, and Clair "would be very funny as a woman who is bored with her husband and looking for adventures with Pirates. In the end, I think, Walter should get together with her husband and settle down in the house, and Ina would become a pirate."[11] Whether this last suggestion was serious or meant as a joke is not clear, but Behrman did not take Weill up on it. In a sense, this suggested twist is the first indication of the latent appeal of the play for gay audiences.

In early 1941, Behrman and Weill resumed work on the project, and Weill was happy to be collaborating with Behrman. But when Lunt and Fontanne were finally ready to commit to the project early in 1942, they handled the collaboration with Weill very poorly. Alfred had a different conception than Weill of what kind of music *The Pirate* needed, but he never clearly told the composer his views. In a meeting of Lunt, Behrman, and Weill in April 1942, the composer argued for a full-blown musical score throughout the play, the use of "a negro band of Calypso singers and players," and an "opening lullaby, the Clarinet-solo for Alfred, the Street Scene, . . . the mysticism-show in the third act." Weill thought his colleagues were in accord, but a few weeks later Lunt sent a message through Weill's servant that the composer "should write him some 'hot numbers'" for the play. Weill was disgusted and ready to drop out of the project. Behrman felt very bad about this development and was apologetic to Weill. At the same time, the playwright had to concede to Lunt's wishes and hoped Weill would still contribute music to the production.[12] But the German composer had had enough. He did not accept the proffered invitation.

Weill's vision for *The Pirate* would have resulted in a major stage musical with a score that crossed the line between popular music and more sophisticated, art music. It would have been a thoroughly integrated production with the words, acting, and music seamlessly woven together. The core audience probably would have been different than for a stage comedy with a few songs dropped into place here and there. But Lunt and Fontanne were not capable of a Weill production; their forte was lightweight popular entertainment, and that was what Behrman's *The Pirate* became.

The Lunt-Fontanne home at Genesee Depot became the headquarters for the production team in 1942. Behrman spent the month of May there, finding it "the most tranquillizing place to which I have ever been," and enjoyed the products of Lunt's culinary arts. He finished the fifth draft of the entire script on June 19. John C. Wilson, who was to co-direct the play with Lunt, also arrived for consultation. Scene designer Lemuel Ayers and composer Herbert Kingsley traveled to the small working farm in Wisconsin to become involved in the production as well. Lunt wanted to use music to create background moods for each scene and for dances.[13]

Lunt worked closely with Behrman on the script, evaluating every line. "'They won't like it,'" Lunt would tell the playwright, referring to the audience, if he found a phrase inadequate. While Behrman studied the Fulda play closely, he worked many distinctive aspects of his own into the new production. Fishing about for a phrase that Serafin could use to threaten Pedro, Behrman adopted "Mene, Mene, Tekel, Upharsin." In the Old Testament, these words were written by a disembodied hand on a wall during a banquet hosted by King Belshazzar. Daniel, an exiled Jew brought in to decipher the words, interpreted this phrase to mean that God had numbered the days of the kingdom of Belshazzar, and it would end. In other words, God had evaluated the king and found him wanting. Behrman came by this inspiration naturally; his father had been "an ardent Talmudic scholar" who taught Hebrew to children part time. "'My father related the Old Testament stories as if they had taken place recently,'" Behrman recalled, "'as if they constituted his personal past.'"[14]

Lunt's idea of adding music to serve as cues to action and dialogue proved to be more difficult to accomplish than expected. Fontanne thought that a full-blown musical comedy would have been easier to create, for one could "'rehearse the dancing in one place and the lines somewhere else and then combine them; but we have to do this all together, and it's been the toughest chew we've ever bitten off.'"[15]

BEHRMAN'S PLAY

A synopsis of Behrman's play is included here so readers will understand how it differed from Fulda's concept and how the various screenplays built on this or varied from it. To keep the discussion streamlined, the focus is on aspects that differ from Fulda's play.

Illustration 1.1. The stage version shows Alfred Lunt (as Serafin) with Maurice Ellis (as Trillo), his black aide-de-camp. The two men are reading Manuela's letter, which is part of a subplot dropped from the film. Behrman included a racially mixed troupe in his play to match the island setting. (Wisconsin Historical Society, WHS-101825)

Illustration 1.2. The film version shows Serafin's troupe, with two black members, listening with amazement to Serafin announcing to the citizens of Calvados that he is Macoco the Pirate. Showing blacks as part of the main storyline, in scenes that could not be easily excised from the film, was extremely unusual for the era.

Behrman's story is set in Santo Domingo in the West Indies in the early nineteenth century.[16] Behrman depicts a racially mixed population and a racially mixed troupe for Serafin to suit this venue.

When Serafin goes to meet Pedro, the mayor, to ask for a license to give a performance, he recognizes Pedro as Estramudo the pirate. Serafin threatens to reveal Pedro's secret background and chants, "Mene, Mene, Tekel, Upharsin" in a seemingly disembodied voice. This terrifies the pirate because he had heard this ghostly chant in Baghdad when he was condemned to death and later on a ship (that Serafin also was aboard) when Estramudo was about to kill its captain. Shaken to the core, Pedro agrees to permit a performance as the price for Serafin's silence.

Serafin then meets Manuela, and he is enchanted. She reveals that she reads stories about Estramudo, whereupon Serafin claims to be the pirate in disguise. Understandably, she does not believe him and leaves. Serafin strings a rope from Manuela's balcony to her neighbor's so he can hang a curtain for his performance. He

Illustration 1.3. In the stage version, Alan Reed (as Don Pedro) is annoyed when Alfred Lunt and Lynn Fontanne (as Serafin and Manuela) ignore him. A similar scene appears in the film. (Wisconsin Historical Society, WHS-101827)

then walks across the rope to Manuela's balcony and bedroom and finds not only Manuela there but her parents, Capucho and Ines, rolling dice. When Serafin tells them he is Estramudo, Capucho rushes out to get Pedro, but Ines encourages Manuela to have a fling with the pirate because she feels guilty about Manuela's loveless marriage to Pedro, purchased to the advantage of herself and Capucho.

Serafin and Manuela have a long conversation, which they continue when Pedro arrives, ignoring him completely. When Pedro demands to know what Serafin has told Manuela and learns that Serafin is pretending to be Estramudo, Pedro is at first confused but then plays along. Manuela demands to know how the two became acquainted, and Serafin improvises a story about how Pedro had captured him once but he managed to get away. Serafin's plan backfires as Manuela now seems enamored of Pedro, calling him a brave man who dared to take on the notorious pirate and is so modest he never mentioned his exploits.

Illustration 1.4. In the film version, Walter Slezak (as Don Pedro) confronts Gene Kelly (as Serafin) in Manuela's bedroom. Judy Garland (as Manuela), Gladys Cooper (as Inez), and Lester Allen (as Capucho) watch nervously. (The film scene matching that shown in Illustration 1.3 has Garland with her back to the camera whenever the three characters are in the same frame.)

Serafin is disgusted with the turn of events and Manuela's apparent fickleness. He leaves the room and walks away along the tightrope. Sensing Manuela's anxiety for Serafin's safety, Pedro becomes very jealous. He slaps Manuela and says that her hero, Estramudo, did not escape with the Sultan's nine wives, as stated in her book, but that he drowned them, and was paid by the Sultan for doing him this favor. Pedro claims to know this because he sold cannonballs to the Sultan. Manuela refuses to believe that Serafin is capable of such terrible deeds. Pedro then spins a story that when he captured Estramudo, he let him go in exchange for all his loot and that some of this treasure is under the floor of the barn at their summer place. Manuela finds the story unbelievable and starts to become suspicious of Pedro.

Pedro then informs Manuela that he is going to the Viceroy to claim a reward of 100,000 pesos for turning in Estramudo. Manuela pleads with Pedro not to do this and promises to remain faithful to him but to no avail. As he goes to the balcony to cut the tightrope so Serafin cannot return, Manuela notices Pedro's lucky rabbit's foot lying on the floor. She picks it up, removes a charm, and reads the inscription. She exclaims in surprise but quickly replaces the charm and gives the rabbit's foot to Pedro when he returns, without revealing that she has looked inside it.

Serafin storms in through the front door to protest the cutting of the tightrope, which he needs for his performance. Pedro tells him that he is leaving for the capital, and Serafin naïvely asks Pedro to arrange a performance for him there. Manuela asks Serafin if he ever gave any jewels to Pedro, which Serafin denies. Sure now that Serafin is not the pirate, Manuela again begs Pedro not to go, but he leaves anyway. Manuela tells Serafin what Pedro is up to and begs the player to flee. She is exasperated when Serafin refuses to leave, but she is determined to save him. She leaves for her summer place without telling Serafin her purpose, but the audience assumes she intends to look for the jewels hidden under the barn.

Serafin prepares for the performance even though his troupe urges him to escape, fearing that he will be hanged as Estramudo. When the Viceroy arrives to arrest him, Serafin begs permission to give his performance, saying that he is in love and wants to hear the lady say she loves him before he dies. He explains that he will use the arts of Mesmer to hypnotize Manuela to get her to admit that she loves him. The Viceroy agrees, in part because he knows Mesmer personally and is fascinated by the science of hypnotism, and also because he does not fully believe Serafin is Estramudo. In fact, he declares that he intends to give Serafin a proper trial later and evaluate all the evidence.

After a dance, a song, and some magic tricks, Serafin tells the captivated audience that he will perform hypnosis and that he needs a "pure person" to volunteer. He bypasses Isabella, who raises her hand, and Ines, who winks at him. He makes a subtle reference to the Viceroy's being the first to admit that as a politician he cannot be pure and a snide remark about Pedro's being the opposite of what Serafin is looking for. Serafin then picks Manuela, who arises "already half in a trance." Behrman writes, "We do not know exactly whether it is a genuine hypnosis." In fact, at the end of the previous act, Manuela is determined to save Serafin at any cost. So, one would assume she would play along with Serafin's plan. Yet, during the performance, she acts as if she is truly hypnotized and often rambles about tangential things.

Illustration 1.5. In the stage play's *only* performance by Serafin and his troupe, Serafin is hypnotizing Manuela. Note the elaborate costumes designed by Lemuel Ayers, costume and scene director of the stage version. (Wisconsin Historical Society, WHS-101828)

Illustration 1.6. In the film's *first* performance by Serafin and his troupe, Serafin is hypnotizing Manuela. Compare the elaborate, revolving mirror used in the film (designed by Jack Martin Smith's crew) with the simple contraption in the stage play in Illustration 1.5.

Illustration 1.7. The stage version shows a long shot of the set during Manuela's hypnosis. Note the complex set designed by Ayers. (Wisconsin Historical Society, WHS-101826)

Illustration 1.8. The film version shows a long shot of the set where Serafin tells the Viceroy about the upcoming highlight of his performance, namely, hypnotism.

Pedro tries to stop the hypnosis but the Viceroy overrules him. After Pedro leaves, claiming to be ill, Serafin motions troupe members Trillo and Bolo to follow him. Manuela then reveals that Pedro is Estramudo and that he drowned the Sultan's nine wives, for which he was rewarded by the Sultan. As proof, she tells of a jeweled medallion that Pedro wears around his neck in a purse, and apparently, the medallion is inscribed by the Sultan, thanking Pedro for his help. (Behrman somehow slipped up on a detail here and changed the rabbit's foot and charm mentioned earlier into a purse and a jeweled medallion.) Manuela also mentions finding famous jewels, such as Catherine's stomacher, hidden under the floor of Pedro's barn.

The Viceroy goes into Manuela's house and arrests Pedro, who pleads for mercy. As in Fulda's play, the Viceroy is unwilling at first to show the ruthless pirate clemency, but then he recalls that a war is being waged against the "fiercely marine" Berbers and thinks that Estramudo might be useful in it. The Viceroy tells the crowd that Pedro Vargas was the captain of a ship that Estramudo scuttled. When the captain went down with his ship, Estramudo took his name. He announces that Manuela is a "widow," apparently because the marriage was not legal, and this frees Manuela. It takes some time for Serafin to awaken Manuela from her "trance," but he manages to do so finally by telling her that now they can love and live together forever. The play ends as he carries her into the house to the accompaniment of a joyful refrain from the crowd.

A Brief Comparison of Behrman's and Fulda's Plays

Some of the differences discussed below were not mentioned in the synopses, but they are included here so readers can see how Behrman changed certain elements that Fulda had created.

Fulda's play was a farcical comedy with shallow characters, but Behrman created a romantic comedy with stronger characters and a tighter plot. Manuela and Serafin are now more likeable and drawn to each other by love rather than boredom on her part and greed on his. Extraneous characters such as the neighbor couple and the beggar are dropped to tighten the plot. Don Pedro is now the Alcade (or mayor), which makes his role more intimidating. Instead of the beggar, Serafin is the one who recognizes the pirate, which is far more effective.

Behrman tweaked the names of supporting characters so that

Manuela's parents are now called Ines and Capucho; Isabel is now Isabella; the pirate is Estramudo; and Lisarda has become Lizarda. Ines and Capucho quarrel constantly and throw dice, gambling against each other. Isabella is essentially the same character, but instead of having a fling with Serafin, she merely has a flirtatious conversation with Serafin before he meets Manuela.

Fulda's play mentions that Pedro and Manuela are supported financially by her parents, which makes little sense because Pedro has an estate and Manuela is the richest woman in town. Behrman's version has Pedro supporting Manuela's parents as part of the marriage negotiations. It helps explain why Manuela is married to Pedro even though she does not love him. While making him rich, Behrman also makes Pedro a superstitious tightwad, giving Manuela more reason to be bored and frustrated as his wife.

Instead of reading romance novels in general as she does in Fulda's play, Behrman's Manuela reads specifically of Estramudo and fantasizes about him, which sets the stage nicely for Serafin to pretend to be the pirate. Moreover, in contrast to Fulda's play, Behrman's Manuela meets Serafin by chance rather than design, and as a result, she does not come across as scheming.

Behrman's play does have some music—when Serafin and his troupe first arrive in Calvados, when a hermit plays a tune that the troupe repeats in order to learn it, and even a dance and a song at Serafin's performance. It was not quite a musical, but different from Fulda's by having at least some music and dancing.

Behrman greatly improved the plot and characters compared to Fulda's original script, but his play does have weaknesses compared to the M-G-M film. These are summarized near the end of this chapter.

LUNT AND FONTANNE ON STAGE

Rehearsals for *The Pirate* began on August 1, 1942, and the play was premiered at the University Theater in Madison, Wisconsin, on September 13. "We have put everything we have into it," Fontanne told a friend, "and Alfred has damned near killed himself, what with playing a great part, learning a dance, a few magic tricks, tight rope walking (not really), and directing the whole thing." Critical reaction was positive. "It is light and frothy and full of laughter," ran one commentary in *Variety*. "It easily could be cleaned up for pictures, although the costume angle may be against it." The critic declared that "'The Pirate,' is sheer unadulterated escape theatre. It has no hidden meanings. It has no reading between the lines. It has no messages." He also believed that "Behrman has never written funnier dialogue. Lunt and Fontanne have never seemed to enjoy themselves as much."[17]

With support from the Playwrights' Production Company and Transatlantic Productions, the Theatre Guild took *The Pirate* on the road to many cities before opening the production in New York. The cast and crew moved a short distance to Milwaukee, then on to Cleveland, Cincinnati, Indianapolis, Pittsburgh, Washington, D. C., Boston, and Philadelphia by November 1942. A good deal of revision took place along the way. In a note to Behrman, Theresa Helburn, one of the founders and a director of the Theatre Guild, strongly suggested that Jack Smart did not create a convincing Don Pedro. "This man is too effeminate even to convince you he was a pirate & he isn't funny! Neither is Trillo or the father. Both rather on the tragic side." Ironically, a Cleveland reviewer thought that Jack Smart "made his role of the husband one of the highlights" of the performance. Nevertheless, Helburn suggested Alan Reed as a replacement for Smart and hoped Maurice Ellis could put more laughs into the role of Trillo. Reed did replace Smart as Don Pedro before the New York opening, and some of Behrman's dialogue was replaced in a seemingly never-ending tussle between Lunt and the writer. In fact, Behrman later acknowledged that *The Pirate* and another of his plays, *I Know My Love,* gave him and Lunt-Fontanne more trouble than any other of their collaborative efforts. "My adaptations of these plays didn't stack up," as Behrman put it. He entirely rewrote the second act of *The Pirate* while the production company was in Washington.[18]

The situation worsened to the point that Behrman and Lunt were "at an impasse" by the time they reached Philadelphia. Lunt often took exception to a particular line, deliberately misreading it on stage to prove to Behrman that the audience reaction justified his criticism. Their biggest argument developed over the ending of the revised second act. "I would submit a rewrite; Lynn would say: 'I don't think Alfred will like this,'" Behrman recalled. "It was not possible to know where the source of the discontent resided." As a result, the production nearly closed before it moved to Broadway.[19]

But Behrman and Lunt resolved their quarrels and opened *The Pirate* at the Martin Beck Theatre on November 23, 1942. The long tryout and the repeated arguments had not been for naught; the audiences loved it, and Lunt had a field day with the varied demands of the play on his talent. He was capable of outbursts of temper, however, if something did not go completely right on stage. Lunt faked walking across the tightrope by standing on a large crate with wheels, the crate covered by a curtain. During one New York performance the curtain fell to reveal everything to the audience. "Lunt stormed offstage and threw his boots at the stage manager," as the Lunts' biographer, Jared Brown, reports. The footwear missed the poor man, and by the end of the performance Lunt had calmed down enough to apologize for his display of temper and frustration.[20]

Critical response to *The Pirate* consistently praised Lunt and Fontanne as well as the design and production values. Although some reviewers found the script to be weak, others thought Behrman's writing was brilliant. Some critics noted that Fontanne's controlled, urbane performance suited Behrman's dialogue beautifully and served as a good counterpoint to Lunt's antics, which one critic likened to Ed Wynn's. "This frolicking fable is a heaven-sent showcase for all the Lunt-Fontanne artistry which has delighted playgoers through the years," wrote another commentator. "West Indian Opulence of Color and Costume Make *The Pirate* a Brilliant Spectacle," proclaimed a headline as Miles White's costumes came under scrutiny. Tom Burley of the *New York Amsterdam Star-News* praised the mix of races seen on stage among the cast members and was delighted that the production "does not stress racial distinctions, and faithfully recreates the history of a period." Elliot Norton of the *Boston Sun-Post* suggested that someone make a full-blown musical comedy of the material.[21] Indeed, the fragile plot and colorful setting seemed suited for such an endeavor. But although M-G-M did purchase the property before the end of the play's run, it was a long time before studio executives thought of making it a musical.

The Pirate ran on Broadway for five months, racking up 177 performances at the Martin Beck Theatre, before closing on April 27, 1943. It was the most profitable play Behrman had written to date. Lunt and Fontanne chose to give much of their earnings to the Stage Door Canteen, which was their pet project at the time. They volunteered time at the canteen whenever possible to feed and entertain servicemen passing through New York. The canteen had opened in the basement of the Forty-fourth Street Theatre on March 1, 1942. Between 3,000 and 4,000 servicemen visited it every night until the end of the war.[22]

Lunt and Fontanne also performed *The Pirate* as a benefit for a young artists' group in Lenox Hill, which sparked a spate of clay modeling of pirates and their ships among the group. The artists hoped to sell the models as Christmas gifts to raise money for their organization.[23]

The Lunts had hoped to take *The Pirate* on the road after its New York run, including visits to military camps, but they canceled these plans when Fontanne became ill and they decided instead to visit England, Lynn's birthplace. *Variety* named Lunt the best performer on stage in 1943, based on its poll of drama critics. The Drama League of New York gave Lunt and Fontanne an award "for the best performances of the season" in March 1943. Despite its problems, the production pleased everyone in some way. Fontanne herself put it well when she said, "We want to entertain and amuse and if the play is a success we shall attain our wish."[24]

Fulda's widow, Helene, was touched when Random House, which published the script of Behrman's *The Pirate* in 1943, sent her a complimentary copy. She especially appreciated "the touching memorial" for her late husband, who had committed suicide only four years before. "I am sure that he would be deeply appreciative of your work if he had lived to see it," she informed Behrman.[25]

In turn, Behrman was fully cognizant of how much he owed to Lunt and Fontanne. This explains why he was so patient with their exasperating ways of dealing with collaborators, something that Weill did not fully realize.

"Berrie . . . worshipped you and Alfred," Behrman's widow, Elza, wrote to Lynn Fontanne, soon after her husband's death. "You and Alfred launched him! For that, he always was—and I still am—deeply grateful to you. Your artistry was a never-ending wonder to him and he felt the greatest of achievements each time that you agreed to 'do' a play of his."[26] The acting couple gave Behrman his first major recognition as a playwright, and Behrman felt great admiration as well as overwhelming gratitude for the Lunts.

SCHOLARLY ASSESSMENT

Theater scholars have noted that *The Pirate* is one of only three productions by Behrman that "escape far into the world of romance, and all three are adaptations from foreign sources." Kenneth Reed writes that Behrman retained "a touch of Fulda in the play, but a little Shakespeare as well," and that in the use of magic, character names, and its "matrimonial theme," *The Pirate* is evocative of *The Tempest.*[27] The praise heaped on Behrman's play is valid. It not only started with an intriguing concept created by Fulda, but was a marked improvement over Fulda's version in terms of characterizations and situations, as discussed earlier.

Film commentators treat the play less generously. They complain of "verbal clutter," where Behrman "stuffs the dialogue with epigrams, straining for the concise wit of Wilde and Shaw," according to film critic Joel Siegel.[28] Ironically, film analysts praise the final screenplay by Goodrich and Hackett as being far superior. However, a careful study of all the scripts shows that Goodrich and Hackett incorporated a huge number of witty lines from Behrman's play into their screenplay (see Chapter 2 and Appendix B).

Some criticisms of Behrman's script are justified. Film curator Stephen Harvey correctly points out that the exposure of Don Pedro as the true pirate is "a distinct anticlimax."[29] There are other instances as well where Goodrich and Hackett improved Behrman's plot as detailed in Chapter 2.

It is true that Behrman's script was not a perfect vehicle for a successful play, especially in terms of plot weaknesses and lengthy conversations. For example, the fact that Pedro is really Estramudo is revealed too early. Several of the subplots involving minor characters, such as Isabella and Serafin's troupe members, are distracting, and many conversations, even between principal characters, are much too long. The Viceroy's not fully believing that Serafin is the pirate is realistic but reduces the tension in the third act. Much of Manuela's ranting under hypnosis is irrelevant to the discovery of the pirate's identity and slows the play's climax. Despite these problems, *The Pirate* became a successful stage play because of its production values, the Lunt-Fontanne performance, and the many gems in Behrman's dialogue that film scholars have overlooked.

Behrman's play held lasting interest. In 1962, an instructor of dramatics at Canal Zone Junior College, located within the American-controlled part of Panama then called the Canal Zone, inquired about the rights to stage the play at his school. "Because it is especially suitable for presentation in this locality," he explained to Behrman, "and because it is such a damn good play."[30]

From Fulda to Behrman to Lunt and Fontanne, the course of creativity brought *The Pirate* story twice to the stage before M-G-M grabbed it to make a movie. But how to transform this unique stage production into a mass-entertainment film posed a problem that was not easy to solve. It would take more than four years just to produce an acceptable script. The preproduction and production phases of the film also turned out to be unusually challenging due to the scope of the project as well as Garland's personal problems.

CHAPTER TWO

Creating the Perfect Screenplay

Behrman's play was in its fifteenth week on Broadway when M-G-M purchased the rights to it for a reported $225,026 in March 1943. The studio wanted to make a sound recording of the play during one of its performances "to gauge its laugh quotient," a process it had already used for *The Philadelphia Story* (1940). But Lunt and Fontanne asked "an extortionate sum for their service," and the deal never was concluded. The Lunts also wanted to star in the film version of their play. The pair had seen their debut in an M-G-M film twelve years before in *The Guardsman* (1931) but had concentrated on their stage career ever since. Studio chief Louis B. Mayer, however, had other actors in mind, including William Powell, Hedy Lamarr, and Charles Laughton. His initial idea was for Joseph Pasternak to produce the film, Henry Koster to direct it, and Joseph L. Mankiewicz to write the script. Like the stage play, the film was intended to be a straight comedy, not a full-blown musical production.[1]

Before the perfect vehicle was created for *The Pirate* film, there were many false starts at M-G-M. A number of talented screenwriters tried their hand at adapting the successful stage play for a cinema audience—but all of their creations were cast aside. This chapter includes a few salient points from the different screenplays and some biographical information about the writers to help readers understand why the process of screenwriting was so unwieldy for *The Pirate*. Full synopses and analyses of the discarded screenplay versions are presented in Appendix A to give interested readers a more complete understanding of the screenwriting process for this film. In addition, Table 1 charts the changes in characters and setting across all the versions written for the stage as well as the screen.

Table 1. Comparison of Key Elements in All Versions of *The Pirate* (stage plays and screenplays)

Version	Fulda	Behrman	Mankiewicz	Connolly-Koster	Blum	Loos-Than	Goodrich-Hackett	M-G-M Film
Year	1911	1942	1943	1944	1944	1946	1946	1948
Setting	Andalusia, Spain, 17th century	Santo Domingo, West Indies, early 19th century	Unnamed Caribbean island, no time period	Unnamed Caribbean island, no time period	Unnamed Caribbean island, no time period	Unnamed Caribbean island, no time period	Unnamed Caribbean island, no time period	Fictitious towns Port Sebastian & Calvados, no time period
Serafin	Strolling player (comical, greedy)	Strolling player, sings songs (funny, idealistic)	Strolling player (flippant, selfish)	Strolling player (flippant, thoughtless)	Strolling player (irrational, tragic)	Strolling player (acrobatic, obsequious to authority figures)	Strolling player (funny, smart)	Strolling player, sings and dances (smart, virile, talented, hammy)
Manuela	Don Pedro's wife (bored, selfish)	Don Pedro's wife (noble, unhappy)	Don Pedro's wife (childish, selfish)	Don Pedro's bride, marriage not consummated	Don Pedro's fiancée (immature but improves)	Don Pedro's fiancée (immature but improves)	Don Pedro's fiancée (immature but improves)	Don Pedro's fiancée (addicted to romance, budding actress)
Don Pedro Vargas	Businessman	Mayor	Mayor	Mayor	Mayor	Mayor	Mayor	Mayor
Pirate's name	Estornudo	Estramudo	Estramudo	Estramudo	Estramudo	Macoco	Macoco	Macoco
Manuela's Mother/Aunt	Mother (Inez)	Mother (Ines)	Aunt (Inez)	Mother (Inez)	Aunt (Trina)	Aunt (Lucia)	Aunt (Inez)	Aunt (Inez)
Manuela's Father/Uncle	Father (Capacho)	Father (Capucho)	Uncle (Capucho)	Father (Capucho)	Uncle (Capucho)	None	Uncle (Capucho)	Uncle (Capucho)

Table 1. Comparison of Key Elements in All Versions of *The Pirate* (stage plays and screenplays) *(continued)*

Version	Fulda	Behrman	Mackiewicz	Connolly-Koster	Blum	Loos-Than	Goodrich-Hackett	M-G-M Film
Year	1911	1942	1943	1944	1944	1946	1946	1948
Manuela's friend(s)	Isabel (prominent role)	Isabella (prominent role)	Isabella	Isabella (black)	None	None	Several friends, all minor roles	Several friends, all minor roles
Serafin's aide-de-camp(s)	Trillo (self-serving)	Trillo (black, devoted to Serafin)	Trillo (lesser role)	Trillo (black, buffoonish)	Trillo (minor role)	Trillo (minor role)	Trillo	Trillo and Coutat
Authority figure(s)	- Alcade (mayor), - Corregidor (chief magistrate)	Viceroy (shrewd, sardonic, dignified)	Viceroy (alert, but not very dignified)	Viceroy (silly, not interested in his duties)	Viceroy (minor role)	- Governor (bullied by Don Pedro), - Viceroy (minor role), - Viceroy's wife (decisive)	Viceroy (shrewd, calculating)	Viceroy (shrewd, calculating, yet dignified)
Other characters	- Torribio (beggar), - Lisarda (Manuela's maid, self-serving), - Mercedes & Hurtado (Manuela's neighbors)	Lizarda (Manuela's black maid, devoted to Manuela)	Lizarda (Manuela's black maid)	Sampson (Don Pedro's black henchman)	Lizarda (part of Serafin's troupe)	- Lizarda (Manuela's sister), - Capucho (part of Serafin's troupe), - Sanchez (Don Pedro's henchman)	Advocate and other citizens	Advocate and other citizens

The Mankiewicz Screenplay

In revising the stage plays for the screen, Mankiewicz seemed to favor Fulda over Behrman.[2] He made interactions between Serafin and Manuela rather flippant and tried to introduce broad humor in several places. He added scenes that weakened the flow of the narrative such as Manuela's lengthy fantasy about the pirate. At the same time, he retained some segments from Behrman's play that created inconsistencies, such as Manuela's suddenly switching from passion to sarcasm toward Serafin in a way that is inexplicable. There are discrepancies in characters, and many subplots do not blend with the main storyline. Understandably, the studio was not pleased with Mankiewicz's work. (See full synopsis and analysis of Mankiewicz's version in Appendix A.)

A look at Mankiewicz's background helps one to understand why he produced such an inferior vehicle for *The Pirate*, despite his talents. Joseph L. Mankiewicz was born February 11, 1909, in Wilkes-Barre, Pennsylvania, and moved with his family to New York at age five. His father was a college professor, and the young Joseph was a precocious child. He finished high school in three years by age fifteen and graduated from Columbia University in 1928 at age nineteen. Mankiewicz had a flair for writing and went to Hollywood, where Paramount released his first screenplay, *Fast Company*, in 1929. His script for *Manhattan Melodrama* was made into an M-G-M film in 1934. Mayer hired him as a producer, but Mankiewicz never felt fulfilled in that role. He preferred to write and direct to secure better control of his projects.[3]

Mankiewicz and Judy Garland developed a romantic relationship in 1942, and Mankiewicz thought that *The Pirate*, converted into a musical comedy, could be an important vehicle for Garland's career. He played a key role in convincing Mayer to purchase the rights to the play, and his relationship with Garland deepened as he crafted the screenplay. Yet, M-G-M had not approved the making of a musical at that time. Mankiewicz tried to become Garland's champion, blaming Mayer for her many personal problems.[4]

Aside from *The Pirate* project, Mankiewicz saw the writing of screenplays as a way to delve into the psychological makeup of his characters, an approach inspired by his academic background in psychology. Motivation figures deeply in his films. It is possible Mankiewicz might have made something more sophisticated of the plot and characters of *The Pirate*, but he came to see the project within the context of possibilities for Judy Garland rather than for his penchant to write serious stories.

When Mankiewicz arranged for Garland to spend time at the Menninger Clinic in Topeka, Kansas, to overcome her drug addiction, Garland's domineering mother staged a showdown for control of her daughter. She and Mayer confronted Mankiewicz—and the result was a vicious shouting match and the end of the writer's career at M-G-M. He finished the first draft of the screenplay for *The Pirate* quickly, near the end of March 1943, but dallied with revisions and submitted the script just before leaving the studio in August 1943. He went on to a sterling career with other studios but always remembered the bitterness surrounding his parting with M-G-M. "Her mother was a dreadful bitch," Mankiewicz recalled of Garland, and said the mother told Judy, in his presence, "'You know you're ugly, you little hunchback. The only thing people want from you is to hear you sing.'"[5]

This background sheds some light on the reasons for the weaknesses and inconsistencies in Mankiewicz's script for *The Pirate*. The tensions surrounding Mankiewicz's interactions with Mayer and Garland's mother seem to have worked insidiously into his creation. Moreover, he knew his promising career at M-G-M had ended, and this must have further wiped away his motivation to produce a good screenplay for M-G-M.

THE CONNOLLY-KOSTER VERSION

After Mankiewicz left the studio, Mayer gave *The Pirate* to writer Myles Connolly and director-writer Henry Koster to work on. While Mayer continued to see William Powell as Serafin, he began to think of Myrna Loy instead of Hedy Lamarr as Manuela. Connolly wrote suggestions and an outline from August to December 1943. Then Koster worked on these from October 1943 to complete a screenplay by January 1944.

Connolly's outline is not available, but Koster created drastic character changes that alone made his revision unacceptable.[6] For example, Koster radically changed Serafin so that he cared little about his upcoming performance. He made Serafin's troupe members black, but he also made them stupid and clownish, possibly to fit racial stereotypes of the era. The Viceroy too is portrayed as a silly character, more interested in learning magic tricks than in serving justice. Koster added illogical subplots that dragged the storyline and introduced many elements of sex and violence that would never have passed censorship codes. (See full synopsis and analysis of the Connolly-Koster version in Appendix A.)

In January 1944, Connolly made minor revisions to Koster's script.[7] A careful reading of the Connolly screenplay shows that he merely made unimportant alterations in a few of Koster's lines, shortened some conversations, and cut some scenes. For example, where Koster had Manuela and Serafin walking through her house and garden during a very long, irrelevant conversation, they now have the same conversation while Serafin is setting up the props for his performance.

Eventually, the Connolly-Koster version was pretty much discarded. Connolly admitted in April 1947, long after filming had begun, that the final script contained none of his material.[8]

Unlike the first screenplay, there is nothing in the archives, interviews, or biographies to indicate why these talented men produced such an unacceptable product. Myles Connolly was born in Boston in 1897 and contributed to the screenplays of many films, including *Mr. Smith Goes to Washington* (1939). He also produced a number of films in the 1930s. Henry Koster was born as Hermann Kosterlitz in Berlin in 1905. He wrote his first scenario for a film at age seventeen. Koster began directing in 1932 but a short time later fled Germany to escape the Nazis. He was involved in dozens of film projects for different studios as both writer and director, and directed James Stewart in *Harvey* (1950).[9]

It is possible that Koster and Connolly were simply not interested in this particular project. Movie studios tended to assign screenwriters to films without considering the writers' strengths or inclinations. Because Connolly's initial outline is not available, it is difficult to know the quality of that effort. Regardless of its potential, it is possible that Koster felt constrained by Connolly's outline and created bizarre aspects simply to put his own mark on the script. Later, when Connolly was asked to revise Koster's script, he made minimal changes and the product remained unacceptable.

Breen and the Production Code

By January 1944 the studio felt it was time to consult Joseph Breen, whose office was responsible for monitoring compliance with the production code adopted by the Motion Picture Association of America. Breen informed Mayer that he was concerned about the premise, "the breakup of a marriage." "Such a basic story could not be approved," he informed the studio chief. Breen noted that Behrman's dialogue also contained "some rather unacceptable statements concerning marriage and fidelity."[10]

Although Mankiewicz's script as well as the Connolly-Koster product had been completed, M-G-M submitted only the Behrman stage play for review in early 1944. This reflects how strongly the studio felt about the poor quality of both submitted screenplays. Mayer seemed ready to go back to Behrman's stage play and start from scratch.

It is strange that Breen felt the production code would frown on the breakup of a marriage to a bloodthirsty pirate, and that too arranged under false pretenses. But he identified a fundamental issue in the development of a suitable screenplay for *The Pirate*, creating another problem for M-G-M in trying to get the project off the ground. Whoever wound up writing the final script would have to find a way to avoid portraying Serafin as a home wrecker while they also tried to adapt Behrman's characters and plot situations into a viable screen offering. None of the writers to date had been able to achieve either goal, but there were plenty of other writers that Mayer could call on to try.

THE BLUM SCREENPLAY

Edwin Blum worked on the screenplay from January 18 to May 12, 1944, although he continued to suggest changes through August 17, 1944. Born in 1906 in Atlantic City, New Jersey, Blum wrote scripts for a number of films, including *The New Adventures of Tarzan* (1935). His greatest achievement was *Stalag 17* (1953), several years after his unsuccessful effort to write a suitable script for *The Pirate*.[11]

Possibly in an attempt to create something quite different from the two rejected screenplays, Blum made some drastic revisions.[12] His overall effort was no better, and in many aspects much worse, than the Connolly-Koster version. For example, Serafin creates a show about pirates, and *real* pirates come to see it, apparently unconcerned about being arrested. After telling the whole town that he is Estramudo, Serafin disguises himself as Pedro and tells everyone that Serafin is innocent, confusing the townsfolk (and anyone who reads his script as well). In the end, Serafin is arrested and—in a shocking conclusion—he is executed. (See full synopsis and analysis of Blum's screenplay in Appendix A.)

Why exactly Blum created this bizarre version is anybody's guess. The ending in particular is most jarring. One wonders whether M-G-M forgot to tell Blum that the movie was planned as a light-hearted comedy. Needless to say, Blum's version was also rejected.

Freed Tries to Make a Musical

Two months after Edwin Blum submitted his final screenplay to the studio, Lemuel Ayers, who had recently worked with Arthur Freed and Vincente Minnelli on *Meet Me in St. Louis* (1944), suggested that Freed take on *The Pirate* and make a musical out of it. Mayer approved of the idea. Head of what was developing as the Freed Unit within M-G-M, Freed was still in the early stages of concentrating on making film musicals. Ayers, who went on to have a long and productive career on Broadway in scenic and costume design, had designed the costumes and scenery for the Lunt-Fontanne stage version of *The Pirate*. He was among those observers who recognized the musical potential of the story and setting. It was October 1944; the project had been acquired a year and a half before, and still no acceptable film adaptation, as a straight comedy, had been developed. Freed was interested.[13]

Already, the studio had asked two other writers, H. E. Rogers and Frances Marion, to offer advice on the script. Howard Emmett Rogers was born in New York in 1890 and was involved in many screenplays as a writer from his first movie in 1926, a silent film called *Tin Gods*. Frances Marion was born in 1888 in San Francisco as Marion Benson Owens. She worked as an assistant to the pioneering female director Lois Weber and wrote films for Mary Pickford. Marion won Oscars for *The Big House* (1930) and *The Champ* (1931). Rogers and Marion turned in a brief treatment (or outline) in October 1944.[14] Although this treatment is not available, it appears that it did not offer much promise, and the studio put it aside.

Freed took his time with *The Pirate*. From the fall of 1944 until December 1945, he worked out who should be the major writers and actors involved in the project. Freed chose the rising director Vincente Minnelli to direct the movie. He had more difficulty choosing a leading lady to play Manuela. In July 1945, after seeing a copy of Joseph Breen's letter warning about the minefield to be encountered on the issue of breaking up Manuela's marriage, Freed concluded that *The Pirate* was "an unacceptable vehicle on any basis for Judy Garland," who had been the star of Freed's lucrative series of musicals opposite Mickey Rooney. The public still perceived Garland as a little girl, and Freed wanted to ease her gently into maturity. He thought of two other projects for her instead: "He Who Gets Slapped," about a failed inventor who became a circus clown, and "The Rosary," a "simple story of faith and service climaxing with the singing of the Rosary by Judy." Both projects would have been remakes of older films. As it turned out, M-G-M never made remakes of either film.[15]

In contrast, Minnelli was enthusiastic from the beginning about the suitability of *The Pirate* as an appropriate vehicle for Garland. He enlisted Garland's enthusiasm for the project early on, although Freed could not see her as Manuela at first, saying, "Judy had never played such a role." But the producer eventually came around to their way of thinking. Minnelli later told interviewers, "I always wanted to do it as a movie." In fact, he took credit for M-G-M's acquisition of the property. That claim, however, has been discounted by historians.[16]

Freed became more serious about developing *The Pirate* as a musical when he engaged Anita Loos and Joseph Than to write a new screenplay. Than went on the studio payroll on November 1, 1945, while Loos began on January 17, 1946. Born in Vienna in 1903, Than had created ABC-Film in Berlin to produce his screenplays and moved his operations to Paris in 1938. He escaped the Nazi occupation of France and came to the United States in 1942. Than had produced seven German movies in Europe, but he made his living in America as a screenplay writer. Anita Loos was born in Sisson, California, in 1888. Her early screenwriting efforts resulted in a number of scenarios for silent films, including several directed by D. W. Griffith. Loos was best known for her comic novel, *Gentlemen Prefer Blondes* (1925).[17]

Before Loos came on board, Minnelli began to work closely with Than on ideas. The notes that the two compiled indicate that they were working hard to tweak the basic scenario, and, in the process, creating some complicated situations and plot narratives.[18] (See details in Appendix A, under the Loos-Than screenplay.)

Minnelli and Than also considered who should play the characters they were trying to create. Possibly to emphasize the cordial racial relations Minnelli wanted to portray, they thought of Lena Horne as a new character, Pepita, who would be Manuela's friend. They were still penciling in Garland only as a potential Manuela as late as December 1945.[19]

Yet, only two months later, because no material progress had been made, other members of the M-G-M staff began to look into the property. In February 1946, M-G-M executive Benny Thau asked that Breen take a look at the original screenplay, the one written by Mankiewicz. Breen evaluated the project in no uncertain terms. He still felt that Behrman's "stage play is unacceptable because it is a story of adultery without sufficient compensating moral values. It is, in addition, a story of the successful breakup of a marriage." He also pointed out that while Mankiewicz's script had no adultery, it did wreck the marriage "with some kind of a flimsy excuse."[20] It is unclear why Breen evaluated Behrman's play as adulterous but Mankiewicz's as not. In both versions, Serafin and Manuela are attracted to each other, and in neither version do the two have a physical relationship.

It is possible that Breen was referring to a twist that Mankiewicz had introduced at a late stage in the screenplay, that Pedro and Manuela had never been physically intimate. This might have been an attempt on his part to keep Manuela a virgin so the censors would not object too much to a married woman's falling in love with an actor. Obviously, his effort failed.

In addition to trying to resolve this persistent roadblock regarding the breakup of a marriage, Benny Thau went further than asking Breen for a mere review. He told Breen "in strict confidence" that the studio planned to use Cary Grant and Ingrid Bergman in *The Pirate*, and that both were "anxious" to do the movie. Obviously, it would have been a nonmusical comedy with that cast. Leon Gordon, according to Thau, was slated to produce the film. Consequently, Breen discussed his reading of the Mankiewicz screenplay with Thau and Gordon, advising them to revise it. Breen also suggested that Pedro have a previous wife in Spain to let Manuela off the hook.[21] Apparently Breen thought such a situation would not violate the code or any sense of public morality.

By February 21, 1946, Benny Thau's effort fell apart when the studio failed to line up Grant and Bergman for *The Pirate*. The deal M-G-M tried to arrange "did not 'jell,'" in Breen's words.[22]

As a result, Mayer was committed to rewriting the story for a musical, and Freed and Minnelli, with Anita Loos and Joseph Than now on board as a team, were hard at work to make that happen. By this time, Freed had agreed to cast Garland as Manuela and apparently the producer and director had chosen Gene Kelly to play the role of Serafin.

Unlike the extensive material available on the casting of the male lead in *Singin' in the Rain*,[23] there was nothing in any primary sources on the casting of Kelly for *The Pirate*. It is likely that either Freed or Minnelli first thought of Kelly for the role, suggested it to the other, and found immediate and unequivocal support, so nothing was ever recorded about the process—not in the Freed papers, the Minnelli papers, the Kelly papers, or even in any interviews. Kelly fits the role of Serafin so perfectly that his casting seems to have been almost uneventful.

There was no doubt who would write the songs for this film musical. Freed wanted Cole Porter for the job, and the songwriter agreed. He required, however, that the name of the pirate be changed from Estramudo to Macoco. Porter said he had a friend named Macoco, who often was called Mack the Black. He had "always wanted to write a comic song about him," in Minnelli's words. It was a condition to which Freed readily agreed.[24]

THE LOOS AND THAN SCREENPLAY

Loos and Than had a preliminary, full screenplay ready by April 15 and submitted a final script in June 1946. An almost legendary incident occurred when Loos and Than were ready to reveal the fruits of their labor to Freed. Other than the pirate's name, which they were told to change, they kept their major changes secret until the screenplay was finished. Freed arranged a dinner party at his house in July 1946 and invited Minnelli, Cole Porter, Judy Garland, Gene Kelly, and Freed's resident musical whiz, Roger Edens. After the meal, Loos and Than narrated their new plotline with great enthusiasm. The story goes that instead of an actor who impersonates a pirate, Loos and Than had the pirate pretending to be an actor to cover his true identity. The small audience was stunned, realizing that a pirate would not be able to pull this off. Everyone thought it was awful, but no one had the heart to tell the writers, at least not that evening. This story is told by Minnelli and Hugh Fordin, the latter in his history of the Freed unit. It is repeated by John Fricke on the DVD version of *The Pirate*, and by Mark Griffith in his book on Minnelli, without mentioning their sources.[25]

This makes for one of the more interesting stories in Freed Unit history, but the archival evidence simply does not bear it out. A close examination of the Loos-Than script, which was completed before the dinner party, revealed that Loos and Than had *not* included this strange plot device in their screenplay. Instead, they had directly copied a scene from Behrman's stage version in which Serafin, who is really an actor, merely pretends to Manuela that he is the pirate, disguised as an actor. It is possible that Loos and Than tried to relate this scene from Behrman's play in an unclear manner, causing a misunderstanding among their audience. It appears that Fordin simply took Freed's version of the incident for granted. As for Fricke's comments on the DVD, they are interspersed with photographs of the Loos and Than screenplay, but apparently no one associated with making the DVD looked closely enough at the script to see that it does not contain any reference to a real pirate posing as an actor.

Ironically, an allusion to the pirate's being disguised as an actor is retained in the final film version of *The Pirate*. Moreover, the allusion is extended in a way that is illogical and contradicts the plot. When Serafin claims to be Macoco, Manuela is confused because she knows he is a strolling player. Serafin explains, "Manuela, even a man desperately in love has the instinct of self-preservation," suggesting that he (as the pirate) was in love with her and became a strolling player to hide his identity. Obviously, this is not consistent with the plot of the film, in which Serafin is a traveling actor *before* he meets Manuela.

It is difficult to reconcile the story about the dinner party at Freed's house with the existing, documentary evidence. At the same time, careful reading of the Loos and Than script explains why their version, which was ready in the summer of 1946, was not acceptable.[26] Loos and Than added unnecessary characters, extraneous subplots, and several instances of lengthy and boring conversations. They also weakened the principal characters. For example, they made Serafin sniveling and obsequious, which is radically different from Behrman's conception of Serafin, as well as from the way he is portrayed by Gene Kelly in the film. Moreover, there is a lack of cohesion from one part of the Loos-Than screenplay to another, and the ending is rather outlandish. (See full synopsis and analysis of the Loos-Than version in Appendix A.)

By midsummer 1946, nearly three and a half years after M-G-M had purchased the rights to *The Pirate*, the studio still did not have a viable script. Already, eight writers had tried their hand at creating a screenplay or treatment, with none coming close to what the studio wanted. The only positive development was that the project was now in the firm hands of the studio's ace producer, Arthur Freed, and his best director, Vincente Minnelli, was on board. The two key roles had been filled as well by the highly talented duo of Judy Garland and Gene Kelly. All they needed was a screenplay.

Goodrich and Hackett Come on Board

Unlike the previous times when writers failed to deliver a usable script for *The Pirate*, Freed and Minnelli moved ahead rapidly to find others who could. Frances Goodrich and Albert Hackett were put to work on *The Pirate* the day after the controversial party at Freed's house.[27]

Frances Goodrich was born on December 21, 1890, in New Jersey. She began to act by her teenage years and never lost the desire to shine before an audience, performing in her first Broadway show in 1917. Albert Hackett was born in Manhattan on February 16, 1900. He began to act from age six. The two met and began to collaborate on writing plays in 1928. Hackett's forte was creating witty dialogue while Goodrich handled organization, structure, and situation. Both preferred comedy, as actors and writers, but their acting careers dwindled as the success of their scripts made a name for the pair. Goodrich and Hackett were married in 1931. It was the third marriage for her. The decade of the 1930s started their sterling career in Hollywood, especially with the script of *The Thin Man* for M-G-M in 1934.[28]

Goodrich and Hackett began working on the screenplay for *The Pirate* in August 1946 for a joint salary of $75,000. They completed their first draft by September 18. According to their nephew, Minnelli asked them to rewrite it to add spice. The pair did so to good effect. The writers recalled that Cole Porter was not very helpful. He merely "gave us the songs and that was that," refusing to rework them in cooperation with the writers.[29]

The Influence of Minnelli and Freed on the Goodrich-Hackett Revision

Minnelli, on the other hand, worked very closely with Goodrich and Hackett, as he had tried to do with Joseph Than. Notes in Minnelli's papers show that he did not simply ask them to spice it up, as their nephew suggests, but gave them minutely detailed feedback to improve the script. This pair of writers, however, was receptive and appreciative of the collaborative effort.

Thirty years later, Minnelli cogently told an interviewer about his working relationship with screenwriters. "I con him or charm [him] into re-writing an awful lot," he admitted. He certainly plied all his skill at collaborating with writers on *The Pirate*. Minnelli considered the basic plot to be a one-joke construct, and wanted something a bit more complex but believable. Unsigned and undated notes filed in Minnelli's papers indicate that "our script is more realistic and less whimsical than the play, and . . . we have made every effort to make all the plot complications reasonable."[30]

This, of course, is the opinion of the screenwriters who made these notes. Behrman's play is actually more realistic and less whimsical, whereas the film version is much more tied to fantasy. For example, Behrman's Manuela is more pragmatic and sensible, his Viceroy is more astute in recognizing that Serafin is unlikely to be the pirate, and Serafin's troupe is understandably vocal in trying to save their leader from being hanged. At the same time, some of the plot twists are more believable in the film than in the stage play, and the screenplay is certainly better paced and more dramatic. Overall, the movie corrects the weaknesses in Behrman's stage play that were discussed in Chapter 1.

Freed and Minnelli Reshape the Screenplay and Film

There are extensive notes in both the Minnelli papers and the personal papers of Arthur Freed regarding ideas for script changes to be made in the first draft of the Goodrich-Hackett screenplay.[31] A comparison of these notes with the revised screenplay as well as with the film showed that the following ideas were fully incorporated into the revised screenplay and also made it into the release print. The producer and director, in other words, played a large role in shaping the screenplay and affecting the final product seen by viewers on the screen.

Freed and Minnelli wanted to emphasize Manuela's infatuation with the pirate early in the script, as had been done in the stage plays. They also urged Goodrich and Hackett to more clearly delineate Pedro's character as "a pompous, pious, and rather dull official" who conducts himself with flourish and self-importance during his first meeting with Manuela. They suggested that the troupe notice Pedro, ask a townsman who he is, and, upon learning he is the mayor, start to take down the tent for a quick getaway. Freed and Minnelli suggested that when Serafin reveals that he knows Pedro is Macoco,

Illustration 2.1. Manuela, Inez, and Capucho listening as Don Pedro threatens Serafin. Manuela clearly looks "tortured," as the Freed-Minnelli notes mention she should.

Illustration 2.2. Manuela, Inez, and Capucho after they hear Don Pedro announcing to the citizens that Serafin's troupe will give a performance that evening. Manuela clearly looks "relieved" that Serafin is alive, and Inez looks "apprehensive," as the Freed-Minnelli notes mention they should.

Illustration 2.3. The Viceroy (played by George Zucco) is flattered by Serafin (off camera). The Freed-Minnelli notes suggested flattering the Viceroy as a way for Serafin to be allowed to give a performance in which he can expose Don Pedro as Macoco.

Pedro should not merely plead piteously for mercy but make an effort to kill the actor first. They also noted that it was important to show reactions by Manuela and Inez while Pedro and Serafin are in Manuela's room. Manuela is tortured by the silence, thinking Pedro has killed Serafin; Inez is uncaring. Later, when Pedro makes a speech to the townspeople, Manuela should look relieved, Inez apprehensive. Freed and Minnelli even came up with the line, "You should try underplaying some time—very effective," for Serafin to say to Pedro, after he tells Inez and Capucho to leave the room.

The producer and director noted that when Manuela discovers that Serafin tricked her and he is not really a pirate, she should "make it impossible for Serafin to forestall her" as she raves about him as Macoco. They suggested that Manuela's belittling of Serafin's acting should be condescending, but when he is hurt, she, not the troupe members, should revive him. In fact, they suggested downplaying the prominence of the troupe in Goodrich and Hackett's first draft, with the result that in the final version, the troupe members barely have a presence as far as dialogue and character development are concerned. Instead, Minnelli seems to have used the biracial troupe more as a backdrop, along with the multiethnic citizens of Calvados and Port Sebastian, to create the cultural atmosphere he wanted.

Freed and Minnelli accurately identified the role of the Viceroy as the pivot on which the plot turns during the latter part of the storyline. They wanted Goodrich and Hackett to emphasize his vanity early on, for Serafin plays on that vanity to reinforce the competition between Pedro and the Viceroy to save himself.

Changes Made to the Screenplay but Not the Film

A further comparison of Freed's and Minnelli's notes with the revised screenplay and the film revealed that other ideas had a different outcome.[32] The following suggestions made it into the final draft of the Goodrich and Hackett screenplay but were not kept in the release print.

Freed and Minnelli wanted Manuela's friends to admire her trousseau and choose pieces of her old clothes (which she will never wear again) for themselves. Inez and an "alterations lady" are present. Lizarda takes the hat that Manuela wore when she met Serafin, but everyone is surprised when Manuela refuses to part with it. After they leave, Manuela sings "Love of My Life" while looking at the hat and thinking of Serafin. Minnelli filmed this sequence but dropped it because the preview audience thought it was silly for Garland to sing to a hat.

The producer and director suggested that Manuela go into great detail about how Serafin had tricked and humiliated her. Goodrich and Hackett wrote such a scene but reading it one can see how it slows the action, so this was never filmed. Freed and Minnelli imagined Serafin intermittently running to the window during Manuela's tantrum to reassure the crowd that all was well, saying, "A lovely girl!" But Minnelli changed his mind during preproduction, planning for a more focused tantrum sequence instead.

When Manuela knocks Serafin unconscious, Freed and Minnelli conjured up an elaborate crying scene to follow. Manuela would display "every variety of crying in the feminine repertoire—from the frame-shaking wails of a woman who must give up her man to the soft, yielding, cooing sobs of a girl newly awakened to love. Our hopes are that this scene, if it is adroitly and closely worked out by writers and director, could result in a blend of drama, tenderness and gentle humor." Instead of this risky plan, Minnelli decided to have Garland sing "You Can Do No Wrong" to the injured Serafin.

Ideas Considered and Discarded

Continuing with the comparison, a third set of suggestions by the producer and director had yet another outcome.[33] Their brainstorming produced some ideas that were not incorporated either into the screenplay or the film. After considering the following ideas, the two decided not to use them.

Freed and Minnelli wondered whether Capucho needed more character as Manuela's uncle and noted that he had been depicted in Behrman's play as rolling dice and using colorful language. They suggested that Capucho, "in his alcoholic stupor be flowery and gallant," using "exaggerated phrases" such as "my exquisite zebra," and "I am gilded by joy." Also, when the townspeople are terrified by the news that the strolling player is Macoco the Pirate, Capucho "should never be able to quite make out what the hell is going on." All of these ideas would have focused greater attention on Capucho, detracting from the fast pace of the storyline. Freed and Minnelli also considered an extended dialogue between Manuela, Pedro, and Inez immediately after Manuela faints when Serafin leaves her house. To do this Inez would have to return to the house, and it would have led to a digression from the flow of the narrative.

Stephen Harvey reports that Freed relied on his "favorite script doctor," Sally Benson, to evaluate the Goodrich-Hackett screenplay for *The Pirate*. Born in St. Louis in 1897, Benson's semi-autobiographical stories for *The New Yorker* became the basis for Freed and Minnelli's *Meet Me in St. Louis* (1944).[34] It is likely that the notes in Freed's papers regarding suggested changes in the script were actually Benson's suggestions, made with Freed's approval. So it is appropriate to include Benson in the list of screenwriters who worked on *The Pirate*.

ANALYSIS OF THE GOODRICH-HACKETT REVISED SCREENPLAY

Goodrich and Hackett reworked their first draft, incorporating Freed and Minnelli's suggestions. Their revision was finished and submitted by December 1946.[35]

There is little point in including a full synopsis of the Goodrich-

Illustration 2.4. The Viceroy and Don Pedro calmly watch the shocked Serafin as he opens the incriminating prop box filled with the pirate's treasure. This subplot is Goodrich and Hackett's creation and is not in Behrman's play.

Hackett revised screenplay because overall it is close to the synopsis of the film, presented in Chapter 1. Instead, it is more useful to discuss the key elements of the Goodrich-Hackett version in comparison with Behrman's play and Fulda's as well.[36]

Goodrich and Hackett discarded many characters, complex scenarios, and plot twists from Behrman's stage play. They dropped the saga of the Sultan and his nine wives, the story about Pedro selling cannonballs, the long-winded rambling by Manuela in a trance, and the idea that the Viceroy grants clemency to Macoco so he can fight in a naval war. It appears that Goodrich and Hackett evaluated all the elements of Behrman's play and changed what they felt was needed to make a good film. Their deletions helped to tighten the plot and move the action along for the much more streamlined needs of a film musical.

The scriptwriters dropped Behrman's lengthy subplot about the pirate's treasure hidden under a barn at Pedro's summer house and Manuela's finding it there. However, Goodrich and Hackett introduced a weakness in their revision when they had Pedro arrange to fill Serafin's prop box with the stolen jewels to incriminate him. Goodrich and Hackett never explain how Pedro had the time to do this (while he was away at the capital), or how he was able to obtain the box (which was guarded by Serafin's troupe). Despite these flaws, the plot change is dramatic and also sets the stage for Manuela's discovery of who Macoco really is in a more streamlined way.

Goodrich and Hackett changed Manuela's character considerably from Behrman's portrayal of her. Whereas Fulda had created Manuela as a rich, bored housewife looking for adventure and romance, Behrman made his Manuela more noble. She dreams of Estramudo only because she is in a loveless marriage, and the pirate is described as a Robin Hood of the seas. In contrast, Manuela in the Goodrich-Hackett script and the film is a young, unmarried woman who is fascinated by Macoco despite stories of his violent and terrible deeds. She seems to lack moral judgment and character at this point. When Behrman's Manuela meets Serafin and he tells her he is Estramudo, she questions him minutely and does not fully believe him. She is also adamant about not getting romantically involved despite being attracted to him because she believes in being faithful to her husband. The Manuela in the Goodrich-Hackett script and the movie, however, is naïve enough to believe Serafin's claim to be Macoco. She is delighted to "sacrifice" herself to him to save the town and puts on a great show of martyrdom. When she discovers that Serafin is not Macoco, she is furious that he tricked her and plots her revenge. Manuela's "sacrifice" and her subsequent tantrum are interesting additions made by the screenwriters and work well in the film. Besides, the good thing about painting Manuela as somewhat naïve, yet selfish and conniving at times, is that one appreciates her growth in the third act of the movie, so to speak. The overlap with Behrman's play occurs when Manuela realizes that Pedro is the legendary pirate, who is not heroic but a cold-hearted criminal, and she plans to expose him and save Serafin from being hanged.

Other changes that Goodrich and Hackett made substantially improved Behrman's plot. After declaring that he is the pirate, Behrman's Serafin had no real plan to get himself out of the fix he was in. He planned to hypnotize Manuela merely to hear her say she loves him, even though he faced the gallows at the end of his performance. It was Behrman's Manuela who revealed that Pedro was the real pirate and saved Serafin. Goodrich and Hackett changed the single performance that Serafin gave in Behrman's play to two performances. In the first, Serafin does hypnotize Manuela to get her to say that she loves him. But this makes sense because he has just fallen in love with her. However, in the second performance, Serafin has a concrete plan to get himself out of the fix he is in—by hypnotizing Pedro to get him to reveal that he is Macoco. When Inez ruins that plan by breaking the revolving mirror Serafin uses in hypnosis, Manuela pretends to be hypnotized, and she and Serafin together goad Pedro into a jealous fit so that he reveals his identity as the pirate.

Despite these plot and character changes, many of them for the better, a great deal of the material in the Goodrich-Hackett script comes directly from Behrman's stage play, something that film commentators do not realize. After all the script revisions that preceded theirs, Goodrich and Hackett went back to Behrman to carefully study what could be used.

Recall that when the Lunt-Fontanne play opened in Madison, a critic wrote, "Behrman has never written funnier dialogue."[37] Yet, as mentioned in Chapter 1, film historians have undervalued Behrman's dialogue and have claimed that the Goodrich-Hackett script is far superior. They seem unaware of how heavily Goodrich and Hackett borrowed from Behrman and that it is his lines that film audiences enjoy. One cannot fault Goodrich and Hackett for drawing on Behrman to such a large extent. In fact, it is odd that most of the script writers assigned to the project largely ignored Behrman's lines in developing a screenplay.

It is to their credit that Goodrich and Hackett rediscovered an enormous number of dialogue gems in Behrman's stage script and incorporated them into their screenplay. Sometimes these lines are said by different characters or in different scenes in the film as compared to the stage version, and at other times entire scenes from the play are retained intact. Appendix B includes a comprehensive discussion of the overlap between the Goodrich-Hackett screenplay and Behrman's stage play. This discussion reveals not only the extent of overlap but also the clever ways in which Goodrich and Hackett changed some contexts for Behrman's lines.

Goodrich and Hackett also drew on Fulda's play in large and small ways. A critical idea the scriptwriters took from Fulda is that Pedro becomes wild with jealousy when Manuela says she is in love with Serafin (who she thinks is the pirate) and Pedro reveals that *he* is the pirate. The difference is that Fulda set this up in a farcical way (see Chapter 1), whereas Goodrich and Hackett made Pedro's revelation dramatic, which is more effective for the screen. In Fulda's play, when the beggar recognizes and confronts Pedro, the ex-pirate clutches his heart because he has become soft from age and easy living. Goodrich and Hackett had Pedro react the same way when Serafin recognizes him and fights back as Pedro tries to kill him. When Fulda's Manuela arrives for Serafin's performance, she looks at him closely and is instantly enamored, referring to his "sinister brow" because she thinks he is the pirate Estornudo. Goodrich and Hackett retained the phrase, but their Manuela is only pretending to be enamored after discovering that Serafin tricked her into believing he is Macoco and that he is not the pirate after all.

There is no question that Goodrich and Hackett produced a fine script. However, no film historians seem to be aware of how much Goodrich and Hackett borrowed from Behrman's dialogue. A huge number of lines were devised by Behrman and placed by Goodrich and Hackett in the film, demonstrating a commendable lack of fussiness about authorship in order to create a good script. No previous screenwriters who essayed a script for *The Pirate* borrowed lines so heavily from the stage versions of the story (especially Behrman's), but this was a key element in the success of the Goodrich-Hackett script. Most of these held over lines are memorable and go to the heart of the story and characterizations. Like any good adaptation, the Goodrich-Hackett screenplay retained what worked from the original, drawing heavily from the brilliant dialogue that had already proven itself in 177 performances on Broadway.

DIFFERENCES BETWEEN THE SCREENPLAY AND THE FILM

Goodrich and Hackett finished their revisions by December 1946, and archival evidence shows that writers Wilkie Mahoney and Robert Nathan worked with Minnelli after the screenwriters signed off.[38] Despite the improved quality of the Goodrich-Hackett script, there are significant differences between their final draft and the release print of the film. Many of the changes were due to the work of Minnelli and his assistants Mahoney and Nathan, with some input from Kelly during the preproduction phase of *The Pirate*. Minnelli had worked with the screenwriters to craft the script, and he continued to work on details of the story and characterizations after Goodrich and Hackett turned in their final draft. These latter changes were not recorded on paper but worked out informally and then used in

filming the movie. For example, Serafin's character was strength-
ened and made more virile in contrast with Alfred Lunt's depiction
for the stage version. Scenes were altered for greater dramatic effect
during Serafin's second performance and to end the film on a high
note. All of the changes made during preproduction (see Chapter 3
under Script Revisions) considerably improved the script turned in
by Goodrich and Hackett.

In addition, some lines were revised and a few scenes deleted from the Goodrich-Hackett script. For example, Pedro's line to
Manuela, "I have watched you going about your little duties," was
changed to "I have watched you growing up," probably to eliminate
the idea that Manuela was pious or dutiful. When Pedro is relieved
to hear that Manuela is not interested in callow youth, he asks Inez,
"She said that?" In the script, the aunt replies blandly, "She did not
need to say it. I know her. I can read her heart." This was changed to
"*I* said it," which is shorter and funnier. Pedro's line to the advocate,
"Don't pay any attention to him. He's just acting," was dropped because Pedro would not risk giving anyone the idea that Serafin is
truly an actor and not the pirate. Any scenes that slowed the action,
such as Manuela's hesitating to pack for her move to Pedro's house,
Serafin's long speech (as Macoco) to the citizens of Calvados before
Manuela comes to him, and Manuela's arguing with Serafin to get
him to escape before the Viceroy's arrival, were dropped during
preproduction. Along with the more substantial changes, such revisions of lines and deletions of scenes tightened and enhanced the
script, resulting in a better film.

A Final Assessment of the Goodrich and Hackett Screenplay

Film commentators have argued that Goodrich and Hackett produced a script far better than Behrman's play. For example, Joel
Siegel correctly notes that Goodrich and Hackett achieved a good
script by "heightening the comic sequences, paring away the verbal
clutter and working Behrman's meanings into the structure of the
story." However, Siegel also claims that the couple "completely ren-
ovated the play."[39] This chapter (along with Appendix B) provides
extensive evidence that such contentions are inaccurate. Goodrich
and Hackett borrowed heavily from Behrman—it is Behrman's lines
that work so well in the film.

Stephen Harvey correctly notes that Goodrich and Hackett portrayed Pedro more powerfully by having him reveal his identity in the throes of passion, when he realizes that his fiancée worships Macoco. Thus, the screenwriters "allow the now-bourgeois brigand a measure of tragic dignity he never possessed in the play." However, Harvey also writes that Goodrich and Hackett made Manuela into "a woman torn between infatuation and propriety," instead of merely "an object of seduction," and that Behrman had Pedro "unwittingly expose" himself during Serafin's trial.[40] Both are inaccurate attributions. Manuela's struggle between attraction to Serafin and propriety is taken directly from Behrman; in fact, Behrman's Manuela is even less an object of seduction and has a higher sense of propriety. As discussed earlier, she was a far more complex character than the Manuela in the film. Also, Behrman's Pedro was actually exposed by Manuela in her "trance" while he had slipped away during Serafin's performance.

In addition to not giving Behrman sufficient credit, most film historians look at the movie and assume it is based exactly on the Goodrich and Hackett script. However, many revisions were made to the script during preproduction—some briefly described in this chapter and others discussed in Chapter 3. As a result, much of what works well in the film was Minnelli's often last-minute contribution, helped by Kelly as well as writers Mahoney and Nathan.

The script revisions Minnelli and others made improved the final product enormously, just as Gene Kelly and Stanley Donen did later with Betty Comden and Adolph Green's screenplay for *Singin' in the Rain* (1952). It is worthwhile to compare these efforts of M-G-M directors with the accepted practice at Warner Brothers Studio at about the same time. Jack Warner did not like the fact that directors and producers rewrote scenes during filming. He saw it "as a waste of time and money" and "harangued all his directors and producers about this issue."[41] In stark contrast, Freed allowed his best directors plenty of freedom.

It is true that Goodrich and Hackett created good plot changes and drew extensively on Behrman's lines to create a much better version than all the previous scripts for the project. But *The Pirate* serves as an excellent example of a director getting deeply involved in revising a screenplay for a much better outcome.

Eventually, thirteen writers, not including Minnelli and Freed, worked on the script for *The Pirate*. From March 1943 to May 1947, five screenplay versions and two treatments (or outlines) were produced, with several rewrites after the Goodrich-Hackett screenplay was turned in. It took more than four years and the efforts of many people to get to the final script that was the basis for the film.

This process of writing a screenplay for *The Pirate* was most unusual for Hollywood. Typically, scripts were written and revised in less than a year, with a few going to two years. In addition, although it was common to use several writers, they were often used for different aspects such as adaptation of a novel or play, adding witty dialogue, polishing, and so on. It was not the practice to assign completely new writers or teams and have them do everything from scratch. Rudy Behlmer provides several examples of the typical Hollywood process of screenwriting. Frank Capra's *Lost Horizon* (1937) had only one screenwriter, Robert Riskin, and the screenplay was drafted, revised, and ready for filming in less than a year. Darryl Zanuck's *The Grapes of Wrath* (1940) also had only one screenwriter, Nunnally Johnson. The screenplay was drafted and revised in only a few months, and the film was released less than a year after acquiring the rights. *Casablanca* (1943), widely viewed as a film with a complex screenwriting process, had one team that adapted the play; the Epstein brothers, who wrote the dialogue; and Howard Koch, who worked on removing problems from the plot and characters. Koch worked on his assignment even as the Epstein brothers continued to revise. Despite all this, the film was released in just over a year after the first synopsis was written.[42]

CHAPTER THREE

Major Players and Preproduction

After the script for M-G-M's *The Pirate* had undergone several revisions from 1943 to 1946, director Vincente Minnelli and producer Arthur Freed were still not pleased with it, and for good reason as detailed in Chapter 2. Nevertheless, even before they assigned Frances Goodrich and Albert Hackett in July 1946 to revise the script again, the movie was well into its preproduction phase of development. The salient aspects of the project were worked out during this phase by Minnelli and the male lead, Gene Kelly. The two men intensely discussed questions regarding character development, costumes, lighting, décor, props, and the overall style of the production. No other actors or technical crew played such an important role in shaping the fundamental and artistic elements of the film as did Minnelli and Kelly.

MINNELLI

Vincente Minnelli was born Lester Anthony Minnelli on February 28, 1903, in Chicago. His parents owned a tent show that traveled circuits throughout Ohio and Indiana, but they eventually settled the family in Delaware, Ohio. Lester appeared in stage plays as a boy and attended the Art Institute of Chicago after graduating from high school. He worked as a window dresser for Marshall Field's and a designer at the Chicago Theatre before going to New York to design stage shows. In New York, Minnelli worked in a variety of roles, including design, lighting, costumes, and even some directing for a variety of performers and producers. "I taught myself as an artist," he later asserted. Minnelli changed his first name to Vincente while in New York.[1]

51

Arthur Freed eventually convinced Minnelli to go to California in 1940. Once in Hollywood, Minnelli spent many months doing any job that was asked of him so he could become acquainted with the working procedures at M-G-M. He doctored scripts, edited, worked with cameras, and learned how to direct for a year before embarking on his first film, *Cabin in the Sky* (1943). This was an innovative picture involving an all-black cast and was both a critical and commercial success. The very next year, Minnelli hit his stride with *Meet Me in St. Louis* (1944), widely regarded as the true start of the Freed Unit's best film musicals. In both *Cabin in the Sky* and *Meet Me in St. Louis*, the salient elements of Minnelli's musicals are apparent. Film historian Douglas McVay summarizes these aspects as "a penchant for fantasy, surrealism, raffish locale, picturesquely formalized figure-grouping, choreographed movement, virtuosic crane shots, and contrastingly contemplative close ups during songs."[2]

Minnelli worked closely with all members of the crew to shape his films in minute ways, but he encountered a problem in working with M-G-M's art department, headed by Cedric Gibbons. "I had to revolutionize them initially," Minnelli recalled. "They were shocked at a lot of things I wanted to do. . . . Their methods were staid and old-fashioned, and they weren't integrated properly." Minnelli tried to coordinate common elements in the visual scene of his shots so that décor and props contributed to the development of characters. "I feel that the surroundings of people are very important. You don't see people isolated. You see them with their surroundings. And the environment and the look that the surroundings have is very important to me. I think it shows character." While *Cabin in the Sky* was shot in black and white, *Meet Me in St. Louis* was Minnelli's first color film. "For me, the colour is primarily dictated by the décor and the costumes and then, as you're shooting the film, by the way you select the colours, put them together, and the sense the composition gives you of colour."[3] Minnelli's *Yolanda and the Thief* (1945) is the film in which he first experimented with vibrant colors.

During this time, Minnelli was also starting to make script changes to shape his films the way he saw them. While preparing to shoot *The Clock* (1945), a black-and-white film about a soldier who impulsively marries a girl he has just met while on a short leave, Minnelli often changed the script without consulting the screenwriter, Robert Nathan. "I used a lot of improvisation," Minnelli admitted, and he developed "new ideas, new situations and dialogue as I went along." Nathan protested such changes but to no avail. Minnelli got his way.[4]

Minnelli's obsession with the correct placing of props to frame his shots could be extreme as well. While filming Lucille Bremer in a bubble bath for *Yolanda and the Thief,* he spent so much time getting a gargoyle in the right place—between the telephone and Bremer's head—that the actress became exhausted and near tears. Freed happened to come on the set just then and became furious with his star director. Shouting, "Come down here, you boom-riding son of a bitch!," Freed engaged in a huge fight with Minnelli.[5]

Minnelli's penchant for taking his camera way up in the air was well known at M-G-M. "I was very much influenced by the movies of Max Ophuls, who moved the camera all the time," he later acknowledged. But Minnelli took the camera up from the studio floor as well as along it, creating one of the trademarks of his film work. He also preferred to use one camera at a time, unless filming complex scenes that included "fires or explosions or something like that." Minnelli stressed preparation during the preproduction phase. "I preplanned the films very carefully," he said in 1969. "I worked with the writers on the scripts in detail. But there was always an area for improvisation as well. I rehearsed a great deal, and then had the minimum of takes." Minnelli depended "on one camera with many moods, many different positions, different compositions."[6]

The overall style of his pictures depended in part on the story to be told: "I try to find the style that belongs to *that* particular film." Minnelli did extensive research to find the right color combinations, costumes, and props—elements that in their own way contributed to the overall style of the film. In many ways, *Yolanda and the Thief* was a dress rehearsal for *The Pirate* because they both shared a common Latin American setting. As Douglas McVay explains, the "Spanish milieu" of both films called for "maximum decorative and atmospheric effect" as well as an appreciation for "colonial architecture."[7]

Most of his colleagues liked working with Vincente Minnelli. Andre Previn, a young musician at M-G-M in the 1940s and 1950s, mentioned that the director could be "nervous and a bit irritable when things did not go smoothly," but he also was "certainly one of the very best directors of musical films ever. His visual sense was immaculate and his taste impeccable. He . . . should have given lessons in how to make a film look beautiful and move gracefully."[8]

Minnelli has been a prime candidate for film scholars who search for an example of the auteur in film musicals. He "represents the director-as-artist," as Albert Johnson has expressed it. Minnelli understood the importance of freedom for individual expression in the highly complex task of filmmaking, one of the most collaborative art projects ever developed. "Once you're on a set," he said in 1969, "it depends on you; most of my films, although made in a studio, have been in a sense independent films." Minnelli saw his work as an attempt to touch the audience in a special way. "The search in films, what you try to create, is a little magic. . . . But the main search is for a little magic in our lives."[9]

STYLE OF *THE PIRATE*

In developing the overall style for M-G-M's version of *The Pirate*, Minnelli was influenced by the Caribbean island of Martinique and the time period of the 1830s. But he deliberately avoided being specific about either the locale or the era in order to create an "artificial flavour." The melding of cultures, races, and color schemes attracted his design sense, and he wanted the venue for *The Pirate* to have an atmosphere of almost anywhere, with just enough specificity to ground the viewer in time and place.[10] As a result, the audience is generally aware of when and where, without being constrained or limited by that sense of time and place. Moreover, Minnelli's artistry in creating colorful crowd scenes of ethnically mixed people was unique among filmmakers and nowhere so evident as in *The Pirate*.

Veteran art director Jack Martin Smith was in charge of the crew that collected props and created the sets and décor for *The Pirate*. He recalled the immense effort to materialize Minnelli's conception of the world inhabited by Serafin and Manuela. For each set, his assistants assembled color samples on a single card to represent the color scheme of the walls and the floor, as well as the colors of the costumes to be worn by the actors. Because the film was to be processed by the Technicolor Corporation for release, three assistants from the company worked closely with the art crew in getting the color shades right for maximum effect. They "would take a sheet and do a collage in flat tones without any shadows or anything showing to see what the presentation was going to be like." Smith also sketched the cart to be used by Serafin's troupe and the street sets for Port Sebastian and Calvados. "We used to go to that

Illustration 3.1. Serafin and Manuela meet near the sea wall—carefully modeled and built by art director Jack Martin Smith's crew. Except for the seaside setting, the entire sequence with all its lines is taken directly from Behrman's play.

extent in those days to formulate an intelligent color scheme," he commented years later.[11]

Smith worked on the portable stage for the troupe, designing a proscenium arch from a book of heraldry he found. To complete his "nice little Baroque theater," he designed simple canvas drapes that could be readily set up and taken down and could fit in the cart for traveling to the next venue. Smith was so proud of his work that he kept the original sketch of the stage for many years, decorating it by cutting swatches of Gene Kelly's costume (red) and Judy Garland's costume (green) to make a mat around the sketch.[12]

The next stage of development consisted of making many models of the interior and exterior sets. Nine assistants helped Smith to construct more than twenty-four complex models. Everything, from the dock at Port Sebastian (where the film introduces Serafin), to the sea wall where Serafin and Manuela first engage in conversation, to the interior of Don Pedro's house, was modeled before the sets were constructed. About ten models of scenes were soon after dropped from production as changes were made in the script, first by Goodrich and Hackett and later by Minnelli. The dropped models included Don Pedro's cellar, a native hut, the decks of a pirate ship and a merchant vessel, and the interior of a church belfry.[13]

Building the sets was a huge undertaking. For the dock sequence at Port Sebastian, Smith used a set 3,106 feet long and 1,336 feet wide. Some buildings on the Port Sebastian set, used for Kelly's "Niña" number, were up to forty feet tall. Altogether, Smith spent $86,660 on building sets for *The Pirate*. All of them were constructed anew, without the use of previously used sets from other M-G-M productions, which was unusual at the studio. In using these huge sets, Minnelli gathered the largest number of extras used in many years in Hollywood, and he deployed twenty speakers around the set so as to be heard by everyone when he gave directions.[14]

For Minnelli, selecting the right color for costumes was vitally important. He used it "for great emphasis, just to punch something up. They're dramatic tricks." *The Pirate*'s wardrobe staff consisted of more than forty people, leading many to predict that costumes would cost more for this production than for any other film in many years. Tom Keough designed the costumes, and Madame Barbara Karinska "executed" them under the general supervision of Irene, the executive designer at M-G-M. Nothing was spared for this production. Garland needed eight major sets of clothing, and for some of these, laces and satins were imported from France. One of them was a "replica of an 1830 Worth gown," according to promotional literature issued by M-G-M, and another was "a white satin wedding dress embroidered with hand-made antique lace. . . . The wedding headdress carries 1,000 pearls." These lavish productions carried a hefty price. The replica of the Worth gown cost $3,462.23 and the wedding dress cut $3,313.12 into the budget. In all, wardrobe costs soared to a total of $141,595.30. Minnelli himself became involved in costume design by formulating the clothes Serafin would wear. For Kelly's first appearance in the film, in the dock sequence at Port Sebastian, the director described Serafin as wearing "form-fitting trousers."[15]

Variety reported that Minnelli used 5,060 props for *The Pirate*, more than any other M-G-M picture had employed. This included a collection of 150 old trunks and garden tools used in the early nineteenth century that were found in junkyards around Los Angeles. Harry Lazarre, the head of props at the studio, employed six assistants to help him find suitable material at antique shops. But the crew could not find everything that Minnelli wanted by perusing junkyards and antique stores and had to make some props themselves. They acquired two beef bladders, probably from a butcher shop, which they dried and painted so that clowns could bounce them off the heads of spectators. Many such props that Lazarre laboriously accumulated or created never made it into the release print of *The Pirate*. But Serafin's revolving mirror, which is prominently used in the film, was built by Lazarre's crew from scratch.[16]

KELLY

The Pirate's male lead also played a huge role in shaping the film. Gene Kelly was born on August 23, 1912, in Pittsburgh, and grew up in a working-class neighborhood of this industrial city. As a boy he was primarily interested in sports, although his mother formed an entertainment troupe of all her children because she was deeply interested in the arts. Many people in the neighborhood considered dancing by men to be "sissy," and the young Kelly struggled with conflicting influences until he discovered in high school and college that he enjoyed dancing. He also loved to teach dancing and taught children at the dance school that his mother eventually took over as a family business. A short stint in law school convinced Kelly that the arts were his calling, and from that point he devoted himself full time to dance. Kelly went to New York in the late 1930s and found his big break as the lead in *Pal Joey* (1940). This stage musical gave Kelly the opportunity to sing, dance, and act the complex role of a man who is a heel, yet likable. His performance wowed the critics and led to a screen career. His first movie experience, co-starring with Judy Garland in M-G-M's *For Me and My Gal* (1942), taught Kelly that dancing for the camera was very different than dancing on stage, and he set about exploring innovative ways to create and project dances on film. His two biggest successes during the next few years were in *Cover Girl* (1944) at Columbia (on a loan-out from M-G-M) and in the best-known film of his budding career, *Anchors Aweigh* (1945), when he was back at M-G-M.[17]

Kelly talked the studio into letting him volunteer for service in World War II. He joined the U. S. Navy and worked primarily at making films before returning to civilian life and facing the daunting task of retooling for Hollywood. "Two years in the Navy, three years off the screen, I shall never be the dancer I was," he told a reporter just when Minnelli began to film *The Pirate*. "I put on eighteen pounds in the Navy and I am only just working them off." Kelly also worried about his relatively advanced age; at thirty-four, he already was older than most dancers were when they hit their prime. "A dancer is like a prizefighter," Kelly explained. "He gets superannuated very early; can't take it nearly so well in his thirties."[18] But Kelly was mistaken, as his lengthy dancing career would show, and performed powerful and athletic dances well into his forties.

Worries aside, Kelly threw himself into the project—the first major film of his postwar career. *The Pirate* offered Kelly an opportunity to rejuvenate his film work and take it in new directions. Serafin was a wonderful, multifaceted role for him. Kelly had seen Lunt and Fontanne in *The Pirate* and thought the stage production and its dialogue were delightful. But he considered Lunt a bit too old even to *pretend* to be a dashing pirate as Serafin does, and he erroneously commented that it had been the only Broadway failure in the illustrious career of that acting couple. Although Kelly was acquainted with Lunt and Fontanne, and they invited suggestions to improve their work, Kelly could never bring himself to tell them why he thought the play was weak because he did not want to hurt Lunt's feelings.[19]

Both Minnelli and Kelly thought Serafin had to be played with more youthful vigor than Lunt had shown in his portrayal. They envisioned the style of John Barrymore, when Serafin was playing himself, a strolling player, and the bravado of Douglas Fairbanks Sr., when Serafin was pretending to be Macoco. They sought a level of pretense that they thought the audience would understand. They wanted people to see that Kelly was sincere in his effort to honor these famous actors by imitating them but "not too obvious, just enough to let everybody in on it." It was a tricky scheme which both men wholeheartedly embraced as a challenge.[20]

While the pair worked closely on developing the character of Serafin, the idea to base him on Barrymore and Fairbanks was Kelly's own. He considered Serafin to be a thoroughly imitative man. Because the strolling player was "such a ham and he's so false," he would inevitably model himself on a great actor who also was a ham. "When he plays the pirate, he'll copy somebody else, because he's still a fraud, in the piece." Barrymore and Fairbanks readily came to Kelly's mind. Fairbanks was a particular hero of his, and his style had influenced Kelly's own, as he often acknowledged. "He was a strong, virile man and yet he used dance movements in his dashing histrionics and proved to me you didn't have to be a sissy

Illustration 3.2. Kelly going up the rope to the crow's nest in the "Pirate Ballet." Note Kelly's short shorts and muscular thighs. Both Kelly and Minnelli were determined that Serafin as Macoco be virile and energetic, in contrast to Lunt's portrayal of him.

to become a dancer," Kelly wrote in an article for *Parade Magazine* in the late 1950s. "He made me become aware of the actual ballet movements used by all athletes, which in turn gave me ideas for new choreography."[21]

Kelly also recalled an earlier association with Fairbanks that influenced his personal development. As a boy, he had once skipped school "because I was mad at the world." His mother had punished him "in a way I thought unjust." Soon after, he went to the theater to see Fairbanks in *The Mark of Zorro* (as Kelly reports it) and was impressed by a line that flashed across the screen in this silent film: "When you are in the wrong admit it—when you are in the right, fight." He left the theater ready to apologize to his mother. It "was the soundest advice I ever received." As a result, "Doug Fairbanks was my ideal from that day on and his dashing athletic prowess was what really inspired me to become a dancer."[22] As it happens, this particular line is not in *The Mark of Zorro*. It is in *Don Q, Son of Zorro* (1925), the sequel to *The Mark of Zorro* (1920), also starring Fairbanks.

Kelly was twelve or thirteen years old at the time, close to the age that he began to be interested in dancing and doing so athletically.

One of the most popular movies that Fairbanks ever made became somewhat of a model for *The Pirate* as well. Fairbanks filmed *The Black Pirate* in the winter of 1925–1926, and there has been much scholarly discussion about a particular stunt in the movie, how it was accomplished, and whether Fairbanks himself or a stuntman performed it.[23]

The Black Pirate (1926) is an adventure film about a man who takes on a ship full of bloodthirsty pirates by using trickery and daredevil stunts. The movie was shot in two-strip Technicolor and had elaborate sets, lavish production, and nonstop action. The famous sequence involves Fairbanks sliding down two large sails in rapid succession by ripping the canvas apart with a knife held in his hands. He later repeats the stunt down a third sail. But one cannot see the man's face as he slides down the sails, hence the speculation about who actually performed the stunt. It foreshadows the shot of Kelly sliding down from the crow's nest during the "Pirate Ballet" of *The Pirate*. The difference is that Minnelli's camera makes it abundantly clear, both when "Macoco" goes up the rope *and* when he slides down it, that Kelly performs these stunts himself.

THE KELLY-MINNELLI COLLABORATION

Kelly and Minnelli found on their first collaborative project that they worked very well together. The two men were quite different in their backgrounds, personalities, and ways of dealing with people. Kelly thought this was an advantage, because each added something to the other's sense of style and technique. Each was completely open to suggestions from the other, and they formed a powerful creative team that shaped many of the key elements of *The Pirate*. They also lived close to each other in Beverly Hills. After dinner with his wife, Betsy Blair, and his daughter, Kerry, Kelly walked through his backyard and over to Minnelli and Garland's home on many evenings to continue work after a full day at the studio.[24]

Kelly recognized Minnelli's strengths, such as his ability to visually compose shots down to the smallest detail. Minnelli shared the joy Kelly felt at working up details of *The Pirate*. For the director, this lay in the knowledge that Kelly understood "there [were] 20 ways to do a scene," and both eagerly explored all the possibilities.

"Gene Kelly is more of an intellectual," Minnelli told an interviewer in 1975. "He is just as much a perfectionist as Astaire, in his own way. . . . But Gene Kelly is more earthy and more romantic. And in all of the things that Gene does, he has the same sense of reality that never leaves."[25]

While both men consistently praised each other, German-born Lela Simone had a different perspective on their collaboration very late in her life. Simone had been a trusted member of the Freed Unit who usually worked on improving the sound tracks of Freed's musicals. More than forty years later, she argued that Kelly and Minnelli had a good deal of difficulty working on *The Pirate* because "temperamentally and as a person, they were *very*, very contrary." According to her, the two remained friends but disagreed on their work. "Kelly's basic tastes, from a viewpoint of what is good and what is beautiful and what is not beautiful are so different from Minnelli's. I mean, Gene Kelly is wide away from serious arts and Minnelli is so close to serious arts that one has to be careful not to be run over with it." Simone claimed she saw behind the scenes how the two men clashed and that she offered a friendly ear to both. "I heard the raving of Gene and the raving of Minnelli. So that [it] was very difficult for me to stay the balance."[26] It is possible, of course, that Kelly and Minnelli disagreed on any given issue, but no one other than Simone indicated that any degree of discord existed between Kelly and Minnelli.

The care with which Kelly and Minnelli approached the shaping of Serafin's character and style in the film is impressive. Serafin is portrayed as a consummate performer and promoter, from his very first scene, where he jumps onto Manuela's trousseau box and rides high with it above the crowd—to the end of the film, when as his troupe members overpower Macoco, Serafin hugs Manuela and happily points to the action as if it is part of his performance. Minnelli also appears to have ensured that Serafin's costumes always projected an image of virility. He wanted to highlight Kelly's athletic physique and to overcome the weakness of the stage production in that respect.

In addition, Kelly took it upon himself to improve his diction. He felt this necessary considering that he wanted "to fuse an image of John Barrymore into an image of Douglas Fairbanks, Sr." And even Arthur Freed was involved in many small details regarding Serafin's portrayal. He insisted that Minnelli film Serafin cracking the whip in the direction of Don Pedro in such a way so that the audience

Illustration 3.3. Serafin, the consummate performer, riding high on Manuela's trousseau box, dramatically invites the citizens of Port Sebastian to his performance that evening.

Illustration 3.4. Serafin points to the overpowering of Macoco as if it is part of his performance. From his first appearance on screen to his last, Serafin is portrayed by Kelly and Minnelli as a consummate performer.

could easily see that it did not actually hit him. Freed's concern was to keep Serafin's character at a level of comparative innocence.[27] Actually, one cannot see the whip in that scene because the camera switches to Manuela. But the very next scene shows Don Pedro unharmed, thus achieving Freed's goal.

GARLAND

As important as Kelly was to the project, Judy Garland was considered the primary star of *The Pirate.* Her reputation was at a peak in the postwar period and attracted a good deal of audience recognition. Kelly was happy to take slightly second billing in order to work with her again. But Garland played no role in preproduction planning, content to let her director-husband and her close friend Kelly work out the themes, styles, and décor for *The Pirate.*

By 1947, Garland was reaching a period of turmoil in her life and career, resulting from a complicated series of problems that had plagued her troubled life ever since "little Baby Gumm" first sang for an audience at the age of two. Born Frances Gumm in Grand Rapids, Michigan, on June 10, 1922, Garland had a unique gift for song that her ambitious mother capitalized on to create a career for her talented daughter. According to some accounts, by the time Frances was ten years old, Ethel Gumm was feeding the young singer pep pills to keep her bright for performances. All observers agree that Ethel was cold, dominating, and manipulative of her daughter as a bankable commodity, the worst example of a stage mother in film lore. Young Frances idolized her father, Frank Gumm, but Garland's biographer portrays him as a troubled man who lusted after young boys, and reports that Ethel obtained a lover, Will Gilmore, who treated Frances cruelly. Frances changed her name to Judy Garland in 1933, near the end of her participation in the singing Gumm Sisters. Only two years later, in November 1935, she was traumatized by her father's death, which left a hole in her life that she tried desperately to fill for the rest of her days.[28]

A short time before Frank passed out of her life, Judy signed a long-term contract with M-G-M on September 27, 1935. She was only thirteen at the time. Her skill at performing before a camera was honed by work in a long string of films that never really showcased her talent, but Freed's assistant, Roger Edens, managed to find the proper musical niche for Judy and helped to shape her screen persona. She attained wild success by co-starring with Mickey Rooney in a series of Freed musicals, as well as in *The Wizard of Oz* (1939).[29]

Garland began a pattern of calling in sick during production schedules as early as *Girl Crazy* (1943), for which she missed seventeen days of filming. She also called in sick for sixteen days during filming of *Meet Me in St. Louis*, and the pattern continued with *The Harvey Girls* (1946). Pill popping has been the most common explanation for these lapses, but other causes included Garland's dislike of her juvenile role as scripted in *Meet Me in St. Louis* and her secret rendezvous in Los Angeles (probably with Joseph Mankiewicz, who reportedly was having an affair with her at the time) while the crew of *Girl Crazy* was filming on location in Palm Springs.[30]

Clearly, Garland was a troubled soul with many different but related problems. The idea that the studio was responsible for her drug addiction has resonated with the public almost to the exclusion of all other issues. It appeals to public taste to think that the big, heartless corporation was merely interested in milking her talent for profit.

But Garland's own daughter saw it in a more balanced and accurate way. Lorna Luft reports that M-G-M gave her mother benzadrine, an amphetamine designed to curb appetite, for the first time in 1938 when the singer was sixteen. Garland became hooked on the drug, but Luft notes that amphetamines were widely used everywhere in America at the time. She writes that once the studio executives realized a problem had developed, they tried in every way possible to help her get off drugs. Garland, however, was clever at finding ways to smuggle the pills through the studio-imposed blockade. Luft reports also that Garland made sincere, if episodic, efforts to quit from 1943 on, but failed every time. Her daughter believes the singer had a genetic disposition to addiction and adds: "Ignorance, not evil, began the process that destroyed my mother's life."[31]

Beyond the problems associated with drug abuse, Garland was a boiling mixture of emotions. Yet, she was loved and respected by fellow performers and crew alike. By the late 1940s, the studio executives also treated her with respect and care, overlooking the many delays she imposed on shooting schedules by her repeated absences.

Kelly, in particular, was ready to do almost anything for her. He felt indebted to Garland because of her pivotal role in giving him his start in films, as Harry Palmer in *For Me and My Gal,* and for teaching him the nuances of acting in front of a camera.[32] She was a troubled genius for whom nearly everyone rooted. But her personal problems of parental abuse and the loss of her father haunted Garland. Moreover, her reliance on drugs simply to feel good worsened over time.

This was the woman with whom Minnelli fell in love while filming *Meet Me in St. Louis,* and the love was mutual. Garland also liked the way Minnelli made her look on screen in that film, as a mature young lady despite the script. At the time, she was estranged from her first husband, bandleader and musician David Rose, who granted her a divorce in June 1944. Garland arranged for Minnelli to direct *The Clock* after deliberately undermining the film's first director, Fred Zinnemann. The couple announced their engagement in January 1945 and were married the following June, spending a long honeymoon in New York.[33]

In fact, it was during this honeymoon that Minnelli concocted some of the ideas he would later use in crafting *The Pirate.* At the end of a farewell dinner the couple hosted for their friends before returning to California, Minnelli was impressed by the way his wife had handled the duties of a host. "'I think I'll keep you,'" he told her. Garland responded in a similar vein of mock self-importance, "'My dear sir, you do me such great honor.'" The remark reminded Minnelli of *The Pirate,* and he started to think about its style and content. Much earlier, he had seen the Lunt and Fontanne stage play and thought the acting couple had "played the improbable farce in a probable way . . . the only way farce should be played. It was great camp, an element that hadn't been intentionally used in films up to now."[34]

After returning to California in September 1945, Minnelli filmed his wife in several segments of *Till the Clouds Roll By* (1947). Now pregnant, Garland had to be placed carefully in some scenes to hide her expanding middle. Liza was born in March 1946, when preproduction for *The Pirate* was in full swing. All seemed bright, at least from Minnelli's perspective. As far as he could tell, Judy had sworn off drugs during her pregnancy and was eager for the work to come. In November 1946, she signed a new five-year contract with M-G-M that doubled her salary to $5,619.23 a week and that required her to make no more than two films per year. The studio wrote in a clause to protect itself from her habit of calling in sick. If she was ill for more than three weeks, M-G-M reserved the right to cancel the agreement. Minnelli had played a huge role in negotiating the terms of this new contract, which went into effect on November 21, the same day she was scheduled to start work on *The Pirate*. But the studio had generously allowed her to start on December 2 if she felt the need to postpone reporting. Not surprisingly, Garland took the extra days and arrived at the studio on December 2.[35]

MUSICAL NUMBERS

With two of M-G-M's top musical and dance performers as stars, Minnelli included seven musical numbers in *The Pirate*. Three of them are major dances, two are performances but not quite dances, and two are songs.

The first dance is Kelly's energetic "Niña," which he performs in the heart of Port Sebastian for an impromptu audience, before he meets Manuela. Next is Garland's "Mack the Black," sung while Manuela is under hypnosis at Serafin's first formal show. This is not actually a dance, although some audience members join in the performance, moving around to the beat. After that is the "Pirate Ballet," a vibrant and complex dance performed mainly by Kelly. It represents Manuela's fantasy about Serafin as Macoco the pirate. Then Garland sings "You Can Do No Wrong" to the prone Kelly— after Manuela's tantrum on discovering that Serafin was only pretending to be Macoco. After the Viceroy permits Serafin to give a final performance before his impending execution, Kelly performs "Be a Clown" as an invigorating dance with the Nicholas Brothers— the first time ever for a white man to dance with black men as equals on film. Following this, Garland sings "Love of My Life" to Serafin (as Macoco) on stage, supposedly while Manuela is under hypnosis. Actually she sings it to goad Don Pedro to jealousy and prompt him to reveal that *he* is the pirate. But the number also expresses the true passion that Serafin and Manuela feel for each other. The final number is a reprise of "Be a Clown" by Kelly and Garland, which shows the audience that Manuela is now part of Serafin's troupe and presumably his partner in life. It is not a dance per se but a performance accompanying a song.

These seven numbers included in *The Pirate* received varying amounts of development in preproduction. Other numbers were considered—some were even filmed and then discarded. The details of this entire process are discussed in the rest of this chapter and the next.

ALTON, KELLY, AND DANCE DIRECTION

Robert Alton, veteran Broadway choreographer and a fairly recent addition to Hollywood, was brought on board as the dance director for *The Pirate*. Although it was not intended from the start, he and Kelly came to share the duties of choreographing and supervising the dance numbers. "Alton was a master at staging," commented art director Smith. He "was also a master at holding his troupe together." According to Minnelli, Alton had the facility of changing entire sections of choreography "within minutes" if he decided that something was not working with the old routine. Kelly and Alton had worked together on Broadway, and the two greatly respected each other. Kelly had a strong desire to choreograph for the screen and offered to help the older man with his work. As it panned out, Alton worked with the groups while Kelly worked with individual dancers. Kelly also choreographed all of his own dances. The two nevertheless worked in close collaboration with each other to coordinate the movements of ensembles and individuals.[36]

Kelly always made a point of asserting that work on *The Pirate* "was strictly a collaboration among as many people." But he also tended to say that he gave Alton co-credit for dance direction in *The Pirate*. Actually, Alton was the senior partner in this collaboration, not Kelly. He allowed the young actor to have a free hand in developing his own numbers and to help Alton in choreographing and supervising the other numbers. As a result, Kelly did end up doing much of the critical choreography in the film as his numbers alone represent the highlights of the movie's dances. Consequently, Freed authorized the addition of Kelly's name to Alton's in the area of dance direction.[37]

The only two dances worked on in preproduction were "Niña" and the "Pirate Ballet." Both had to be planned in great detail—the first mainly in terms of props and the second in terms of the sequence itself.

Kelly wanted a lot of props and set designs to facilitate the creation of his role as Serafin in the "Niña" dance. He needed footholds to give himself a boost up to the second stories of buildings, ledges to dangle on, and slippery poles for sliding back down to ground level. The carousel that serves as the venue for the most intense part of the dance was designed with revolving poles to allow him the opportunity for inventive choreography. Lazarre and Smith were willing to do whatever he required. Arthur Freed too was

68 • Chapter Three

fully supportive, specifically telling Smith to give Kelly whatever he wanted.[38]

The insertion of a ballet into *The Pirate* seems almost to have been a foregone conclusion. Minnelli had been fascinated by the concept since his work on Broadway in the 1930s. He was heavily influenced by surrealism and liked to explore the unreal aspects of reality through dream ballets. Minnelli had done this on the stage, and he had done it again on the screen. The "Limehouse Blues" segment of *Ziegfeld Follies* (1945) and the dream ballet in *Yolanda and the Thief* (1945) are wonderful examples of the "film ballet"—elaborate surrealist dance sequences in film musicals. "It just seemed right in musicals—dream sequences and things like that—to do them in the form of a ballet. Even in dramatic pictures there are dream sequences," Minnelli pointed out in a 1975 interview, citing his own work in *Father of the Bride* (1950). In fact, Minnelli complained that studio bosses did not give him enough latitude to explore this fascinating aspect of filmmaking. "They felt that it would confuse the audience, and things had to be made very clear."[39]

Efforts to chart a course of action for the ballet in *The Pirate* began before Goodrich and Hackett completed the final draft of their screenplay in December 1946. Minnelli and Freed wrote story notes to guide the action as follows. Serafin struts down the main street of Calvados toward Don Pedro's house, with shots of frightened townspeople cowering behind shutters and doors intercut in the sequence. Serafin's costume changes to match whatever fantasy of the pirate each townsperson holds. As Serafin's dance down the street ends, church bells peal and Trillo tells his boss that Pedro and Manuela are getting married, sparking Serafin's desperate ringing of a triangle and his demand that Manuela be delivered to him immediately. Goodrich and Hackett dutifully wrote up this basic idea in the final draft of their screenplay.[40]

Based on this idea, Alton worked up a detailed scenario in January 1947, about three weeks before the onset of filming the movie. Alton's scenario started with Serafin yelling "Macoco!" and proceeded in a series of episodes as Serafin tries to convince the townspeople that he is the real pirate. Although this idea comes from Freed and Minnelli's story notes, Alton envisioned the scenario as taking place in very straightforward, blunt terms: Serafin ties a citizen to a post in the street and sets fire to his beard, but cuts off the beard before the flames injure the man's face. When another man accidentally knocks a flowerpot off a balcony, Serafin becomes enraged, even though the pot misses him. The man throws a spear in self-defense, but Serafin catches it in midair, dances with it, and then throws it into the air. The spear lands point first in the ground near his feet as Serafin again yells, "Macoco!" As Serafin dances around the spear, a woman looks at him and imagines the actor physically growing into a huge monster, to make a heavy-handed point about his threatening character.[41]

Alton went on to suggest more, rather bizarre, antics: Serafin obtains knives from a knife sharpener and throws them in a way so as to pin the dress of a girl to the wall and stop her from fleeing. He throws more knives around her as he dances. He then pulls her from the wall, kisses her, and cuts off her braids before she breaks away and runs for her life. A child then hides in a barrel and Serafin menaces him by reaching into the barrel with a knife. The camera angle shows the actor's bloodthirsty face but also clearly shows that he is only pretending to slash the child. Serafin next goes to Pedro's house, which is guarded by eight soldiers. The actor taunts them. "He snatches off medals, steps on their toes, snaps his fingers in one's eyes, clips off side burns and whiskers," in Alton's words. When they threaten him with guns, "there follows a most exciting and violent ju-jitsu routine," which constitutes the climax of the ballet segment. After defeating the soldiers, Serafin fires the guns, giving the Macoco yell again, before he enters Pedro's house.[42]

It is clear when comparing the Minnelli-Freed-Alton scenario with the finished ballet in *The Pirate* that some drastic changes were made in this extended dance sequence, and it most likely was due to Gene Kelly's influence. Minnelli obviously agreed to the changes. The most important change is that the previous scenario is hardly surrealistic—except for the point about Serafin's growing big in the imagination of the woman observer and the change of costumes to match the townspeople's imagination of a pirate. Additionally, the Alton version is not only crude compared to the Kelly-Minnelli screen version, it is too violent, and bordering on the sadistic, to fit the rest of the film. Kelly understood, and Minnelli agreed, that suggesting violence through symbolic action was better than depicting it through literal action. As a result, they created a dreamlike, or surrealistic, effect for this segment instead of the episodic dance down the street of Calvados that Alton had proposed.

Moreover, the Minnelli-Freed-Alton scenario involved a public

Illustration 3.5. Serafin knocks off the guards' hats in a show of bravado to impress Manuela, who is watching from her bedroom window. This is the prelude to the "Pirate Ballet" as fantasized by Manuela.

performance to convince the townspeople that Serafin really is the pirate. Manuela and the other principal characters were not observers. It would have wound up being like another "Niña," a romp through the streets for public viewing. Kelly and Minnelli wisely crafted an alternative scenario that involved only Manuela's perception (or fantasy) of Serafin, a more appropriate audience of one for this dream ballet. But Kelly and Minnelli retained several aspects from Alton's proposal—the Macoco yell, the idea of Serafin dancing circles around an object (in their case a white mule instead of a spear), and the idea of Serafin dancing *with* the spear as well. In fact, Kelly brings that particular idea to life brilliantly in the ballet. Cutting off the girl's braids, as Alton envisioned, seems to be translated into cutting off the ends of a girl's bandana, and the fight with the guards that Alton described is obviously in the Kelly-Minnelli version but as a prelude to the actual ballet. The final form of the dream ballet was worked out long after filming began. Meanwhile, Freed and others concerned themselves with the songs to grace *The Pirate.*

PORTER AND THE SONGS

Everyone associated with the project felt they had accomplished a coup by convincing Cole Porter to write the songs for the film. He had not been associated with the stage production in any way, and it was not usual for the successful songwriter to work on a brand-new project for Hollywood. Porter's work had centered on stage musicals, but his witty lyrics and easily hummed tunes were tailor made for mass consumption on the silver screen.

Born in Peru, Indiana, on June 9, 1891, Porter grew up with wealth and advantage. His domineering grandfather, J. O. Cole, had made the family fortune in California but continued to live most of his life in Indiana. While J. O. wanted Cole to succeed him as director of the family's fortune, Porter early on developed his skills as a writer. He attended Yale University and wrote his first stage musical, which was produced in 1916 in New York. He served in the ambulance service during World War I and married Linda Lee Thomas in 1919. Thomas was a woman of wealth, traumatized by an abusive first husband and content to live with the worldly, suave Porter in a relationship that many could not understand. It was widely known that Porter was homosexual, and many believed Linda was a lesbian. Porter's biographers tend to conclude that Linda was, at the least, not interested in sex and did not mind her husband's male liaisons as long as they were not too prominently displayed for public view.[43]

Linda encouraged the budding career of her husband, who was eight years younger, and the pair was devoted to each other for many years. By the 1930s, Porter had established himself as a songwriter with sharply defined lyrics that often threatened staid conventions of morality. He had, as a boy, found risqué books for sale in a shop in Peru and admitted that "'some of my lyrics owe a debt to these naughty books.'" Porter usually wrote the lyrics first, then the music, and often worked very fast. One of his most successful songs, "Night and Day," originally written for the stage in *Gay Divorce* (1932), was composed in only two days. Porter also liked to talk producers into letting him name characters in plays for old friends of his, as a nod of appreciation for their friendship.[44]

Personal tragedy struck Porter in October 1937, when a skittish horse he was riding fell on him, resulting in compound fractures of both legs. Porter insisted on painful treatments for the rest of his life rather than amputation, and suffered enormously. But he continued to write and be active in social circles, both of which were important to his life. To facilitate his work in Hollywood, Porter rented a house in 1943, at 416 North Rockingham in Brentwood.[45]

M-G-M hired Porter to write the songs for *The Pirate* for the princely sum of $100,000. As mentioned in Chapter 2, he agreed on the condition that they name the pirate Macoco so Porter could write a song called Mack the Black to acknowledge one of his friends. The studio's willingness to hire Porter at a hefty price underwrote its support of Minnelli as well, because the director "liked to feel that numbers should be given as much importance as dramatic sequences" and sought to weave the songs "into the story completely." Porter wrote the songs for *The Pirate* in 1946, a year in which he was also involved in other projects for which he had high hopes. Early that year, Porter worked with Orson Welles on making a stage musical out of Jules Verne's *Around the World in Eighty Days*. It was a massive undertaking, a greatly overblown production with many problems when it opened on May 31, 1946. Welles had dropped several of Porter's songs, and the songwriter lost interest in the project. He left for California by plane in late May to work on songs for *The Pirate* and returned to New York in early November. Meanwhile, *Night and Day* (1946), a Warner Brothers biographical film about Porter's life with Linda, premiered on August 1, 1946. Although Porter had been involved in this project from the start, he was disappointed with the result. About the same time, *Around the World* closed after only two months on Broadway.[46]

Despite these disappointments, Porter's track record had earned him status and renown, and he often tried to bank on it. But prestige or not, Porter found that the people who were making *The Pirate* did not passively accept whatever he wrote. Porter completed six songs in less than one month while staying in the Los Angeles area during 1946. His first four songs disappointed Freed, who asked for rewrites. Porter graciously agreed to do that. Related to this, Richard Barrios incorrectly concludes that Porter was in a slump when he was brought on board to write the songs for *The Pirate* and that it was Freed's intention that this film could be a comeback for Porter. Mark Griffith echoes this erroneous conclusion and writes that Porter was eager "to take on *The Pirate*" after his *Around the World* failure. There is no primary evidence for any of this. Porter was riding high when he was hired, and this is why he was paid generously. *Around the World* was deemed a failure two months after Porter had left for California to work on *The Pirate* songs, and *Night and*

Day opened around the same time, as mentioned above. In any case, these setbacks did not affect Porter's standing.[47]

Freed's problems with the first four songs are unclear, but an examination of the lyrics in the M-G-M archives provides a possible explanation.[48] Porter wrote twelve verses for "Mack the Black" with a different refrain for each one. In the final version of *The Pirate*, Garland sings only verses 1, 2, and 7 and their related refrains. Actually, these are about the only good verses among the dozen. The nine unused verses have significant problems. There are tortured rhymes in plenty, but that is not the worst of it. There are sexual allusions, for example, "Mack'd wave his cutlass and his cutlass was big," in verse 5. Also, most of the dropped verses are filled with graphic violence. Verse 9 is about mothers singing lullabies to their babies with the lyrics, "If yuh wake and cry or laugh, Mack the Black will whack yuh and he'll whack yuh in half." Another verse added late in 1946 by Porter is about Macoco's setting a ship on fire with people on it, which ends with "What a pretty fun'ral, pretty fun'ral pyre."

It appears that Porter tuned the lyrics of this opening number to the images of graphic violence that both Loos-Than and Goodrich-Hackett had written into the start of the film in their respective screenplays. Fortunately, both the images and the lyrics were dropped, and the only three verses that were salvageable from Porter's song were later used.

By early January 1947, Porter had submitted seven songs to M-G-M's Music Department for *The Pirate*. These included "Love of My Life," "Be a Clown," "You Can Do No Wrong," "Mack the Black," and "Niña." The other two songs, "Voodoo" and "Manuela," were later dropped. According to a memo written by an M-G-M executive, Porter had already received his full $100,000 in the form of loans, and his contract required him to write a "new and complete musical score including all original songs and incidental and background music for our picture."[49] For unexplained reasons, Porter did not write the score or incidental music for the film. Roger Edens performed that important task and also arranged Porter's song scores for M-G-M's orchestra. It is possible that Porter saw no incentive in fulfilling these aspects of his contract because he had already received his full payment.

Regarding the two deleted songs, "Voodoo" was filmed but dropped after negative reaction at the previews. "Manuela" was apparently never incorporated into the film, or even recorded.

A close look at the lyrics in the M-G-M archives helps shed some light on why these two numbers were dropped.[50] Some of the original lyrics for "Voodoo"—for example, "On the topmost tip of a tamarind tree, dwelt a Voodoo God called Jim"—sound inane. And although Porter completely revised the lyrics in early 1947, the preview audience did not like the number. As for "Manuela," one possible reason for dropping the number is revealed by listening to the "guide tracks"—recordings made to aid singing and dubbing. The guide tracks by Roger Edens on the DVD version of *The Pirate* reveal that the song was supposed to be sung by Serafin, but the style of the music does not fit the rest of the songs in the film. Moreover, the lyrics, such as "Manuela tell a fella what to do," are at odds with Serafin's decisive character.

A further look at the lyrics in the M-G-M archives reveals that in the number "You Can Do No Wrong" which Manuela sings to Serafin, Porter's line is "I can barely wait, 'til you make me your permanent date."[51] This line was changed in the film, possibly by Minnelli, because the original line borders on the juvenile and is anachronistic in using the word "date" for the 1800s. In the film the line is "I can barely wait, till I know that we'll share the same fate," which avoids the anachronism and better reflects the maturation of Manuela's character. It also nicely ties to the plot because at this point Manuela is still engaged to Don Pedro and is unsure whether everything will work out for her and Serafin.

PORTER AND KELLY

The story behind Porter's writing of "Be a Clown" involves Gene Kelly. As a young, aspiring dancer on Broadway, Kelly had met Porter while working on *Leave It to Me!*, his first stage show in New York. Kelly had a small, insignificant part, and he spent much of his time between rehearsals reading Aldous Huxley's novel *Point Counter Point*. Porter visited the theater often and became curious about the young man. "'What's that one boy over there doing reading all the time,'" Kelly recalled Porter asking about him. "'The other kids are talking, laughing, and running around. . . . I'd like to know what he's reading.'" Robert Alton introduced them, and a lifelong acquaintance developed.[52]

Kelly wanted a peppy song for a segment of *The Pirate*, "a *lift* number," as he called it, because "everything had gotten too classy and elegant." He consulted Freed, who suggested that Kelly go to Porter's house on North Rockingham to pitch the idea to him.

Edens normally would have performed this task, but he was in the middle of a row with Porter about the arrangement of "Niña." Porter sat in a corner of the room as Kelly explained what he needed, and the next day called Kelly back to the house to hear the result. "When he was through, he turned to me and asked me whether it was the sort of thing I had in mind," Kelly recalled nearly thirty years later. "Had in mind! It surpassed anything I could have imagined. It was brilliant. Each verse was more stunning than the last." Kelly showed the song to Freed and Minnelli. They liked it as much as Kelly had and decided to use it twice in the film. For Porter, "Be a Clown" brought back memories of his fascination with the circus as a boy in Peru, Indiana. In fact, at one time he had wanted to become a circus performer.[53]

Porter did far better work on "Be a Clown" than on "Mack the Black." In comparing the verses in the M-G-M archives with the songs used in the film, there are nine unused verses out of twelve for "Mack the Black" but only one unused verse out of the five that Porter wrote for "Be a Clown."

Kelly believed that in quickly writing "Be a Clown," Porter had deliberately kept the music within a range of notes comfortable for Kelly's voice. Although Porter never mentioned this, Kelly appreciated the gesture a great deal. Porter did mention to Kelly years later that he would have liked to have infused more West Indian flavor into the music of "Niña." Kelly concluded that his own somewhat limited singing ability was the likely reason Porter did not attempt it, and he felt bad. Kelly thought, however, that he could have handled the spice if Porter had given it to him.[54]

However, Kelly shortchanged his own singing talent. He was not a world-class vocalist, but his singing was fine and very appealing to audiences. Comparing his performance with the way Roger Edens sang the same songs on the guide tracks of *The Pirate* DVD makes Kelly's talent abundantly clear.

Approving the Lyrics

It was necessary to submit the song lyrics for review by the Breen office. That process for *The Pirate* started in late July 1946 and continued as Porter completed each song. Strangely, Joseph Breen approved the lyrics for "Mack the Black" in July, despite the somewhat suggestive tone of some phrases. It is possible he did not notice the sexual innuendos and was unfazed by the violence, given the context of pirates. He passed on the lyrics for "Voodoo" and "Manuela" in August and for "You Can Do No Wrong" the next month. Breen had no difficulty with "Be a Clown" when the lyrics were sent to his office on October 31, or with "Love of My life" in early November.[55]

But Breen did have a problem with the lyrics for "Niña." As he informed Louis B. Mayer in late August, "the repeated expression, 'Till I make yuh, till I make yuh, etc. etc.,' is unacceptable because of its sex-suggestiveness and could not be approved." The studio submitted the lyrics again, apparently with some minor changes, in early November. Breen again found fault with this line, which, as he put it, "must not be read suggestively." The studio submitted the lyrics a third time, in mid-November, and this time Breen passed on them.[56]

It is unclear exactly why Breen changed his mind, for the song still contains the suggestive line in the final version of *The Pirate*. It is possible that Edens was willing to shorten the number of times the line was repeated to win Breen's reluctant approval.

GARLAND'S TROUBLES DURING PREPRODUCTION

Garland began to prerecord the songs on December 27, 1946, starting with "Love of My Life." She followed with "Mack the Black" the next day, but neither recording was satisfactory. The former was dull and the second one shrill, and both had to be redone.[57]

Garland had already caused delays and difficulties in the final weeks leading up to the start of filming. Internal M-G-M memos sent by Al Shenberg, the production manager for *The Pirate*, show different reasons offered for these delays and reveal the difficulties they caused. For example, the studio asked Garland to come in for costume fitting on November 6, almost a month before she was to report for work on December 2. Garland's secretary called the Wardrobe Department on November 6 and reported that she was too ill to come in, but she would try the next day. On December 5, three days after officially reporting for work, Garland again missed her costume fittings due to illness. This time, her mother, Ethel, called in for her. Two days later the star failed to report at all, and when the studio called her home, Ethel told the staff member that Judy was still asleep "because the alarm clock failed to ring." On December 17, Garland's maid called the studio to report that her boss would not be in that day. No, she was not ill, it was "just that she couldn't make it." Minnelli called in for his wife on December 30 to explain that she was not feeling well. Judy called in sick herself on January 31, 1947. On February 14, Garland reported so late to Wardrobe that a fitter had to work overtime "to take care of her."[58]

On some of the days that she did report, Garland was given permission to do other work instead. She performed on radio broadcasts several days in late 1946 and early 1947, and Kelly also received permission for this kind of work outside the studio during the same period.[59]

APPROVING THE SCREENPLAY

Joseph Breen had a good deal of difficulty with the overall content of *The Pirate,* as seen in Chapter 2. When the studio initially submitted the Behrman play for his review in January 1944, as well as when it finally submitted Mankiewicz's screenplay in February 1946, he voiced his objection to the idea of a married woman's falling in love with a man other than her husband. The screenplay versions that were created later overcame this problem, but the studio did not submit any of them to Breen except the first draft of the Goodrich-Hackett script in September 1946. Breen's original objection about "adultery" was no longer relevant, but he warned the studio to be careful about costumes for the female roles, and he wanted the Wardrobe Department to make sure that Manuela was "quite properly covered." Breen also did not like the "rather brutal" scenes slated to start the film and designed to establish the legend of Macoco. "There seems to be quite a slaughter of older women and others in these opening scenes," he sarcastically commented and suggested they be rewritten.[60]

Indeed, the Goodrich-Hackett screenplay began in a way similar to Loos and Than's, with Macoco and his pirates. One difference was that the pirates pretend to be women in distress and then they attack their rescuers. More scenes of violence follow. As the pirates drag young women, kill older women, and throw men into fiery infernos, "Mack the Black" is sung in the background. Macoco appears in every scene, but his face is hidden. Minnelli dropped this entire sequence in response to Breen's objection, and it was never filmed.

Breen also had difficulty with several lines in the script. "We must ask that Serafin definitize the purpose for which he wants Manuela brought to him," so as to dispel the assumption "that the girl is going to sacrifice her virtue." He wanted the studio to cut several lines that bordered on sexual suggestiveness, including Manuela's "I shan't even mind not being the first." Breen recommended rewrites for several other lines, such as Manuela's "Women can't resist you, can they?" and Serafin's "You're supposed to be sacrificing yourself to me."[61]

M-G-M made many of the changes that Breen suggested and submitted the rewrites for approval in November 1946 and even in February 1947, after Goodrich and Hackett were off the project. These changes met Breen's interpretation of the Production Code and were approved. But the studio balked at a couple of changes that Breen felt strongly about. As late as February 19, two days after the start of filming, Breen scolded the studio for again failing to clarify or, as he put it, "definitize," why Serafin wants Manuela brought to him. He suggested they could skirt the problem by changing the line so that Serafin would be "requesting that she be brought to a banquet." Minnelli still had not changed Serafin's line, "You're supposed to be sacrificing yourself to me," and Breen insisted that it be done "because of its direct pointedness." In the end, Minnelli did drop the latter line but retained Serafin's demand for Manuela with little change. In fact, even the village elders praise Manuela for her "sacrifice." Nevertheless, M-G-M got away with all this in the form of overall approval by the Breen office when the film was released.[62]

Script Revisions during Preproduction

In addition to dropping the violent beginning in deference to Breen, several changes were made to Goodrich and Hackett's script during preproduction. For example, Goodrich and Hackett had retained scenes from earlier scripts about Serafin's troupe complaining of hunger and Serafin's lackadaisical response to this. Instead, Minnelli and Kelly planned Serafin's first appearance on screen to be dramatic and virile as he leaps onto Manuela's trousseau box while it is being hoisted above the crowd at Port Sebastian. The scene has obvious implications for the plot. Serafin's riding high on Manuela's trousseau box foreshadows his stopping her upcoming marriage to Don Pedro and winning her for himself.

Goodrich and Hackett deserve credit for having Serafin awaken Manuela from her trance with a kiss. In Behrman's play, Serafin simply passes his hands over Manuela's face and talks of their love. Serafin's kiss is analogous to the fairytale Prince Charming's kiss to awaken Sleeping Beauty—because it is the only thing

Illustration 3.6. Serafin is about to kiss Manuela to awaken her from her hypnosis. This touch was added by Goodrich and Hackett and enhanced by Minnelli to symbolize the awakening of Manuela's passion for Serafin. Note the ethnically mixed audience.

that snaps Manuela out of her hypnosis. However, the Goodrich-Hackett script does not indicate that Manuela responds to the kiss, other than to wake up. Minnelli's added touch was for Manuela to react passionately, suggesting that Serafin's kiss not only awakens Manuela but also awakens her passion for him.

In the Goodrich-Hackett script, Serafin asks Inez, Capucho, and Manuela for assurance that they will keep his true identity as the pirate secret before he lets them go. Minnelli and Kelly realized that this did not fit with the bravado of the Macoco character that Serafin was trying to create. Also, it was illogical because Serafin talks to the townspeople shortly afterward, posing as Macoco. Understandably, the scene was dropped.

Goodrich and Hackett placed Manuela next to Pedro for Serafin's "last" performance so she could urge him to look into the revolving mirror. With good directorial insight, Minnelli placed Pedro far away from the family and the Viceroy, for dramatic visual effect in the scenes that follow.

Minnelli also added a scene in which Serafin persuades the Viceroy to let him perform before the momentous event of his hanging by using the analogy of a sumptuous banquet that should be savored, not pounced upon like a peasant. Even in their early notes, Freed and Minnelli had wanted Serafin to win over the Viceroy through flattery. This scene helps to establish the basic character of the Viceroy and also allows Serafin to attempt his plan to hypnotize Don Pedro into revealing that he is Macoco.

The screenwriters had Pedro draw two pistols before he leaps onto the stage yelling, "Macoco." As he is about to fire at Serafin, the latter "releases the rope that holds the trap door," and "Don Pedro, guns blazing harmlessly, drops out of sight, with a strangled roar." Instead, as fans of the film know, Pedro jumps onto the stage, rants and raves, and then pulls out two pistols. There is no trap door; Serafin disables Macoco by throwing Indian clubs at him, after which bustling troupe members subdue the pirate. It appears that Minnelli and Kelly changed this sequence to highlight Kelly's prowess in throwing the clubs rapidly and accurately and to allow Serafin, the consummate actor, to point to the action as if it is part of his performance.

Goodrich and Hackett had Serafin sing to Manuela as he came across the rope to her balcony. Minnelli dropped this idea because the ropewalking scene needed to move fast in order to be effective. The screenwriters also had Serafin's entire troupe sing "Be a Clown" to end the film, with Manuela simply as part of the troupe. Minnelli dropped the other troupe members to make the final number a duo for Serafin and Manuela. This change not only led to a memorable number but allowed for the unique ending of the film—a close-up of Kelly and Garland laughing naturally, as themselves.

Supporting Cast

M-G-M had a stable of stock players to provide actors for bit parts in the films the studio churned out—at the rate of about sixty a year in the immediate postwar era. Many of them were veteran character actors who appeared in several films every year. The studio also had contracts with actors who had worked their way up the career ladder in roles that more closely supported the principal players. As a result, *The Pirate* did not lack good actors and actresses who could provide sharply defined characters, even if those characters appeared only briefly on the screen. (See Appendix C for mini-biographies of everyone who played a part, however small, in the creation of *The Pirate*.)

Selecting the right person to play the real pirate was crucial to the success of the film. Jack Smart had started as Estramudo in the Lunt-Fontanne stage play. But he was not considered menacing enough in the off-Broadway run, so Alan Reed replaced him for the New York performances. M-G-M selected Walter Slezak for this critical role. Born in Vienna on May 3, 1902, the son of a famed operatic tenor of Czech heritage, Slezak made his first visit to the United States at age seven when his father fulfilled an engagement to sing at the Metropolitan Opera. Back in Europe, Slezak initially intended to study medicine. According to his own story, the twenty-year-old student met director Michael Curtiz at a beer garden and from that chance encounter was steered into an acting career. He gained success playing romantic leads on stage and in German films during the 1920s until gaining so much weight that he was forced to do character roles.[63]

Slezak came to the United States in 1929 and, after quickly learning English, found renewed success on Broadway. A multitalented man who enjoyed painting and playing the piano, he had a good sense of humor and a facility for quickly establishing a character. By 1942, when his Broadway career had hit a slump, director-producer Leo McCary brought him to Hollywood for film work. Slezak achieved his greatest success playing the heavy in *Once Upon a Honeymoon* (1942) and *The Princess and the Pirate* (1944). He came most prominently to the attention of moviegoers with a riveting performance in his third film, Alfred Hitchcock's *Life Boat* (1944). Slezak played the arrogant skipper of a German U-Boat who tries to dominate a lifeboat filled with the survivors of a ship he has just destroyed. He spoke only German in the film.[64] The role demonstrated his ability to handle serious, as well as comical, parts.

The German skipper exemplified the type of role Slezak excelled at creating, the smart, suave, bad guy, or, as the publicity men at Twentieth Century-Fox put it, a "glamour villain." At six feet tall and 240 pounds, he looked the part. "He also eats enormously," according to a publicity release from Paramount, "things like limburger cheese by the half-pound, cherry pie by the pan, corn on the cob by the dozen and onion soup by the tureen." He married Dutch-born singer Johanna van Rijn in 1943 and enjoyed visits to the farm in Bucks County, Pennsylvania, that he had purchased in the 1930s. By the time M-G-M slated him to portray its pirate, Slezak had to deal with the declining health and death of his beloved father. He traveled to Germany in the summer of 1946 but arrived too late for a last visit with him. Visa problems forced the actor to return by a roundabout way before reaching the United States but he was well in time for the filming of *The Pirate*. His second child, Erika, was born in Hollywood, in August 1946, and later became a well-known soap opera star on television.[65]

M-G-M publicity writers asserted that Slezak did not mind playing a pirate for the fourth time in his film career. Actually, Slezak had acted in three prior films about pirates and had played the heavy in each of them but not the role of a pirate. It is true, however, that he was content to portray bad guys with a twist. "Its [*sic*] more profitable being a bad man," he said. "After all screen heroes can go on just so long. But a movie villain can go on forever." Slezak told a reporter in 1958 that character acting was harder than playing the male lead. "I know, because 20 years and a hundred pounds ago I used to play leading men in Germany and New York. I was nauseatingly beautiful and only played lover boys until I was forced at 33 into character parts—and, believe, me, I learned to act."[66]

The studio selected Gladys Cooper to play the role of Aunt Inez, Manuela's comically matriarchal aunt. Born on December 18, 1888, in Lewisham, England, Cooper began acting in her teenage years and became something of a demure pinup model before and during World War I. In fact, thousands of British soldiers considered her the ultimate postcard girl. She performed in her first film in 1917 but preferred stage acting for many years, traveling occasionally to the United States for some of her stage roles. Not until 1939 did Cooper go to Hollywood for a small part in Hitchcock's *Rebecca* (1940), and at that point she decided to stay and make films her main source of income.[67]

Cooper took an unconventional approach to her screen acting. A self-assured, dignified lady who was a product of the British stage, she always felt a bit uneasy with her screen persona. When viewing the rushes of herself in *Rebecca*, Cooper was shocked at the experience. "'What I saw was a hump-backed creature in an ill-fitting tweed suit, out of whose mouth such a frightful grating noise was coming that I thought at first something must have gone mechanically wrong. That *can't* be me, I said to myself. But it was. And in horror I walked out.'" Cooper rarely saw any of her own films and was happy merely to learn her lines without involving herself in the rest of the film's story. Her detached attitude toward film work did not hamper her career, for the English lady role was widely popular in Hollywood in the postwar era.[68]

As work on *The Pirate* loomed on the horizon, Cooper's personal life reached a traumatic crisis. Her third husband, the English actor Philip Merivale, became ill and passed away on March 12, 1946. Her previous marriages had ended in divorce, and she had several children and stepchildren. Despite her loss, she soldiered on with her work on *The Pirate* without a murmur.[69]

Veteran character actor Reginald Owen agreed to play the advocate, a small but significant role in *The Pirate*. It is the advocate who spearheads the citizens' effort to convince Manuela to save the town by offering herself to the supposedly bloodthirsty pirate. Owen was another English actor who found a niche in Hollywood. Born in Wheathamstead, on August 5, 1887, he gained experience on the stage and in British and French films before coming to the United States in 1923 for a Broadway career. His movie work began in 1929. Owen was a contract player with M-G-M from 1935 on, and perhaps his best role was as Scrooge in the studio's version of *A Christmas Carol* in 1938.[70]

George Zucco filled the prominent role of the Viceroy in *The Pirate*. He was another English expatriate, born on January 11, 1886, in Manchester. Of Greek heritage, Zucco served as a lieutenant in the British army during World War I and was shot in the right arm. Subsequent surgery could not fully restore the use of two fingers and the thumb of his right hand—it shows in some scenes of *The Pirate*. Zucco returned to the British stage after the war. He first engaged in film work in England and traveled to the United States in 1935. His forte in Hollywood was not only the authority figure but the master villain such as Professor Moriarty in *The Adventures of Sherlock Holmes* (1939). The crew at Universal Studios called him "One Take Zucco" to honor his facility for getting the character right immediately.[71]

The most innovative casting decision for *The Pirate* was Freed's and Kelly's desire to use the Nicholas Brothers. Fayard and Harold Nicholas had achieved fame as a pair of specialty dancers in a succession of films marketed to both black and white audiences. Born of parents who were jazz musicians (Fayard in Mobile, Alabama, in 1914 and Harold in Winston-Salem, North Carolina, in 1921), the brothers danced as children under the name, The Nicholas Kids. By 1929 they were performing professionally and appeared in their first film in 1932, the same year they appeared at the Cotton Club in Harlem.[72]

The brothers reached a peak in their career in the 1940s, but their dance routines were difficult for scholars to classify. They mixed a wide range of dance steps and devised acrobatic stunts with help from choreographers like Nick Castle to enliven the steps. Their somewhat bizarre mix of moves often appears to be less a dance routine and more an exhibition of physical agility. Fayard described the routine in a 1988 interview: "When we tapped, we added a little ballet to it, plus a little eccentric, a little flash, and we used our hands a great deal. With style and grace we used the whole body from our heads down to our toes." It was "the lacing together of tap, balletic leaps and turns, and dazzling acrobatics" that seemed to define the brothers' success, according to their biographer.[73]

The Nicholas Brothers were among the relatively few black performers whose work could be seen in films with white actors, designed for distribution primarily to white audiences. The brothers' spectacular performances enabled them to cross the race barrier in entertainment, at least to a limited degree. Their routines were inserted ad hominem in these white films as discrete segments that wowed audiences, but their characters were never seen again in the film. In this way, the segment could easily be clipped from the distribution prints sent by the studio to theaters in the segregated South if necessary. As long as the brothers were not seen touching or talking to whites in the film, they could enjoy furtive appearances in white films. Only rarely did this vary. Fayard was proud of the fact that he and Harold had extended roles in *The Big Broadcast of 1936* (1935), with dialogue and character development, so that their dances could not so easily be excised.[74]

With a career spent crossing the race line, Fayard Nicholas often spoke about respect and equality. He and Harold wanted to be accepted for their talent rather than constricted by the color of their skin, and they insisted on staying in good hotels and being allowed to socialize with anyone they chose. The brothers wanted to demonstrate that black Americans could live in style and with a degree of class. These feelings intensified to the point that Fayard often suffused his later interviews with self-praise: "'My brother and I, we were doing our thing long before we saw Fred Astaire, and long before there was a Gene Kelly.'"[75]

Kelly played the key role in selecting the Nicholas Brothers for *The Pirate*. He had developed a sensitivity to any form of racial or ethnic prejudice in his days as a student at the University of Pittsburgh, where segregated fraternities for Catholics, Jews, and Prot-

Illustration 3.7. Kelly's daring pose—not just touching but physically (and symbolically) supporting the Nicholas Brothers in "Be a Clown"—challenges racial conventions in the 1940s. Note that Harold even has his foot wrapped around Kelly's neck.

estants were the norm. Kelly and some friends tried to break down that system and failed, but the experience created a lifelong abhorrence in him for any form of discrimination. Moreover, Kelly often talked about a certain attitude among truly professional performers that impelled them to respect anyone who had talent, regardless of their race or ethnicity.[76]

Freed supported Kelly's desire to use the brothers and pointed out that *The Pirate* was a good vehicle. The Lunt-Fontanne stage production had a multiracial cast, and Minnelli had also established his preference for a color-blind approach to this film by mixing people of all races in the crowd scenes. According to Fayard, Kelly had long wanted to work with the brothers but could not find "the right story. He didn't want us to come on like we were servants, and all of a sudden I'm whistling and tapping a little bit, and he says, 'That's nice, how do you do that?'" To a degree, the Caribbean setting of *The Pirate* helped to obviate that difficulty. According to Fayard, "There was nothing American in it, so you couldn't think about prejudice and all that jazz." The brothers would play members of Serafin's troupe and perform a dance with Kelly, breaking the tradition of not allowing blacks to perform in dance routines with whites. M-G-M offered the brothers a contract in January 1947 shortly before filming began. They were to report for work about mid-March and were guaranteed eight weeks, with the studio paying their travel expenses to California. Late in his life, Fayard spoke appreciatively of Kelly's and Freed's efforts to help him and Harold.[77]

It may be difficult to appreciate this casting decision from the standpoint of the early twenty-first century, but it was a daring statement within the context of 1947. Previous films marketed to white audiences had done a poor job of bringing any hint of the equality of races into the all-white world on the screen. Successful black actors took on roles as porters, janitors, maids, slaves, or comics, often using squeaky voices and personifying laziness to make audiences laugh and to gain acceptance. These stereotypical roles, with "cheerful and shameless subservience to whites in films" and "bug-eyed expressions," were the key to their success. Richard Maynard gives several examples of black stereotypes used in the 1930s and 1940s: in *The Prisoner of Shark Island* (1936), black prison guards were "portrayed as grotesquely subhuman"; in *Ghost Breakers* (1940), a Bob Hope comedy, Willie Best was used as a stereotypical scared "darkie," providing many gags; *The Charlie Chan Series* (1931–1949) often used Mantan Moreland for "his ability to roll his eyes to show fear."[78]

In addition, there had been a bizarre trend for white musical performers to don blackface in the early 1940s. Judy Garland and Mickey Rooney did it in *Babes on Broadway* (1942), an Arthur Freed production, and Bing Crosby did it in *Holiday Inn* (1942) to celebrate Lincoln's birthday. In both cases, the results appear nothing less than hideous from today's perspective. Against this background, the tasteful way in which Freed and Kelly planned to use the Nicholas Brothers in *The Pirate* was remarkable.

Preproduction for *The Pirate* took much longer than usual for a motion picture at M-G-M, according to Minnelli.[79] But finally, everything was worked out—the sets, the props, the costumes, the dances, the songs, the approvals, and the casting of supporting roles. After more than a year in preproduction, *The Pirate* was ready for filming in February 1947.

CHAPTER FOUR

Filming Challenges

Filming of *The Pirate* began on February 17, 1947, with the opening scenes of Manuela, her friends, and Aunt Inez on the patio of Manuela's home. Minnelli continued shooting those scenes the next day, in addition to scenes that took place in Manuela's bedroom. The first daily rushes were shot beautifully by Harry Stradling, the cinematographer on the project, and Minnelli was pleased.[1]

Internal M-G-M memos reveal that even though production had started, many details associated with hiring additional cast and crew members, and with Kelly's schedule, still had to be sorted out. Kelly rehearsed and prerecorded some of his numbers for up to three weeks after the start of filming. He had suffered a sprain while rehearsing, sometime prior to this point, which set back his schedule a bit. Walter Slezak generously agreed to give one week free to the production if he was called for added scenes or retakes within two weeks after he completed principal photography. Lenny Hayton was hired starting February 25 to help with musical arrangements. Character actors were lined up for prominent secondary roles starting in March. The studio hired Ben Lessy for the role of Trillo (one of Serafin's two main assistants) at $750 a week. Cully Richards was signed on for the role of Esteban (also a troupe member) at $1,000 a week. O. Z. Whitehead was hired to play Hurtado (one of the citizens) at $500 a week. In April, M-G-M recruited Lester Allen at $600 a week for the role of Manuela's Uncle Capucho, which placed him prominently in the visual field but offered him only two short lines. George Zucco was hired in May and received $1,500 a week to create the role of the Viceroy.[2]

It appears that the roles for the character actors were switched around from what was mentioned in the M-G-M memos. Ben Lessy played Gumbo (a troupe member) and Cully Richards played Trillo. O. Z. Whitehead played the prominent role of Coutat (the other of Serafin's two main assistants), but he did not receive on-screen credit.

GARLAND

Judy Garland was a source of delay and vexation from the start of filming. In past projects, she had often not shown up for work but seemed to have a sense of how many days she could do this without upsetting the overall schedule too much. Now she seemed to have lost touch with that sense. She and Minnelli fought more often as soon as filming began, and both sought refuge at the home of Ira and Lee Gershwin when they felt the pressure was too much at their own house. The Gershwins offered a spare bed to either one whenever they asked. Minnelli also felt trapped in the middle when dealing with Garland's repeated refusals to go to the studio. As her husband, he wanted to be supportive, but as her director, he later regretted that he was not more demanding of her. "These were agonizing times," Minnelli remembered.[3]

Al Shenberg, the production manager, kept careful records of how many days Garland missed. As during preproduction, either her mother or secretary, and sometimes her maid, called in to report that the actress felt ill and could not come in to work. Or, she arrived much later than expected without any notice. Filming of the "Voodoo" number and wardrobe fittings for Judy were postponed thirteen times because of such delays.[4]

Minnelli also called in for his wife. On February 22, he phoned Wally Worsley, the assistant director, to say that he and Judy had been on their way to the Culver City studio but she suddenly felt too ill to work, so they returned home. Garland was "nervously exhausted and run down after spending a sleepless night," in Worsley's words. Consequently, "Company call for today was cancelled," as Shenberg informed Freed. On the morning of February 27, Kelly called to report that his wife was quite ill and he preferred to be with her most of the day. But he promised to arrive at 2 p.m. to rehearse the "Voodoo" number with Garland. Minnelli, who also seems to have taken the day off, called at 2 p.m. to say that Garland was too ill to perform, but she would come to the studio to watch the company rehearse "Voodoo." Kelly arrived at 2 p.m. but Garland did not show up at all, and no explanation was offered. The actress continued to call in sick for many days to come, and each time rehearsals for "Voodoo" were canceled. Alton and Kelly worked instead on "Niña" on some of these days, but the company simply went home on other days that Garland failed to report for work. On May 19, Garland and Minnelli started for Culver City but returned when she felt unable to work, just as she had three months earlier, forcing the studio once again to dismiss the entire production crew for the day.[5]

The reports filed by Worsley indicate that production of *The Pirate* was shut down for at least twelve days because of Garland. Despite efforts to keep drugs away from her, she was quite inventive in her efforts to circumvent the blockade. On May 26, Garland called Dr. Jones, the studio physician, to her dressing room and told him she had a toothache and needed pain pills. The doctor complied without question and Garland continued to work that day.[6]

Kelly reportedly covered for Garland as much as he could. According to Hugh Fordin, he pretended to be ill for a week to give her an extended opportunity for rest. It is true that Kelly missed June 12–14 and June 16, 20, and 21 because of illness. Whether he pretended to be ill for Garland's sake or truly was sick is impossible to know. Kelly regularly caught some bug and missed several days of work during production of other films as well. Kelly also took advantage of Garland's absences to finish some filming for another movie, *Living in a Big Way* (1947).[7]

Despite their deep friendship and Kelly's efforts to understand and support her, Garland began to feel jealous of his role in the production phase of *The Pirate*. Kelly and Minnelli were absorbed in their work and enjoying the most stimulating collaboration of either man's career. Garland resented the time they spent together on the set. Minnelli later saw this as an unfortunate development that he could have avoided, writing, "We excluded her from our discussions. I'd felt it wasn't necessary for Judy to have to deal with such problems, but she felt neglected." Mark Griffith, in his book on Minnelli, twists this professional jealousy that Judy felt, recorded in Minnelli's interviews as well as by Garland's biographers, into a baseless assertion that "Judy accused Vincente of having an affair with Gene." There is no evidence in any primary or secondary material for such a presumption on Griffith's part.[8]

Garland tried to break up this collaborative union by insisting that Kelly stage her musical numbers. Minnelli recalled that "Gene helped as much as he could. He was caught up in a domestic squabble, and tried not to offend either one of us." But Garland came to realize, according to Minnelli, that "she was being unreasonable, and her negative mood abruptly changed." Despite that, "an unspoken barrier remained between us," Minnelli wrote in his memoirs. "How had we come to this state of affairs where suddenly I could do nothing right in Judy's eyes?"[9]

The Kelly-Minnelli collaboration was a wonderful experience for both men. It was "the most intense professional association I'd ever had with an actor," wrote the director. "One idea would meld into another, and little difference who started the train of thought. I wondered aloud why our talents complemented each other's to such an extraordinary degree. 'It's because my approach is less esoteric and more gutsy,' Gene said, 'while yours is evanescent and ethereal.'" Kelly had been choreographing his own numbers from the start of the project, but as filming progressed he "became involved in all facets of production." Minnelli still recalled their collaboration with awe as late as 1980, only six years before his death. "Working with Gene was wonderful . . . wonderful. He understood what I wanted to say without my having to say it. He was as crazy about work as I was."[10]

A wife who was emotionally self-confident would not have felt threatened by such a collaboration between her husband and her friend, but Garland could not accommodate Kelly's intense working relationship with Minnelli. Her biographers have agreed that Garland turned on Minnelli with a vengeance during the filming of *The Pirate,* and for several different reasons. She accused her husband of giving the film to Kelly as a vehicle for his talents rather than for her own. At the same time, Stephen Harvey believes that Garland now resented Minnelli's efforts to shape and nurture her acting, efforts she had previously accepted and encouraged. Gerald Clarke believes Garland also resented Minnelli's role regarding her signing a new contract with M-G-M. She felt trapped by her own reluctance to face the camera, yet was urged on by her husband-director, who seemed to have become more of a studio whip than a supportive spouse.[11] Her efforts to find a strong, protective man to substitute for her father seemed to have failed with Minnelli.

Garland was experiencing the worst personal crisis of her working life thus far, and started to see sixty-five-year-old Dr. Ernest Simmel on a regular basis early in 1947. She seemed to trust him, but confessed to hairdresser Dorothy Ponedel, who was also a close friend, that she sometimes invented horror stories for his benefit, overemphasizing things done to her as a child. When he learned of Garland's troubles, Louis B. Mayer hired a psychoanalyst to be on the set. Dr. Frederick Hacker went on the M-G-M salary list and reported for work every day. Hacker was ready to offer advice, and he even watched the daily rushes with the other cast and crew members.[12] It may well have been the first time that a psychiatrist became a regular part of a film studio's labor force.

Hacker's presence failed to shore up Garland's fragile emotional state. She became convinced that someone, either the studio or her mother, was tapping her phone conversations. One day, when Hedda Hopper visited the set of *The Pirate,* Garland became hysterical with anxiety about the eavesdropping and had to be carried home. Louella Parsons broke the news of Garland's emotional state in her newspaper column on July 12, 1947, describing it as "'a complete nervous collapse.'"[13]

Lela Simone's view of all these troubles was sharp and uncompromising. The German-born musician thought Garland looked "emaciated" and on the verge of collapse almost every day. The production crew could not rely on her to show up, much less to perform in a way that would ensure progress in filming. "We never knew what we were going to shoot the next day, which track was going to be used, the new one, the old one," Simone said. The uncertainty created enormous stress among dozens of crew members who were committed to a tight production schedule. "It was awful," Simone recalled in 1990. "It was a nightmare."[14]

At times, Garland could joke about her addiction to pills. One evening before dinner at their house, Goodrich and Hackett recalled that Garland arrayed an assortment of pills on the table and said, "'I'll have one of those, and one of those, and one of those.'" But there was no joking on another day when she arrived at the Culver City studio in near hysterics and accosted the crew members and extras, saying, "Give me marijuana!," as Lela Simone rather dramatically recalled. According to Simone, Minnelli had to grab Garland "very sharply" by the wrist and take her to a studio car for transport home. That shut down production for the day. Simone mentioned that there were many days when Garland was on the set and worked well, but there were many other days that were hellish.[15] Shenberg and Worsley kept Freed up to date on Garland's repeated absences, but he apparently knew little about the more sordid side of her troubles on the set.

A persistent rumor has floated for decades about an incident in Garland's personal life during the filming of *The Pirate.* One day on returning home, she allegedly found Minnelli in bed with a man of her acquaintance. Garland reportedly tried to slash her wrists but Minnelli stopped her from doing too much damage. She appeared at the studio the next day with bandages on her arms and is said to have confided to a friend what had happened. This salacious story appeals to many readers, and thus a number of authors have accepted it at face value. But no one has ever identified the source of the story or offered anything in the way of proof. Garland's latest biographer, Gerald Clarke, takes it for granted that Minnelli was gay, names several of his purported male lovers, and fully believes this story. Minnelli's latest biographer, Emanuel Levy, refers to him as bisexual but does not mention the story at all. Garland's daughters, Liza Minnelli and Lorna Luft, insist that Minnelli was neither gay nor bisexual.[16]

Regardless of whether Garland found her husband in bed with another man, there is no doubt that their marriage broke apart during the filming of *The Pirate*. Clarke puts the worst spin on this issue, referring to them as "an odd and, in the long run, ill-matched couple," separated in age by twenty years and held together only by their work and their daughter.[17]

The Garland-Minnelli marriage can be viewed as something more positive than Clarke's assessment. The couple had a strong, mutually supportive relationship before 1947, but it was threatened by a resurgence of Garland's drug problem, a monster she could never control. Another monster that also endangered the marriage was Garland's lack of emotional self-assurance when assaulted by doubts regarding her relationships with men. Kelly's collaboration with Minnelli threatened Garland in ways that Kelly could not have foreseen and, given his respect and friendship for both Minnelli and Garland, in ways that would have troubled him deeply if he had realized what was happening underneath the surface.

It needs to be stressed that, on the days she was feeling well and on the set, Garland performed magnificently. The film could not have been made if not for this blessing. In fact, she probably performed better in *The Pirate* than in any movie she had yet made—and in a comparatively unfamiliar role tinged with a great deal of sly comedy. Garland never looked better on film than she did in this picture, thanks largely to Minnelli and Stradling, and her pairing with Kelly was, as always, memorable.

It is ironic that she experienced so much personal turmoil and yet delivered such a good performance. It is possible that, by this stage of her life and career, Garland needed either an environment of crisis or some type of external challenge to force her to dig down deep and give her best performance.

When filming *In the Good Old Summertime* (1949), producer Joe Pasternak tried to keep Garland on schedule by arranging for the property man to leave a red rose in her dressing room with a card saying, "Happy day, Judy." This daily ritual, from an anonymous friend as far as Judy knew, worked well. She sailed through the production schedule without trouble, and the film was successful commercially.[18]

But *In the Good Old Summertime* compares poorly with *Shop Around the Corner* (1940), an M-G-M product upon which it was based, and Garland's performance is far from her best. In fact, she moves about so poorly while singing "I Don't Care" that one wonders if dance director Robert Alton was taking a break when it was filmed. There is nothing wrong with Garland's vocalization in this number, but her attempts to "dance" as an accompaniment to the vocals lack grace, charm, and appeal. Apparently, she needed something more than comforting compliments to create memorable numbers on the screen. In *The Pirate,* Garland was surrounded by top-notch talent that drew something extra from her when it was time to roll the cameras. While Van Johnson and her other colleagues on the set of *In the Good Old Summertime* were talented, they did not have the ability to draw that extra something out of Garland. She was as good as she was in *The Pirate* precisely because of the talent present on the set (especially Minnelli and Kelly) of that memorable film. Overcoming her personal crises during the filming may have also helped her to find something in herself that brightened her depiction of Manuela.

Minnelli marveled at his wife's talent long after they parted. "You might tell her twenty things to change in this performance, . . . and you didn't know whether you were getting through to her or not. But everything would be perfect. She would remember everything. She was fantastic." Minnelli enjoyed working with his wife, for she understood "that there were different ways of playing a scene." Yet, according to Stephen Harvey, *The Pirate* ended up as "the most emotionally taxing film of his whole career" for Minnelli and a "trouble-ridden project from the start" due to all the troubles with Garland.[19]

"Niña"

"Niña" was the first musical number to be filmed. Although no one has mentioned this, "Niña" is the Spanish word for *girl,* making it the perfect title for a dance in which Serafin is energetically pursuing a large number of beautiful girls in the heart of Port Sebastian. But Minnelli and Kelly pretended not to know the meaning of Niña.

Illustration 4.1. Kelly leaps acrobatically to climb a wall during the "Niña" number as the barber and the man being shaved dodge him. Art director Smith had walked around with Kelly to precisely plan the footholds Kelly needed for his acrobatic moves.

When the barber asks Serafin right before the dance why he calls all the girls Niña, Kelly shrugs and says "Why not?" They probably decided to go for laughs instead of informing the audience how appropriate that name was for this number.

"Niña" was important in many ways. It was Kelly's first dance in *The Pirate*, planned as an impressive showcase for Serafin's energy and talent. In choreographing the number, Kelly concocted a scenario in which Serafin would use the entire plaza in the heart of Port Sebastian as his playground, demonstrating Kelly's immense capacity for athletic dancing. Such a setting needed to be studded with props, hand holds, and foot holds, many of them inconspicuously placed so as to blend in with the everyday life of the town. It demanded many hours on the set for Kelly and Jack Martin Smith, but the setting they created is a unique venue for a major dance in a Hollywood film.

"I used to go with Kelly," Smith recalled years later, "and we'd make hand holds and diving boards and foot emplacements and

Illustration 4.2. Kelly flies high as Dee Turnell spins below him on the spinning poles Kelly requested from art director Smith for the "Niña" number. Kelly's choreography and athletic dancing required unusual devices. Smith was instructed by producer Arthur Freed to give Kelly anything he needed.

move rocks so that he could jump from place to place and put sandpaper on the roof and fix the vine so he could climb up and all that. . . . He was like a monkey himself." Kelly often thought up ideas and presented them to Smith, who, as a former gymnast, loved helping him on this project. "He'd say, 'I need to go over here.' . . . We'd work it out. He got whatever he wanted. He was a big star then." Eventually the pair fixed the entire set so that Kelly "could run up and down it like a cat."[20]

Smith designed the pavilion that Kelly used for the climax of "Niña." He fixed poles with ball bearings on top and bottom and foot rests attached to them. Kelly and the "Niña" dancers could jump on the foot rests and "sail round and round and round. When they grabbed on that [pole] they were secure, and they had the centrifugal force to take them around."[21] No other dance in a Hollywood musical had a similar contraption.

Careful viewing of the number revealed seventeen "Niña" girls, as they were called, with four major dancers, and three secondary

Illustration 4.3. Ethnically diverse "Niña" girls watch Serafin dance. Minnelli carefully framed the shot with two girls in the foreground—one in an Indian sari and another in a Spanish shawl to suggest a multiethnic population.

dancers. Piecing together various bits of information in the assistant director's reports, we found eleven dancers who had been hired, so four secondary dancers did not *dance* in the final version. They seem to simply have been included in the non-dancing group. The names of all seventeen "Niña" girls, including non-dancers, are included in Appendix C.

It is worth noting that all the "Niña" girls were white despite Kelly's daring insistence on dancing with the Nicholas Brothers in "Be a Clown." Similarly, Fred Astaire's number "I Left My Hat in Haiti" in *Royal Wedding* (1950) was set in Haiti but used only white dancers. After all, this was an era when whites and blacks did not dance together on the screen. But in "Niña," the way the dancers and non-dancers are depicted is consistent with the cultural backdrop of the story and the suggested period. Although the population in Port Sebastian is ethnically mixed, there are racial distinctions if one observes closely. The well-to-do citizens are mainly white, whereas blacks are mostly depicted as maids, barbers, and sellers of produce or seafood. The few black women seen during the number are

Illustration 4.4. Without any props to help him, Kelly jumps high above the admiring "Niña" girls, who are carefully arranged by Minnelli to frame Kelly's spectacular jump.

either standing off on the side or among the vegetable sellers who Serafin waves away from the area where he plans to dance. To Minnelli's credit, even these vegetable sellers are racially mixed, with one white woman and one Hispanic in the group. The only black girl in the "Niña" dance arena is a bored-looking little girl, a maid to a white woman, and Kelly could hardly dance with a little girl in such a suggestive number. The young women who watch Serafin (or who join in the dance) are mostly attired as British, French, or Spanish women might dress during that period; but one is in a sari and another wears a Dutch hat, all of which creates a sense of diverse ethnicities even though all the "Niña" girls are white.

"Niña" was fun to do for everyone involved because of its complexity and inventiveness. It also was very hard work. While Roger Edens engaged in a long-distance feud with Porter about the musical accompaniment for the song, the rest of the cast and crew engaged in repeated rehearsals beginning on February 26 and continuing off and on until March 31. Wally Worsley provided a behind-the-scenes look into the prerecording, rehearsals, and filming of this number through his reports. Kelly prerecorded the song for "Niña" on March 20–22, and again on March 24, working on his dance rehearsals at the same time. While the other dancers continued to rehearse, Kelly did more retakes for *Living in a Big Way* on March 26–27. After fifteen days of rehearsal, the company filmed "Niña" on April 2–5 and 7–9. Kelly had trouble with his wig each day of filming, and Minnelli had to stop shooting for a few minutes when a low-flying plane buzzed the studio and created too much noise on April 8. When filming of "Niña" continued on April 11, Kelly's mustache was ruined during a particularly vigorous segment of his dance and it had to be replaced.[22]

A close observation of the background during the "Niña" number reveals some tricks that Minnelli used to help one of the extras. While Kelly is dancing on the marketplace stage, the duenna who earlier tried to hit him with a fan is watching him from a balcony in the background. As the dance progresses, another woman steps in for the duenna, who leaves, probably because it must have been exhausting for an older lady to simply stand in the background while several takes of the dance were being shot to get it perfect. Later, the second woman is replaced by a mannequin, and at the end of the dance, as Manuela and Inez enter through the archway in a carriage, the woman who looks down on them from that balcony is yet another person. It appears that although the director could not allow more prominent people in the background to leave during the shooting, he could certainly make allowances for those less likely to be noticed. The number of times this one person was replaced indicates how lengthy each shooting period must have been to create a short segment on the screen.

This is borne out by a piece that Kelly wrote for Dorothy Kilgallen's "Voice of Broadway" column in the *New York Journal-American* about the filming of "Niña." On a set fifty yards long, "I do a number in which I dance (and sing) down one side of the street, climb a couple of balconies en route, then up to the top of a building, a leap to another building, then down a water spout and a dance down the other side of the street." It was fun, but "do that fifty times a day, counting rehearsals and camera takes and one gets somewhat tired by the end of the day."[23]

Kelly's article on the filming of "Niña" was meant to be a teaser, a publicity piece to whet audience appetite for the film's release. It is an intriguing parallel that the number itself was Serafin's teaser for his upcoming performance. Serafin is putting on "an act" when he dances "Niña," and his flitting from girl to girl is part of his ploy to interest as many people as possible in attending his performance. When Serafin sees Manuela shortly afterward, he acts very differently. He is sincere about his attraction to Manuela, in contrast to his "pretended" attraction to all the girls in the "Niña" number. In addition, he calls the other girls "Niña" and makes it clear that he does not care to know their names. But when he meets Manuela, he wants to know her name right away. When she refuses and asks why it matters to him, Serafin says, "It is as vital to me as the beat of my heart." Later, he gets her to reveal her name (and the name of her town) during her hypnosis at his performance that evening.

The fact that "Niña" was meant to be a teaser has eluded most scholars and critics other than Joseph Casper, who notes that it is a wonderful advertisement for Serafin's show that evening. In contrast, most film historians tend to conclude that "Niña" is Serafin's character sketch and displays his roving eye or fickleness. For example, Harvey calls Serafin "an equal-opportunity seducer" in "Niña," Thomas refers to his "Don Juan treatment," and Taylor and Jackson write that Serafin dances "in search of yet one more flower."[24]

"Niña" can indeed be construed as Serafin's character sketch, but in a different way. Rather than being fickle, Serafin is a consummate actor who uses the dance to promote his performance. He cozies up to as many girls as possible to interest them in the show to come and gets most of the girls to dance with him. Moreover, they all show up that evening in the plaza of Port Sebastian and even participate in the "Mack the Black" number.

"Voodoo" and "Mack the Black"

The next number to be filmed was "Voodoo," although rehearsals for it had started much earlier. The filming plan called for Serafin to hypnotize Manuela as part of the troupe's show in Port Sebastian, followed by a performance of the song "Voodoo" by Garland. Minnelli followed that plan, but during previews of the film before its general release, audiences indicated that they were not impressed by "Voodoo." As Minnelli later recalled, it "wasn't exciting enough."[25]

Minnelli and Freed decided to replace the song with a rousing rendition of "Mack the Black." Originally, Garland had simply sung this number at the start of the film, but that was also to be dropped based on preview audience reaction. Alton staged the new format

Illustration 4.5. Garland sings the rousing "Mack the Black" number with lively participation from the audience at Serafin's performance in Port Sebastian. This was a great improvement over the "Voodoo" number shown to the preview audience.

for "Mack the Black," including enthusiastic participation from the Port Sebastian audience, and it was filmed. Minnelli kept as many sequences of the hypnotism and the awakening after the number as he could from the original filming.[26] The new number was a huge improvement over "Voodoo," and it all flows together seamlessly as if "Mack the Black" had been slated for that spot all along.

The difficulties associated with the original "Mack the Black" number that began the movie went beyond audience reaction. The musical accompaniment for that version had been written by Kay Thompson, another of Freed's staff members who dabbled in many different areas of production. But Thompson's arrangement was complex, "all kinds of waverings and changes of tempo and changes of rhythmic patterns," according to Lela Simone. "It was busy, it was overdone. Sound-wise, it was disagreeable and awful. And unusable. I mean, a madhouse song, you know." Simone thought the piece seemed more like an aria from a grand opera, while Freed called it "'A Chinese Circus.'" Garland prerecorded this version, but it sounded inappropriate for a mass-entertainment film and had to be reorchestrated.[27]

Similarly, the problems with "Voodoo" were not merely related to poor lyrics and music (as discussed in Chapter 3) or to negative audience reaction at the previews. The assistant director's reports show that rehearsals for "Voodoo" extended over a long period of time and the filming process was difficult due to Garland's repeated absences and other issues. Rehearsals began as early as February 18, the day after production started, and continued for thirteen days to mid-March. Garland prerecorded "Voodoo" on April 10, and filming of the number began on April 12. It continued through April 14–16. Garland complained of not feeling well during makeup on April 16 and arranged for a doctor to visit her in late morning. But she felt worse during lunch and left for home. Scheduled filming had to be canceled on April 18 because of her condition but resumed on April 22. That day, Worsley reported that Garland had to rest between takes because of the "strenuous dance," and eventually filming stopped at 5:25 p.m. because she was worn out. Shooting continued on April 25, which included Garland's reaction shots for the number.[28]

Hugh Fordin writes that while filming "Voodoo," Garland broke down with paranoia about the working conditions she had to endure. The set was filled with open flames because of the night setting, and she came to the conclusion that her life was in danger. She became so agitated that work had to be shut down for the day.[29] But Worsley does not even mention the incident in his reports. Either the story is an exaggeration of what took place or because, like the rest of the crew, Worsley felt uncomfortable witnessing Garland's extreme anxiety and chose not to report what had happened.

"You Can Do No Wrong" and "Love of My Life"

Cole Porter was not present when Garland prerecorded "Love of My Life" and "Mack the Black" in December 1946. Both versions were deemed unacceptable. The songwriter also missed Kelly's prerecording of "Niña" and Garland's prerecording of "Voodoo." But apparently his absence at all of these recordings was not considered to be an issue.

Porter came out to California later, during the filming of *The Pirate*. He sailed on the *President Polk* from Jersey City, New Jersey, on April 13, 1947, and reached California via the Panama Canal on

Illustration 4.6. Manuela sings "You Can Do No Wrong" to the injured Serafin. She has finally acknowledged to herself and to Serafin that she loves
him.

April 27. He visited the set on May 13 when Garland prerecorded
"You Can Do No Wrong." An argument developed between Garland and Porter over how the singer pronounced *caviar,* with Porter
wanting her to stretch it out into three distinct syllables. Edens had
to intervene to talk Garland into listening to the songwriter. Porter
had no difficulties with Garland's second recording of "Love of My
Life," which she also made during his visit. He made a few small
suggestions but overall was quite pleased with her rendition.[30]

Goodrich and Hackett had planned for "You Can Do No Wrong"
to be sung before Manuela's tantrum. This can only mean that they
expected the song to be sung in a sarcastic way. They placed the
song in the scene in which Manuela harangues Serafin about how
he had tricked and humiliated her. This scene, originally suggested by Freed and Minnelli, was dropped in preproduction because
it slowed the action. But Minnelli still kept the song in at this point.
Related to this, when Minnelli realized the elaborate crying scene he
and Freed had envisioned for Manuela would not work, he apparently planned a sincere version of "You Can Do No Wrong" after

the tantrum. As a result, Garland recorded two renditions of "You Can Do No Wrong" (a sarcastic and a sincere one) and Minnelli filmed both versions. In the end, only the sincere rendition sung to the injured Serafin after Manuela's tantrum was used in the film. Minnelli wisely dropped the first, sarcastic version even before the previews.

Garland also recorded two versions of "Love of My Life"—the first sung by Manuela to her hat after her friends leave (as described in Chapter 2) and the second to Serafin when Manuela is supposedly in a hypnotized state. The second version was meant to be the reprise, and initially both renditions were included in the film. But the song to the hat was dropped after the preview (for reasons detailed in Chapter 5). Only the second rendition, sung to Serafin (as Macoco) near the end of the film, was kept in the release print.

The filming of this version of "Love of My Life," however, caused some trouble with censorship issues. It was a passionate sequence in which Manuela sings of her love for the pirate to arouse Pedro into revealing that he is Macoco. Of course, Manuela's passion, at this late stage in the movie, is openly directed toward Serafin, the

Illustration 4.7. Serafin and Manuela in the sensuous "Love of My Life" number.

Illustration 4.8. Don Pedro's palpable jealousy, as he watches Serafin and Manuela's passion, is the key to his revealing his identity as Macoco the Pirate.

false pirate, in a delicious, twist-and-turn effect. Perhaps because Manuela and Serafin do not perform a typical love dance in the film, Kelly and Garland used this song as an opportunity to physically express their characters' passion for each other. Also, their constant movement across the stage in this number makes it a bit closer to a romantic dance than just a love song.

The number fits very well with the plotline for another reason: the two have just declared their love for each other, but instead of being assured of a happy future together, the very real possibility that Serafin may be hanged as Macoco looms over them. So they are not merely trying to goad Pedro into a fit of jealousy; on another level, their passion for each other comes across as very real and poignant because they realize that it may well be their last time together. In fact, the two look quite startled when Don Pedro shouts "Macoco!," suggesting that they are deeply immersed in their passion for each other.

As a result, in Kelly's words, they "were doing a little bit of over-groping. It was a sensual and sensuous sequence—both words are applicable." It had to be edited a bit, according to Kelly, but he did not mind because he thought the sequence was originally a bit too long anyway. Stories by writers Joel Siegel, Tony Thomas, and Roy Hemming that Louis B. Mayer himself insisted on cutting an overly erotic section of the film's ballet are confusing the scenes of "Love of My Life" with the ballet.[31] There is no credible evidence in the archives or interviews that any concern about censorship issues arose in connection with the "Pirate Ballet."

Whether they overdid it or not, the passion in "Love of My Life" was necessary to make the scenario work. As Douglas McVay writes, "The carnal power of her vocal rendition and the repeated intercut close-ups of Walter Slezak's perspiring, lustful, jealous face, make Pedro's culminating furious outburst of self-disclosure completely persuasive."[32]

Filming the Nonmusical Scenes

Apparently more preparation was needed before the remaining three numbers, the "Pirate Ballet," "Be a Clown," and the reprise of "Be a Clown," could be filmed. Instead the crew focused on filming the rest of the movie.

As in the case of "Niña" and "Voodoo," Wally Worsley's reports offer an insider's look at the everyday challenges involved in filming the rest of *The Pirate*. The assistant director's reports also add a human touch to the frenzied, technical process of photographing the film because Worsley often noted the actions of various people as a way to explain why filming was delayed. For example, Kelly had trouble with his wig while filming sequences on the dock at Port Sebastian on March 31. When Kelly and Slezak filmed their fight sequences, Kelly needed to have his ankle taped, probably because he had aggravated his earlier injury. The studio used a stunt double for Slezak's tumble when Kelly (as Serafin) threw Pedro during the fight sequence on April 19. Two days later, a whip expert was on the set to snare the chair. He, of course, was off camera, pretending to be Pedro. When shooting scenes of Serafin's meeting with Manuela on the sea wall on April 23, the crew had to hose down the set several times to create the effect of a masonry wall swept by sea mist. Many scenes were filmed in the interior of Manuela's bedroom, the hall of Manuela's house, and the interior of Pedro's house in late April and early May. Slezak experienced makeup problems during shooting on May 2 but presumably they were fixed, just as Kelly's wig

Illustration 4.9. Alfred Lunt (as Serafin in the stage play) pretending to walk the tightrope. During the play, Lunt stood on a large crate hidden behind a curtain. The crate had wheels and was moved across the stage to fake his walk across the tightrope. (Wisconsin Historical Society, WHS-101824)

had to be adjusted on several occasions. On May 8, Gladys Cooper unintentionally delayed filming when she told everyone she wanted an opportunity to peacefully drink her coffee. Worsley recorded the time, 9:10 to 9:25 a.m., and when Cooper was finished, someone

Illustration 4.10. Kelly (as Serafin in the film) actually walking the tight-rope. Kelly performed all his own stunts whenever he could and did so throughout this film. It is easy to see why a song would not have worked here as Goodrich and Hackett had suggested.

noticed that she had the wrong hairstyle for the scene to be filmed. That necessitated a delay while her hair was altered.[33]

A few days earlier, on May 3, the production took a short break from 4:11 to 4:39 to celebrate Slezak's birthday with cake and ice cream. The cast was dressed for filming, with Garland in Manuela's bridal gown. The crew had made a large poster with a poem about how Slezak typically played "heavies" but in reality he was a sweet guy. Garland helped Slezak cut his birthday cake and she, Kelly, and Slezak shared many laughs. Everyone had a good time. It was a brief respite from the hectic filming schedule and a time of cama-raderie and joy.[34]

Alfred Lunt had faked Serafin's walk along the tightrope in the stage version of *The Pirate,* but Kelly had no intention of doing that. A superb athlete who wanted to do all his own stunts as far as pos-sible, Kelly meant to really walk the rope to make it look authentic. He practiced a good deal and then shot the sequence with wires at-tached to his back and mattresses on the floor below, in case he fell.

A stand-in double, probably Russ Saunders, filled in for Kelly as Minnelli set up the shot. Then the wires were adjusted on Kelly, and the camera rolled to capture the sequence on May 9. Minnelli resorted to trick photography in only one scene of this sequence, where he wanted Kelly to look a bit unsteady to create excitement.[35] Careful viewing of the film shows a gap between Kelly's feet and the tightrope for a moment when Serafin almost loses his balance. By having Kelly walk on a low tightrope for this brief segment, and then doubling this image onto the high tightrope, Minnelli could give the impression that Kelly was about to fall without endangering the actor.

Scenes between Manuela and Coutat in Pedro's salon (parlor), where Manuela finds out that Serafin tricked her, were filmed on May 28 and 31. Manuela's tantrum, a rousing fight in which she throws bric-a-brac at Serafin, was filmed on May 29 and June 2. It was a demanding sequence for Garland, who had to rest between takes, as crew members swept up the debris from the set many times to prepare for the next take.[36]

Hugh Fordin reports that Garland invested more than ordinary emotion in this sequence. Without citing the source of his information, he argues that she took it as an opportunity to vent frustration and anger (perhaps at Kelly for spending so much time with her husband) and that Stradling had difficulty photographing Garland close up because her face looked haggard and worn. During one particular take, according to Fordin, Minnelli had to physically restrain Garland when she became too involved in the frenzy of the moment.[37]

As with many other stories associated with Garland and the filming of *The Pirate*, one does not know how far to trust a report like this, which is not supported by any evidence other than Fordin's word. Garland's performance in the tantrum sequence is intense, but fully in keeping with the broad humor of the film and with the character she has successfully created up to that point.

Garland's daughter Lorna Luft writes that her mother often broke household items in tantrums in the 1950s. "When the chemicals hit her bloodstream, she could just pick up anything within reach and throw it. She was amazingly strong under any circumstances," but when she overused drugs, "the adrenaline rush made her even more powerful. . . . She could hurl almost anything across a room with deadly accuracy: big ashtrays, heavy books, lamps, anything handy. . . . There's a scene in *The Pirate* where she hurls most of the props in the room, including several large vases . . . ten or fif-

Illustration 4.11. Manuela getting ready to pay Serafin back for tricking her into believing he was Macoco. This shot is the prelude to the frantic tantrum sequence, and the vase that Garland holds is the first item to be shattered.

teen feet across the room at Gene Kelly. She never misses. I've got a pretty good idea where Vincente Minnelli got the inspiration for that scene. He was married to Mama at the time."[38]

Whether Minnelli was truly inspired by Judy's behavior at home while they were married, or whether Judy only began to hurl things a few years later after they split up, is something we do not know. Perhaps she learned to do this from Manuela's tantrum. After all, Luft's experience with her mother's throwing arm occurred several years after *The Pirate* was filmed. Also, even though Garland does hurl objects with great force during the tantrum sequence, she is not shown in any scene in which thrown objects directly hit Kelly (or anything he is hiding behind) across a room. This suggests that someone else off camera was doing the throwing in these scenes, and the accuracy and speed can be attributed to this person or persons. It is likely that several people off screen threw things in rapid succession to create the air of Serafin being bombarded by bric-a-brac.

Sixteen-month-old Liza Minnelli was slated to play a bit part in

Illustration 4.12. Manuela walking through town to "sacrifice" herself to Macoco as townspeople stand by respectfully.

The Pirate. Her parents had her christened at the Episcopal Church at the corner of Santa Monica Boulevard and Camden Drive in Beverly Hills during the time *The Pirate* was being filmed. They also did a screen test to see how she would play in the picture. Garland suggested using Liza for a scene in the sequence that depicts Manuela walking bravely to Pedro's house, which Serafin has commandeered. She was supposed to save the town by "sacrificing" herself to Serafin, who had convinced all the townspeople, including Manuela, that he was Macoco. The idea was that she would either pat a baby on the head or place a child on her shoulders as she walked past the awed townspeople. In either case, Liza was a natural. The little girl visited the set on several days during the filming, as revealed by many publicity photographs. Garland put a brave face on her crumbling marriage by telling reporters that she and Minnelli wanted "to have at least two boys and one more girl."[39] In the end, however, the scene involving Liza was cut from the release print.

A great deal of the picture was filmed by the time scenes oriented around the gallows in the square of Calvados were shot from June 4 to 7. The assistant director's reports mention that the climax of the film, Pedro's revelation of his true identity, was shot on June 9. Slezak suffered a cut lip when Kelly (as Serafin) threw Indian clubs at him to stop Macoco from firing his guns. Slezak had to go to the hospital for three stitches. He then returned to the set, where make-up artists touched up the injury a bit, and Minnelli continued filming. Still photographs for the film's posters were shot on June 11, the day that production was considered to be half-finished. The project had already cost $2,725,516 to date, which would have been considered a hefty total sum for any Freed musical. A large percentage of that cost must have gone into film stock. Minnelli exposed 115,355 feet of film by July 5, but only 10,996 feet of it were slated to be incorporated into the release print.[40]

Part of the cost, of course, was due to Garland's repeated absences. But other reasons for the higher bill for this film were the large number of elaborate sets, the expensive costumes, and the fact that changes continued to be made even as production staggered along. Minnelli worked with writer Wilkie Mahoney on setting up rewrites of dialogue and scenes in late March 1947. Script changes, as well as changes in the lyrics of "Voodoo," were submitted to Joseph Breen for his approval in April. Further changes in the movie's script were submitted in mid-May 1947, nearly halfway through the shooting schedule.[41]

The cast and crew party for *The Pirate* production took place on June 10. Chasen's restaurant of Beverly Hills, very popular with movie folk for many years, catered the affair, and nearly everyone who was involved with the film attended.[42] It is unusual that the party was held halfway through instead of at the end of filming. The reason might have been that Minnelli wanted to boost morale at the midpoint of production, considering the many delays and frustrations associated with the project.

"BE A CLOWN"

What still remained to be filmed were three major musical numbers. Although the "Pirate Ballet" appears much earlier in the film than "Be a Clown" and its reprise, it was left for the end and the team took on "Be a Clown" next.

The first performance of Porter's "Be a Clown" in *The Pirate* was a unique event. It was not only the debut of what became a classic show business tune but the first time that black and white dancers performed together in a major Hollywood musical. As mentioned earlier, Kelly's insistence on using the black dancing team the Nicholas Brothers, and dancing *with them*, was something no other film musical had done to date. It was an era when dances in films were segregated by race and a time when it was acceptable for musicals to use white dancers wearing blackface. The Broadway version of *The Pirate* also included racial mixing, based directly on Behrman's plot and script, but it included no dancing and was performed only in the North. Kelly's desire to challenge prevailing racial attitudes, strongly supported by Minnelli and Freed, was the wellspring of his decision to dance with the Nicholas Brothers. Mayer predicted, and Freed accepted, the strong possibility that southern theater managers might demand that the number be excised from the release print sent to their city.

Kelly worked with the Nicholas Brothers in choreographing the dance. As Minnelli later put it, "Be a Clown" was "an audience number and quite acrobatic." While the director thought that Kelly and Alton were primarily responsible for developing the steps, everything was done with the brothers' own style in mind. In fact, the well-established styles of Kelly and the Nicholas Brothers mixed very well, so there was little difficulty incorporating "splits and handsprings and turnovers and so forth" into the routine. Kelly's own style, according to Minnelli, contained "good old standby, flag-waving steps." Wilkie Mahoney had suggested in his script changes in March 1947 that the number be punctuated with shots of Manuela showing love in her eyes, of the Viceroy enjoying the dance, and of Pedro becoming enraged.[43] Kelly understandably ignored these suggestions in the interest of the integrity of the number as a continuous, spectacular performance.

One of the more impressive stunts of the Nicholas Brothers was a "flying split," which both of them perform at the start of the number. Fayard had seen it in vaudeville when he was eight years old, but the dancer had performed the stunt while going down to the floor. Later, Fayard tried it while going up from the floor "without using his hands," and then performed the split by jumping into it rather than just sliding. Harold learned all this too, and the pair performed the stunt repeatedly in their film work. George Balanchine taught the brothers to extend this stunt by sliding under each other's legs and then snapping back onto both feet. They perform the split exactly this way at the start of "Be a Clown."

Near the end of the number, the brothers and Kelly perform another unique stunt. They join Kelly as he "bounces sideways on his

Illustration 4.13. Kelly and the Nicholas Brothers dance acrobatically in "Be a Clown." Kelly incorporated this particular step, which the brothers had performed in *Orchestra Wives* (1942).

hands and toes—body extended in push-up position," like a crab moving across the sand. The brothers claim that Kelly had been influenced by them in developing this step. "Gene had seen us in New York and told us that some of the stuff we were doing was what he'd like to do," recalled Harold.[44]

However, Kelly's biographer, Clive Hirschhorn, reports that Gene emceed for The Revuers in New York and also performed in the show in the summer of 1939. "The 'big finish' to his act was a highly effective combination of dance and acrobatics as he sprang across the floor, bouncing on the palms of his hands, with his legs stretched out behind him."[45]

In trying to figure out who influenced whom, it is worth noting that Kelly also used the stunt in the first number he performed in his first film, *For Me and My Gal*, in 1942. It was one of the most enduring elements of Kelly's dance repertoire.

For the Nicholas Brothers, "Be a Clown" was a departure from the norm. Their routines tended to consist of one spectacular stunt after another, three-minute circuses to wow an audience with comparatively little dancing in them. But Kelly and Alton worked up a true dance routine for "Be a Clown," even if a handful of stunts were incorporated into the choreography. The result is part Kelly, part Nicholas Brothers, but the whole is well crafted and rounded out to be a true dance number.

"It was the first time we did straight dancing," Harold recalled more than fifty years later, "no tricks, or tumbling or anything. But it was interesting because the three of us synchronized our moves."[46]

Yet, during rehearsals of "Be a Clown," Harold thought the routine was too easy and slacked off. He had a habit of not putting his all into rehearsals anyway, but Kelly could not understand that attitude. According to Harold, Kelly confronted him one day, saying, "'Man, we're working our heads off, and you're just moping along.'" Harold insisted he knew the routine well, but Kelly challenged him to do it. When Harold performed it perfectly, Kelly "'was so mad, he didn't know what to do!'" as Harold recalled and as Fayard recounted years later.[47]

The point Harold, Fayard, and their biographer missed is that Kelly took his own work very seriously and always made sure his performance was the best it could be. It was fine that Harold knew the routine, but slacking off was something Kelly could not understand. He gave his all to everything he did, and it is understandable that he expected any performer worth his salt to do the same.

Reports made by assistant director Worsley reveal that the performers rehearsed "Be a Clown" for a total of fourteen days from June 17 to July 8. The first day of filming took place on July 9, with the three working from 9:00 in the morning until 7:25 in the evening. They waited one hour as Kelly completely changed his wardrobe and makeup in the early afternoon. Minnelli supervised Kelly's makeup to make sure it was perfect. The three changed into "fresh wardrobe" at 7 p.m. and took half a dozen more takes before quitting for the day. They had shot an astounding sixty-three takes that day, and yet the number was not finished. The grueling pace continued on July 10, with a total of seventy takes. While Minnelli sometimes shot only one or two takes back to back, he also filmed as many as eleven takes without a rest between. This frenetic activity forced Kelly to change his wardrobe again in midafternoon, and he also stopped for a rest while "baking leg under lamp," as Worsley reported.[48]

"I saw Gene Kelly, one day, dance those Nicholas Brothers into the ground," recalled Jack Martin Smith. "They're like spiders, those guys; they were like monkeys. Kelly kept after them and after them, and he finally had them tuckered out. I never was so amused in my life."[49] But Kelly had no personal agenda in any of this. He was as hard on himself as he was on his colleagues, insisting on perfection and pushing himself and those around him to achieve it.

Although the dance as a whole is excellent, there is a marked difference between the Nicholas Brothers and Gene Kelly in terms of grace and control. When all three perform the same step, the brothers' arms flop while Kelly's are straight and controlled. Fayard and Harold curve their bodies when they do a brief handstand, whereas Kelly holds his body perfectly straight like a classic dancer's. When they are sitting and lift their legs in the air, Fayard's and Harold's legs are wide apart, while Gene's are close together and graceful, with the heels almost touching. One reason for these differences is that the Nicholas Brothers had no formal dance training, whereas Kelly was trained in both tap and ballet. Another reason is that Kelly was far more muscular than the brothers and could exercise better control over his body.

In fact, the only problem Kelly has in the number is trying to keep his hat on. It seems on the verge of slipping off several times, probably because it sat on top of a curly wig that Kelly wore to create the role of Serafin. One wonders why the costumers did not fasten the hat more securely. Also, when the three dancers are holding hands in a circle and each takes a turn being lifted off the studio floor, Kelly seems to be leaping to help the struggling Harold pull him along. In contrast, Fayard seems to fly off the floor when Kelly pulls him pretty easily. Despite these subtle differences, the three worked very well together and the result is a thoroughly enjoyable routine.

REPRISE OF "BE A CLOWN"

Porter's song was such a sure hit that it was slated to end *The Pirate,* with Kelly and Garland performing their only duet in the film. Garland, however, did not like it. When Porter visited the set on July 7 to hear Kelly and Garland prerecord "Be a Clown," Garland openly criticized the song. "'She pointed out that there were hardly any laughs where I had attempted to provide an infinite number,'" Porter recalled. "'It was very embarrassing to have it pointed out.'" Minnelli helped to win his wife over by walking through the choreography Alton suggested, incorporating a gag involving

Illustration 4.14. Harold Nicholas clearly has to struggle to pull Kelly aloft. Nimble and energetic as they were, it would not have been easy for either brother to lift the muscular Kelly off the floor.

Illustration 4.15. In contrast to Illustration 4.14, Kelly pulls Fayard Nicholas easily off the floor. Strong and athletic, it would have been no trouble for Kelly to swing aloft either of the small and slender Nicholas brothers.

Illustration 4.16. Kelly is hit on the head with an Indian club as Garland laughs—to add a touch of vaudeville humor to the "Be a Clown" reprise.

Indian clubs. This tickled Garland's fancy, and she became enthusiastic about the number. Her mood also brightened at the thought of wearing a colorful clown's costume suggested by Lester Allen, the character actor who portrayed Manuela's Uncle Capucho. Allen had worn it in a Broadway musical revue called *Rufus LeMaire's Affairs* exactly twenty years before. Described in *The Pirate's* exhibitors' campaign book as a "long black coat [actually it is green in the film], baggy trousers and size 25 shoes," the costume was far too large for either Allen or Garland, who were nearly the same size. Because it held sentimental value, Allen insisted on being present while Kelly and Garland filmed the number. While Garland's costume was set, Kelly's clown regalia had to be approved by Freed. The prop department found eighteen Indian clubs in an antique shop in Watertown, Massachusetts, a couple of which had already been used to film the capture of Pedro after he reveals himself as Macoco (and had caused the cut in Slezak's lip).[50]

These eighteen clubs, examples of a fitness fad dating from the late 1800s, would play a large role in the success of the reprise of "Be

Illustration 4.17. Kelly and Garland laughing as themselves (instead of as Serafin and Manuela) at the end of the "Be a Clown" reprise. This is one of the most discussed moments of the film.

a Clown." The clubs are used by someone in the wings to hit Kelly on the head each time he comes near. Kelly reacts strongly and Garland laughs every time, creating a bit of humor and adding a vaudeville element to the reprise. Kelly even switches places with Garland at one point so she can be hit instead, but the gloved hand bops him anyway and then bops the laughing Garland. Finally, an avalanche of clubs is directed at the duo as they dive for cover.

Filming of the reprise began on July 15. The assistant director's reports show that Kelly and Garland spent more than two hours, from 10:30 to 1:15, in makeup (including a break for lunch), and then they began to film. The company took a break from 5:18 to 5:49 p.m. because Garland felt ill. Everyone went for dinner at 6:15 and worked for more than two and a half hours before resting from 9:49 to 10:29. The company continued filming until almost 12:30 a.m. when Garland became too tired to continue. She and Kelly had done twenty-six takes that long day. Garland felt too unwell to perform the next day, but she was ready to finish the reprise on July 17 with a total of thirty takes. Sixteen of those takes were shot between 6:13

and 6:45 p.m. After two days and a total of fifty-six takes, Worsley noted that the reprise was "in the can."[51]

The ending of the reprise is a priceless moment in film history, for it ends *The Pirate* with a unique look at Kelly and Garland apparently laughing as themselves rather than as Serafin and Manuela. Douglas McVay was the first to note this in 1959. In 1971, Joel Siegel built on McVay's observation and wrote: "Suddenly their eyes meet and both dissolve into gales of what must be unrehearsed laughter. This final shot, which combines the statement that the artistic imagination is the source of happiness with Garland's and Kelly's very obvious love of performing together, ends the film on a blissfully high note."[52]

Indeed, it was a fitting way to end the film, and both McVay and Siegel are right on the mark. But whether the moment truly was unrehearsed is open to question. Minnelli writes in his memoirs that even though Kelly and Garland "would look like clowns, they also had to look like themselves in this, the last scene of the movie."[53]

In fact, the two look like themselves throughout the number and no longer like Serafin and Manuela. This is partly because they are dressed as clowns and do not look like the characters they played before. But Minnelli's comment suggests that the dropping of the mask, so to speak, was intended, and done in a very natural and appealing way for the audience to see the actors enjoying their work.

THE "PIRATE BALLET"

The details of the "Pirate Ballet" had not yet been worked out before production of the rest of the film ended about mid-July 1947. Minnelli and Kelly had rejected the earlier Minnelli-Freed-Alton idea to involve the townspeople in the number and had decided that it would be Manuela's fantasy. Exactly what she would fantasize was yet to be determined, but both men were set on making it an exercise in surrealism. Minnelli filmed Garland's reaction shots before the number—her fantasy—was shot or even finalized. After taking care of the reaction shots, "Gene and I went into a huddle and made this thing up," Minnelli told an interviewer in 1973. They worked out a portrayal of a "ruthless pirate" as imagined in the vivid fantasy of a young, repressed village girl who has a flair for the dramatic.[54]

Kelly started rehearsing the ballet on July 18, the day after he and Garland finished filming the reprise of "Be a Clown." Rehearsals continued for many days—on the set with Edens and Alton, or

Illustration 4.18. Kelly with other dancers in the "Pirate Ballet." Kelly's costume and athletic moves were inspired by the clothes and antics of Douglas Fairbanks in *The Black Pirate* (1926).

at Kelly's house in Beverly Hills. A troupe of five dancers rehearsed with Kelly, to dance with him in a short stretch of the ballet. As recorded by Wally Worsley, they were Ellis Jenkinson, Fred Jenkinson, Howard Dunham, Harold Ramser, and Bruce Tegner. They rehearsed with Kelly for at least nine days. Only four of the five actually danced with Kelly in the film, but it is not clear which four as they did not receive credit. All told, Kelly and the cast rehearsed the ballet for fifteen days from July 18 to August 8, 1947. The M-G-M orchestra prerecorded the music, which had been arranged by Edens from the music of Garland's song "Mack the Black" on August 7. Lela Simone played the piano parts in this arrangement.[55]

An internal M-G-M memo shows that Freed hired dancers Jack Bruce and Jeanne Coyne to start July 22 and 24, respectively, at $135 per week. That salary had been increased from $111.17 per week to include lifts, throws, and catches. Bruce reverted to his base salary by August 14, apparently involved no longer in lifts, throws, and catches.[56]

Tony Thomas and Jeanine Basinger have written that Jeanne

Coyne was a dancer in *The Pirate*.[57] However, Coyne was hired after the filming of all the dances except the ballet. Moreover, careful viewing shows no evidence that Coyne is in the ballet or any part of the film. It appears that she and Bruce were hired to help Kelly and others prepare for the ballet.

Coyne had been a young student at the Gene Kelly School of the Dance in Pittsburgh, and had followed her former teacher to Broadway and then to Hollywood. Later to become Kelly's second wife, Coyne often helped Kelly teach the routines to other dancers, and by the time of *The Pirate* production, she had worked her way up to full-time dance assistant to Kelly.[58]

Minnelli designed Kelly's costume for the ballet, basing it on the clothes worn by Douglas Fairbanks Sr. in *The Black Pirate* (1926). Fairbanks wore "nothing but a doublet and ragged, thigh-length trousers for most of the film," as his biographer Gary Carey reports.[59]

Accordingly, Minnelli designed a pair of short trousers for Serafin, but to show off Kelly's extremely muscular legs, he made them much shorter and tighter than the ones Fairbanks had worn. It was, in fact, the only time in Kelly's film career that he wore short trousers.

A comparison of both films also shows that Kelly's sleeveless black top, black boots, one earring, and single metal armband worn in the "Pirate Ballet" were similar to what Fairbanks wore for his role as a pirate. Moreover, no scholars seem to have noticed that, other than the shorts, Kelly wears the exact outfit, including a black head scarf, for Serafin's first performance where he hypnotizes Manuela. The only difference is that he wears baggy striped pants for the hypnosis segment instead of the tight black shorts he wears as a pirate. This seems to be a subtle connection indicating that, despite being hypnotized at the time, Manuela accurately recalls later how Serafin was dressed. Just as her passionate response to Serafin's kiss under hypnosis suggests that Manuela is deeply attracted to Serafin despite her denials, clothing the pirate of her fantasy in Serafin's outfit also indicates a deep connection. She conjures up Serafin's image from his performance but changes the trousers to make him more pirate-like and also more alluring.

Minnelli began filming the ballet on August 9. The assistant director's reports show that stages 5 and 6 of the M-G-M studio in Culver City were used, with only sixteen takes the first day. Production was halted briefly as prop men had to fix Kelly's sword handle and bracelet, reload smoke canisters, and fix explosives between takes.

They also had to rehearse the tricky process of timing explosives right before Minnelli rolled film. The production crew rehearsed the scene in which Kelly slid down the rope from the ship's mast toward Minnelli's waiting camera on August 11, and then shot thirteen takes of the scene. The next day, the crew continued filming the ballet with twenty-four takes. This complex production demanded care and time, but Harry Stradling worked through the many complicated lighting problems with professionalism. As Minnelli wrote in his memoirs, Stradling was "responsible for one of my best lighted and most beautifully photographed pictures."[60]

The "Pirate Ballet" is a tour de force of both Kelly's and Minnelli's work. Beth Genné writes that "Minnelli's mobile camera transports us freely through a space that . . . seems almost limitless. We view the action from multiple angles." Genné points out that Kelly conceived the dance with the camera in mind, making it an effective cine dance as opposed to a traditionally choreographed number that could have been performed on a stage with a proscenium arch and that the camera happened to catch on film.[61]

In choreographing the dance, it is obvious that Kelly also drew on scenes from *The Black Pirate*. His slide down the rope was an example of bravura moviemaking in the style of Fairbanks. In fact, as discussed in Chapter 3, it is reminiscent of Fairbanks sliding down the sails of a ship by slicing them with a knife in *The Black Pirate*.

Minnelli reported in his memoirs that Kelly insisted on performing his own stunts in the ballet, and that he wanted them to be spectacular to underscore the fact that the ballet was meant to depict Manuela's fantasy of a pirate. Minnelli staged the rope descent in one take and had Kelly land near the camera so the audience would have no doubt as to who performed the feat. Kelly rehearsed the rope stunt and filmed it on August 11 in thirteen takes. To achieve a camera angle designed to emphasize Kelly within the frame when he landed, Minnelli used an extension with a mirror attached to it. The cameras were far too bulky and heavy to go down within a few inches of the floor. This device, called a Ubangi, used a long mechanical arm to place a mirror at the desired location. Then, the camera could shoot into the mirror to record the target image from a much lower angle than normally possible. Kelly often is credited with the idea for the Ubangi, working with the camera experts at M-G-M, although there is some discussion about whether it was devised for his routine in *Words and Music* (1948) or for *The Pirate*.[62]

According to records in the M-G-M archives, *Words and Music* was filmed from April to July 1948, whereas filming for *The Pirate* ended in August 1947.[63] These dates make it clear that the Ubangi was indeed devised for *The Pirate* and used the following year again for Kelly's dance with Vera Ellen in *Words and Music*. The Ubangi is not mentioned in the literature for filming other musicals or non-musicals, but it is possible it was used routinely whenever needed after *The Pirate*. In fact, that sort of long mechanical arm is commonplace today on film cameras for shooting low-angled views and is sometimes referred to as a Ubangi camera.

Kelly's dance steps incorporated a good deal of classic ballet, for example, what Jerome Delamater calls "large *jete* turns" around the white mule. But, true to his overall style, Kelly mixed in moves taken from many traditions. Working with the white mule was not easy. On August 13, Minnelli tried to use the animal but it would not cooperate. Worsley recorded in his report that it "would not sit down." Perhaps the mule was reluctant to listen because prop men had taped its ears. Minnelli allowed the animal to sulk for a while as Kelly had his boot re-glued. Then he brought the mule back, and the crew tried to make it sit down again, to no avail. After waiting nearly ten minutes, they tried a third time, but the beast would not do as told. This finally convinced Minnelli to use a fake, stuffed mule instead. He filmed Kelly's interaction with the sitting mule on August 14, after the crew rigged wires on the stuffed animal's ears to move them according to cue. Kelly filmed his "jetés" around the fake mule from 12:30 to 9:05 p.m. that day.[64] As this was the last day of production for *The Pirate*, it seems that Kelly took an extra amount of time to make sure the last segment to be filmed was perfect.

The entire ballet was fun to do, according to Jack Martin Smith. The pyrotechnics alone seem to have made it memorable, or, as Smith said, "We pretty near burned down the studio putting it on." It was "a hell of a number, I thought," Smith continued, "savage, beautiful, piercing music."[65] Kelly and Minnelli crafted a ballet that was a coherent work within a work, and all of its elements contributed to its overall, mesmerizing effect.

Although film scholars tend to think of *The Pirate* as Minnelli's film, Kelly clearly played a critical role in its conception and filming. In fact, in his interviews and memoirs, Minnelli gave full credit to Kelly for his contributions. As a result, *The Pirate* does not illustrate the auteur in filmmaking. This film thrived on a close collaboration between Minnelli and Kelly, and benefited significantly from the contributions of a host of talented people ranging from Garland, Freed, and Porter to all the bit players and supporting crew.

And yet, when production finally ground to an end in mid-August, it was a time of strong and mixed feelings for Minnelli. Despite his great enjoyment in working with Kelly on the various aspects of the film, the unexpected weakening of his marriage to Garland made *The Pirate* a grueling project for the director.

CHAPTER FIVE

Postproduction and Reactions to the Film

With the end of filming, *The Pirate* entered several months of post-production work before it was ready for general release. Many people tackled a range of technical and artistic issues and developed a strategy for advertising and marketing before expectant audiences were able to feast their eyes on the product. Much of what the public would see on the screen resulted from this last phase in making *The Pirate*.

Color, Sound, and Editing

The Technicolor process was complicated, and Vincente Minnelli had learned that it was profitable for him to become involved in it. Gene Kelly came along as well, and learned a great deal about how to manipulate the color processing to achieve greater results on the screen. Minnelli and Kelly spent hours in the lab with the Technicolor employees. The three-strip process that Technicolor had developed, which involved the employment of green, red, and blue, was adjusted by increasing one color over the others. "We could sit down in the lab *with* the Technicolor people and *control* the color," Kelly later recalled, "so it's . . . almost like a painting." When commenting on the process nearly thirty years later, Kelly still thought *The Pirate* was a magnificent example of how Technicolor could create color combinations on the silver screen.[1]

Lela Simone was in charge of fine-tuning the sound track. On September 3, 1947, she compiled a list of chores to be done. Judy Garland's recording of "You Can Do No Wrong" posed some problems. As Simone recalled it many years later, she had to manufacture a better ending for the song by splicing other takes to artificially create the last eight bars, because Garland had not been able to re-cord it in one take to perfection. Minnelli called Simone one day and told her that Garland had not sung the manufactured ending and that she was unhappy with it. Minnelli understood the necessi-ty of what Simone had done, but he and his wife nevertheless were upset. In addition to the items on Simone's list, the Sound Depart-ment at M-G-M had already asked various cast members to redo sound recordings that had not turned out well during filming. Kelly and Dee Turnell, who played Louisa in the "Niña" number, re-recorded some lines on August 15. Cully Richards, who played Trillo, re-recorded some "Wild Lines," as noted in the assistant di-rector's report, on September 19. Postproduction also involved re-filming problem scenes and dubbing dancers' taps. Gladys Coo-per and Cully Richards re-filmed some scenes in the exterior of Pe-dro's courtyard for about an hour on August 27. Kelly dubbed his own as well as other dancers' taps for "Niña" and "Be a Clown" for two and a half hours on the afternoon of August 18. Dubbing taps was a tedious procedure that required great skill. One needed to listen to the music, watch the footage, and add the taps precisely where needed. Kelly always dubbed his taps, and often those of his dance partners, to make them come out perfect.[2]

The Pirate was edited by veteran editor Blanche Sewell, with con-siderable input from Arthur Freed. The producer compiled a list of things for Sewell to do after he saw her initial suggestions for com-bining the many scenes into a smoothly flowing narrative. Freed thought Sewell was taking the viewer too suddenly into "Niña." He wanted to reinstate the bit between Serafin and his troupe about the cigar and walking up the street of Port Sebastian "a la Barrymore" before easing into the number. Freed found the "Voodoo" number too lengthy and wanted it shortened. He asked Sewell to keep Kel-ly's run up to the upper-floor balcony to begin his walk across the tightrope to Manuela's bedroom in one "take", i.e., not to intercut any other scenes into the sequence. For the introduction of the "Pi-rate Ballet," Freed wrote, "Let's see Kelly knock off hat of 2nd cop. Laugh will be bigger on look then." He also wanted to keep Kelly in full figure after he yelled, "Macoco!" and until he began to fence with the sitting mule. Near the end of the film, Freed thought Walter Slezak's speech, in which his character reveals himself as the real pi-rate, was too long. He also noticed some splicing of scenes that was illogical. "Shouldn't cut of Kelly and juggler be in after Slezak pulls pistols, not before?" he wrote.[3]

Illustration 5.1. Kelly strutting down the street in Port Sebastian à la John Barrymore. Whereas Kelly modeled Serafin's posing as Macoco on Fairbanks, he modeled Serafin's own demeanor on Barrymore, both imitations made tongue-in-cheek.

Arranging the credits, their size, and placement in relation to all the actors' names was a sensitive issue in Hollywood. For *The Pirate*, Garland and Kelly received top billing, their names slated to be 100 percent. Walter Slezak and Cole Porter received second billing at 50 percent, that is, their names appeared in lettering that was half the size of that used for Garland's and Kelly's names. Gladys Cooper, Reginald Owen, the Nicholas Brothers, Albert Hackett, Frances Goodrich, S. N. Behrman, Arthur Freed, Vincente Minnelli, and the Technicolor Corporation received third billing at 35 percent. The rest of those lucky enough to have their name on the credits were at 25 percent or 15 percent.[4]

Despite his prominent role as the Viceroy, George Zucco did not receive special billing but was simply listed in the cast of characters. In fact, the majority of those who worked behind the scenes on *The Pirate*, including Roger Edens, received no on-screen credit at all. Apparently, as employees of M-G-M, it was not deemed necessary to give them public acknowledgment for their work.

Illustration 5.2. One of the paintings of pirates by Doris Lee, who worked in the costume department at M-G-M. Manuela flips through this storybook about Macoco the Pirate to open the film.

Freed made a couple of changes to the planned credit list by adding Kelly's name to Robert Alton's under the heading of Dance Direction. Alton alone had originally occupied that category. Freed mandated that change on July 3, near the end of production. In early September, he also gave credit to Doris Lee for executing the paintings that depict Caribbean pirates in the book about Macoco at the beginning of the film.[5]

Joseph Breen's office had to examine the release print of *The Pirate* and judge whether it met the standards set by the Production Code of the Motion Picture Association of America. A private company called Lynch-Durland-Houghton handled the review. An employee identified as L. Greenhouse watched the film on October 13, 1947, and filled out a standard one-page form. He mentioned that the movie contained 10,292 feet of film and showed Spanish and Negro characters. Under the heading of Liquor, Greenhouse merely wrote, "Girl lead's uncle sips wine at home," referring to Lester Allen, and under the heading of Drinking, "Very little." Greenhouse noted little else, and Breen issued the standard certificate of approval the next day.[6]

SCREENINGS AND PREVIEWS

Freed held two private screenings of *The Pirate* for small groups of invited guests in September. The motion picture was not yet ready for general release because Freed considered it a bit too long and the music was still not complete. The first screening, which took place on or before September 4, included Freed, Garland, Minnelli, Cole Porter, and Irving Berlin among the audience. Freed and Berlin loved it, but Porter merely said, "'We shall see.'" He left for his New York home on September 5. Howard Strickling, a publicity executive for M-G-M, liked *The Pirate*, too. "The picture is different, refreshing and moves at a terrific pace even in its present overlength." Strickling also reported suggestions he had overheard at the screening. Some attendees thought the "Voodoo" number was the least interesting part of the film, and they "particularly didn't like Judy in this." Others wanted to see "more sincere romantic interest and perhaps a few hot love scenes with Judy and Gene after the fight or somewhere in the latter part of the picture." The second private screening took place on or before September 22, and included Gus Eysell and Ira and Lee Gershwin. According to Minnelli, the invited guests loved the film, complimenting it as "the best thing any of us has done. Felt they had seen something completely new on screen." But Minnelli "was jolted by a couple of cuts" in the film and wanted to speak with Freed about them.[7]

The invited guests at a private screening could be expected to praise the film, but preview audiences at a Los Angeles area venue were free to be more critical. The first preview of *The Pirate* took place at the Academy Theater in Inglewood on October 10, 1947. John Fricke's implication on *The Pirate* DVD that this preview was poorly received is misleading. He says people walked out and others filled in comment cards asking, "What are you doing?" The truth is, among the audience members, 121 (84 percent) indicated they enjoyed the film while 23 (16 percent) did not. Rating it for overall entertainment value, 65 audience members (43 percent) considered it excellent, 54 (36 percent) thought it was good, 21 (14 percent) rated it fair, and only 10 (7 percent) thought it was poor.[8]

When asked to list what interested them the most, viewers noted the dances, Garland's comedic acting, Kelly's "Niña," the "Pirate Ballet," and the first performance of "Be a Clown." "Gene Kelly is outstanding, superb," wrote one viewer, "and at his very best in this picture." Several thought *The Pirate* as well as Kelly deserved Oscars. Some said it was the "best picture" they had ever seen. "Let's have more like this please," wrote an appreciative member of the preview audience. Another asserted, "Don't ever let Gene Kelly stop dancing or Judy Garland stop singing. You have a terrific team in these two and they combine to make a terrific picture. Well done, MGM!"[9]

On the other hand, some preview audience members found fault with *The Pirate*. They thought the music was too loud (which might have been a problem associated with the sound system of the Academy Theater rather than a studio problem), and they identified several scenes that did not click as well as others. Several viewers did not like the opening sequence in which Judy sang "Mack the Black." Others thought Manuela's tantrum was "overdone." Several commentators did not like the "Voodoo" number, which they found boring. Others believed the transition from Pedro's revelation that he was the pirate to the reprise of "Be a Clown" was too abrupt.[10]

A second preview took place at the Academy Theater on November 7, 1947. This time, 43 members of the audience (57 percent) audience rated *The Pirate* as excellent, 22 (29 percent) as good, 6 (8 percent) as fair, and 4 (5 percent) as poor. Both versions of "Be a Clown," "Niña," and the tightrope sequence were among the most favorite segments. The "Voodoo" number once again made the list of least favorite parts, although this time a couple of people said they liked the dance a lot. The audience also listed the tantrum sequence and "When Judy Garland was singing to the hat" among their least favorite scenes. Many people thought Manuela's line, "He asked for me!" was the funniest of the film. "There should be more of Gene Kelly dance numbers," commented several viewers, while one remarked that "Gene Kelly is out of this world!" and another wrote, "I want Gene Kelly for Christmas." One viewer was either confused about who Kelly was or expected typical tap dancing. "I thought Gene Kelly was going to do several numbers during the picture which never happens," the individual complained, "Why not!" Another viewer seemed to have heard rumors about a number being cut after the first preview, which did not actually happen. This viewer assumed it was Kelly's number and pleaded, "I understand one dance was cut after first preview, please put it back in. He [Kelly] is so wonderful and gay and charming and adds so much sparkle to the story!" Overall, *The Pirate* rated very well with this second preview audience. They thought it "a very delightful show" and "a swell picture."[11]

REVISING THE FILM

The results of the two previews convinced Freed to make changes in *The Pirate*. Minnelli had already completed some previously planned retakes of scenes with Slezak, Cooper, and Allen on October 22 and 27. Planned retakes with Garland on October 23 were canceled when she called in sick. These efforts to obtain better versions of scenes that were not up to par continued on November 18, but the changes inspired by preview comments demanded more time to plan. Robert Nathan finished a script incorporating these changes by December 8, 1947. Three numbers were dropped based on feedback from the preview audiences. The first was Garland's rendition of "Mack the Black" from the start of the film. The other two were "Voodoo" and Manuela's singing "Love of My Life" to her hat.[12]

The audio outtakes of all three dropped numbers on the DVD version of *The Pirate* allow an understanding of some of the problems with these numbers. "Voodoo" is completely out of character with the rest of the film's music. It starts on a shrill, plaintive note, then gets a bit creepy, and the rest of the song is very dull. It is not surprising that preview audiences disliked the number. The original "Mack the Black" number is far too long for starting the film. Moreover, some of the lyrics are lurid and disturbing and introduce Manuela as a crazed person rather than the naïve young woman in the final release print. Even Garland's renditions of verses kept in the new "Mack the Black" number do not sound so appealing in the audio outtakes. Only part of the chorus for this number is good, and this is the part retained in the film; it is what audiences hear as the opening credits roll. The version of "Love of My Life" that Garland sang to the hat is longer and less expressive than the same number kept in the film, in which Garland sings to Kelly on the stage. The music is also slightly different. The main reason to drop this number, however, was that it would be unbelievable to watch someone sing a love song to a hat, as the preview audience rightly observed.

Changes had to be made with the dropping of these numbers. Instead of Garland's original "Mack the Black" number, Manuela would thumb through the storybook on Macoco and read aloud about his exploits to start the film with the aura of a fairytale. Doris Lee, who worked in the costume department at M-G-M, was asked to make paintings of pirates attacking ships or capturing maidens. The people in the paintings—whether pirates or their victims—

Illustration 5.3. Manuela appears to be thinking about the last time she wore the hat—by the sea in Port Sebastian, where she met Serafin. This scene is part of the shorter sequence that Minnelli used to replace Manuela's song to her hat.

were to be shown as multiethnic to create the atmosphere Minnelli wanted.

A new, vibrant "Mack the Black" number by Garland would replace "Voodoo," as discussed in Chapter 4. Like "Voodoo," "Mack the Black" would follow the hypnosis sequence but would have the audience in Port Sebastian become part of the exciting performance.

The song to the hat, Garland's first rendition of "Love of My Life," would fall on the cutting room floor along with the lengthy scene with her friends that led up to the song. All of this would be replaced by a shorter, more meaningful scene: When a pensive Manuela, in her bridal gown, wonders aloud to Inez whether she will be happy, Inez responds, "But you will be, my dear, if you wish for it *hard enough*. You can make anything come true by wishing for it." Manuela thinks about this, runs to her cupboard, and gets her hat box. She pulls her hat out and laughs happily, obviously at the memory of her encounter with Serafin when she wore that hat. She holds the hat to her cheek and smiles nostalgically. But then she looks disturbed and confused—after all she is about to be married to someone else. She quickly puts the hat back even as loud music announces the arrival of Serafin's troupe right outside her home. It is a subtle, yet clever, sequence to show that even though she seems upset at his arrival, deep in her heart, Manuela wished for Serafin *hard enough* and made him appear.

A spurt of renewed filming took place to accommodate these changes. Rehearsals for the new "Mack the Black," hurriedly choreographed by Alton, took place on December 1. Garland reported herself too ill to attend, according to the substitute assistant director, Marvin Stuart. More than a week later, on December 11, Garland reported for work but complained of having a fever after only two hours. Dr. Jones, the studio physician, came to the set and "found no temperature," according to Stuart. Nevertheless, Jones advised Garland not to work for the rest of the day or the next, and the actress went home. Garland eventually recorded the "Mack the Black" song on December 15, rehearsed the dance the next day, and filmed it on December 17. Dorothy Ponedel often had to fix Garland's long-haired wig during the filming of the strenuous dance. Stuart reported that Garland took a break for forty-five minutes at midday to do costume fitting for her new film, *Easter Parade*, before continuing to work on "Mack the Black." On December 18, with yet another substitute assistant director, Dolph Zimmer, the filming of the number continued. Zimmer reported that Kelly needed a new wig in midafternoon, but the company managed to finish shooting the number that day. On December 19, Minnelli filmed a new version of Garland interacting with friends on her balcony to follow Manuela's reading from the book on Macoco.[13]

Production of *The Pirate* finally ended on December 20, 1947. Sixty-seven days of filming, twelve more than originally planned, had been required to get the film in the can. Filming had been six days behind schedule and retakes were another seven days behind the original schedule. Even rehearsals had been fourteen days behind. All these delays had been caused by Garland's repeated absences, which also accounted for most of the twenty-nine days of unplanned layoffs. The project was budgeted to cost $3,541,054. As of December 18, it had cost $3,703,825, with $32,671 more expected to complete the film. At a total estimated cost of $3,736,496, *The Pirate* would be $222,442 over budget. After the retakes were finished, the release print of the picture totaled 9,136 feet of film.[14]

The Trailer and Merchandising

Studio staff devoted a good deal of thought and time to the trailer, the all-important teaser for film audiences. Frank Whitbeck, publicity chief at M-G-M, suggested the trailer emphasize Kelly as the pirate, not as Serafin, because "a daring man is more apt to set feminine hearts aflutter. Certainly a bold pirate is the more impressive figure, of the two." He then wanted to switch to scenes of Garland breaking things over the pirate's head. "It's a contrivance that will, we hope, intrigue the ticket buyer—young, old, meek and bold." The trailer consisted of various scenes of Kelly as Macoco, giving the viewer the suggestion that he truly would be a pirate in this film. "Here's the MADDEST, MERRIEST, MELODIOUS COURTSHIP ever on the screen," "A COLORFUL CARNIVAL of LAUGHTER and SONG!" the trailer proclaimed. The studio promised viewers "The LOVELINESS of the CARIBBEAN" as well as a rollicking pirate show. The footage of the trailer amounted to 208 feet of film.[15]

Despite its emphasis on Kelly as the pirate, the trailer includes a brief scene between Serafin and Manuela that hints that things may not be as they seem. This was a good idea because it keeps the trailer from being too deceptive and also adds a touch of intrigue.

A brief segment of Garland's original "Mack the Black" number, which had opened the preview version, is retained in the trailer, even though the number was dropped after the previews. The trailer also includes a segment from Garland's new "Mack the Black" number, which replaced the dropped "Voodoo" dance. It appears that the old segment was kept to make the trailer more colorful and exciting by showing Garland singing the same song, with a quick change of costumes and settings.

Using segments cut from the film in trailers was a common practice at the time. In a few places, the trailer for *The Pirate* used different takes than were used in the movie. Serafin's close-up before the reprise of "Be a Clown" and the way Kelly says his lines here is one example. The take of Serafin looking at Manuela when he sees her for the first time is also different. Moviemakers had many takes of each scene on hand, and they wanted to use takes that were good but that did not make it into the release print.

M-G-M produced two programs for *The Pirate*, one in English and another in Spanish. Lobby cards could be ordered from the studio. These were color posters advertising the film that could be placed in theater lobbies. *The Pirate's* "exhibitors' campaign book," issued by M-G-M, was created by Bill Ferguson, a studio advertising executive. He suggested a wide variety of ideas, including offering a free cruise and creating a pirate float for a local parade. Ferguson also suggested that theater owners create a number of scenarios in their lobby, such as daring local girls to walk a low plank into the arms of a young man dressed as a pirate, and offering free tickets to the film for those who accepted the dare. The same young man could toss candy kisses to girls waiting for tickets in the lobby, or watch over a pirate's chest filled with prizes of various merchandise. He also could dare girls to kiss him. Apparently, Ferguson did not think only young women were a prime audience for the film. He expected women of all ages to be fascinated with pirates and suggested tie-ins to local store displays for women's scarves and bandanas, advertising them as "Pirate kerchiefs."[16]

Another obvious target among film viewers was children. Ferguson produced pirate coloring books with pictures of Kelly and Garland, and suggested that theater owners organize coloring contests for younger members of the audience. He also thought writing contests on subjects such as "Why I'd Like to Be a Pirate" and "Best definition of a Love Pirate in 25 words" would work. Suggested prizes included M-G-M record albums, store merchandise, cash, and guest tickets to the movie. If that did not work, perhaps a pirate's parrot displayed in the lobby would attract attention. Despite Ferguson's coverage of all angles, Minnelli later said he thought the merchandizing for the film was not up to par.[17]

More Audience Feedback

The many changes in the film required yet another preview, which took place at Loew's Seventy-second Street Theater in New York on March 23, 1948. The Motion Picture Research Bureau conducted interviews with 314 audience members (159 males and 155 females), and 92 percent of them considered Kelly "as the player they especially enjoyed." The Bureau reported that, "This is the highest rating of this kind an actor ever received in a preview survey." The "Pirate Ballet" was the highest-rated dance among five that viewers mentioned, with the reprise of "Be a Clown" next, followed by "Mack the Black," the first version of "Be a Clown," and "Niña." A few viewers criticized the "Pirate Ballet" as "too long and too drawn out." Others called the opening sequence on Manuela's balcony "dull and slow" and characterized the tantrum sequence as "too much furniture throwing." Nevertheless, 92 percent of those surveyed said they would recommend the movie to friends. Many of the New York audience echoed the same comments already voiced by the audience in Inglewood: they wanted more dancing from Kelly. Overall comments were highly positive: "Wonderful," "Should make more like it," "They should team Kelly and Garland more often," and "Smash hit."[18]

The Motion Picture Research Bureau provided M-G-M with more detailed analysis than the studio's own research department typically did for preview audiences. For example, the bureau concluded that males liked Kelly's dancing more consistently than females did, while females liked Garland's "Mack the Black" better than did males. Both genders equally enjoyed the Nicholas Brothers in "Be a Clown," while males liked the reprise of "Be a Clown" much more than did females. Even though 208 participants in the survey (66.3 percent) were less than thirty years old, and 106 (33.7 percent) were older than thirty, the Bureau apparently found no significant differences in the segments of the film that different age groups enjoyed.[19]

The Loew's audience liked the photography and the color of *The Pirate,* but some viewers made critical remarks about the film. One did not enjoy the music. "Was too realistic," according to one person, who probably meant to write, "unrealistic." Similarly, another wrote, "Too magnified, too theatrical," and another found "Picture as a whole hammy," all three missing the point that it was supposed to be so. Another audience member thought the motion picture was "too long."[20]

The third preview taught M-G-M relatively little about what was good and bad in *The Pirate* that it did not already know from the other two previews. All that remained was to send this project, despite some mixed reactions by preview audiences, out into the world. M-G-M did so on May 20, 1948, with a release in New York and another on June 11 everywhere else. Freed's friends and acquaintances liked the film. Edward Chodorov of Twentieth Century-Fox called it "such a beautiful picture . . . the most skillful production job I have ever seen."[21]

REACTIONS FROM CRITICS

Newspaper critics were mostly positive, some of them even ecstatic about the film. "The simplest way to describe 'The Pirate' is WOW!" proclaimed *The Hollywood Reporter,* "For it is that kind of show—

bright, fast, witty, and wonderfully entertaining." Declaring that "the plot is cute; the musical numbers sensational; and the performances out of this world," the *Reporter* predicted a large box office take for M-G-M. Ann Helming of the *Hollywood Citizen-News* called it "the gayest, liveliest, most exciting and colorful musical film in many, many months." *The Pirate* seemed "a riot of Technicolor comedy, costumes, and cream-of-the crop Cole Porter tunes" to a reporter at *Cue.* It was "as gay and charming entertainment as anyone would care to see," according to critic Edwin Schallert, who predicted it would be enormously popular with "discriminating audiences for musicals."[22]

Many reviewers called *The Pirate* an example of well-rounded entertainment. A *Newsweek* critic thought the film was a "rare and happy combination of expert dancing, catchy tunes, and utterly unbelievable plot which manages to achieve pure escapism without becoming either sentimental or corny." Cecelia Ager praised Minnelli in *P.M. Daily* because, in directing *The Pirate,* he "keeps its splendors within bounds, relates them to one another, and stays confidently within its own frame." Ruth Waterbury summed up this theme by declaring that, "The best elements in good picture making got together here."[23]

Tom Donnelly of the *Washington Daily News* urged readers to see *The Pirate* "for its visual beauty and Gene Kelly's extraordinary dancing." Several critics echoed this assessment. At least one argued that it was the best musical of the year, and another thought the entire family would enjoy the show. "It is a grand audience treat that will have theater seats shaking, box offices tingling, and Leo's coffers bulging," commented *Box Office Digest.*[24]

Many critics noted the unusual acting style in the film. They recognized that Kelly was trying to imitate Fairbanks and Barrymore. *The Hollywood Reporter* referred to it as the "devastating satire of the swashbuckling adventure yarn." Ernie Schier of the *Washington Times Herald* even recognized that the costume Minnelli designed for Kelly in the "Pirate Ballet" was "a facsimile of the black tunic and arm bands" Fairbanks wore in *The Black Pirate.* Ager thought Kelly did not pull off the Barrymore imitation with "the Barrymore class," but she did not mind. A "half-way imitation of the Great Profile is hard to resist." Several commentators were happy that the movie did not take itself too seriously. "It even appears to be kidding itself," as Rose Pelswick put it in the *New York Journal-American.*[25]

Critics who knew the stage version of *The Pirate* had often commented that the story needed dancing and singing, and they were grateful that Freed had taken on the project and made it into a musical. Many writers thought Porter's songs were good, "among the composer's best," as *Cue* put it. *The Hollywood Reporter* quoted Lee Mortimer of the *Daily Mirror* as saying that the film was "loaded with prospective juke box hits."[26]

The costumes, set design, and the lush color of Minnelli's film drew the attention of many critics. Pelswick thought *The Pirate* held "some of the most beautiful Technicolors yet photographed. In this one the colors aren't merely pretty tints; they're used with dramatic effect." Kate Cameron of the *New York Daily News* believed it represented "the greatest advance in the Technicolor process of photography since Walt Disney's 'Fantasia.' The screen seems to have taken on a depth that accounts for the third [three-] dimensional look photographers have been aiming at for years. The colors are bright and gay, unusually distinct, each keeping itself in place and thus showing no tendency to blur." While *Time* found fault with other aspects of *The Pirate,* it thought Minnelli's color "equals the best on movie record (*Vanity Fair, Colonel Blimp, Henry V*), and is the one unqualified triumph of the show."[27]

Minnelli's depiction of an interracial society, which mirrored Behrman's stage production, caught the attention of Sidney Burke. He found it a "refreshing display of naturalness for the screen." Referring to Kelly's dance with the Nicholas Brothers as well as to the mingling of different races throughout the film, Burke wrote, "No point is made of this in the film; it's just there as though it didn't mean a thing and was an everyday occurrence."[28]

Critics also noted how well Minnelli had staged his crowd scenes. They cited the "Pirate Ballet" as the highlight of the film, one comparing it to the burning of Atlanta in *Gone with the Wind.* Others thought the Kelly-Garland version of "Be a Clown" was the highlight. Schallert called it a clever ending for *The Pirate,* noting that it was "practically like the beginning of a new show," tempting audiences to want to see the second installment in a *Pirate* sequence.[29]

Virtually all critics were united in proclaiming *The Pirate* as Kelly's film. He had "the part of his career as the Casanova with ham in his heart and romance on his lips," commented *The Hollywood Reporter.* "Kelly sails into it with undisguised vigor and literally stops the show cold with his Pirate dance." Oscar Davis, in an article titled "A Swashbuckler Leads, Oh, Such a Strenuous Life," called Kelly's dancing "imaginative and superb." Karl Krug, in Kelly's hometown of Pittsburgh, thought the film was rather overstuffed and boring because of Minnelli's direction but that Kelly saved it with his dancing. A reviewer at *Cue* wrote, "If there has ever been any finer dancing on screen other than Mr. Kelly's, I can't recall it." *The Pirate,* according to Ernie Schier, "should prove that even Kelly's most ardent admirers have been underestimating his flair for interpretation and the authority of his dancing." The critics universally proclaimed *The Pirate* to be the ultimate film of Kelly's career, using phrases like "dancing sensationally, performing brilliantly" as they strove for words to describe their reaction. "Gene Kelly is doing some of the fanciest gymnastic dancing of his career in 'The Pirate'—and he's good, very good, indeed," concluded a *New York Herald Tribune* writer.[30]

Kelly's contribution to the artistic success of *The Pirate* amounted to more than his spectacular dance numbers. Many critics thought his performance as Serafin was quite effective. Darr Smith concluded that Kelly had "been brushing up on his acting fundamentals," and it showed in an improved performance compared to his previous screen efforts. The link with Fairbanks and Barrymore was not lost on these critics, but they compared Kelly with those actors in a favorable, not critical, way. The *Washington Daily News* noted that, just like the character created by Fairbanks, Kelly's Serafin was "swashbuckler, rope climber . . . able to defend himself in all clinches, romantic or combat." Kelly "gives it all he has," commented one writer, "which is considerable and worthy of attention." Howard Barnes summed it up well when he wrote, "Kelly has a particular triumph in the production. . . . He dominates the doings in 'The Pirate' in no uncertain manner."[31]

Garland also came in for some well-deserved kudos from critics. They expected her to sing well and were not disappointed. But "she surprised us by coming through with a fresh comedy talent we didn't know she had." Darr Smith wondered if husband Minnelli was responsible for it.[32]

Those critics who looked favorably on *The Pirate,* and they were many indeed, called it one of M-G-M's "top musicals, . . . a gay, giddy Technicolor gambol." Cecelia Ager described it as "the best big-time musical show presented on screen, or on stage, in years." She thought Minnelli's film was "fun, fast, rollicking; it's lush with taste, color, movement, mood."[33]

But the critics were not united in praise of *The Pirate.* A vocal minority found fault with the movie, and on several different levels.

Alton Cook was disappointed that it did not duplicate the "sly impudence" of the Lunt-Fontanne stage play, and thought the original material had been "smothered under the elaborate trappings of a very expensive musical spectacle." Eileen Creelman agreed by calling it "a big overstuffed musical, with songs too serious, dances too long." She even went so far as to call it "something of a bore." *Motion Picture Daily's* Red Kann praised Kelly's dancing and the overall production values, but thought the film's "entertainment values never approach the same level."[34]

Some New York critics were particularly pointed in their criticism, terming *The Pirate* "a Technicolor nightmare that even the dancing of Gene Kelly and the music of Cole Porter do not redeem." James Agee, the often acerbic critic who wrote mostly for *The Nation,* liked the film's color and Garland's performance. He thought Minnelli's direction "gives the whole business bulge and splendor." But he thought Kelly's performance in imitating Barrymore and Fairbanks was "very ambitious, painfully misguided." Overall, Agee felt sorry for the principals involved in the motion picture, "for they're all really trying something—and in musical comedy, whose wonderful possibilities are too seldom realized by 'artists,' good or bad. Many people admire *The Pirate,* but it seems to me to have the death's-head, culture-cute, 'mirthful' grin of the average Shakespearean comic."[35]

A writer for *Time* agreed with Agee that Kelly's acting was ambitious and flawed. "His performance is so sharply mannered that it is a continuous muted dance." The imitations of Barrymore and Fairbanks were "apt and eager," but "as unhappy to watch as any other forged masterpiece." Pairing Kelly's performance with Garland's, Alton Cook admired the "bravura energy" of the two but could not tell whether "their exaggerations were intended as poetry or comedy but in either case, they miss the goal." Garland specifically came in for some harsh criticism at the hands of a few critics, who nevertheless praised the film, Minnelli, and Kelly. These critics did not like the tantrum sequence and considered Garland's performance "too shrill, too 20th Century . . . to fill the bill this time." Cole Porter came in for his share of the poor reviews as well from critics who liked the film's other aspects very much. In contrast to their praise for the rest of the movie, they called Porter's songs "poor" or at best "ordinary."[36]

Other critics saw both sides of the controversy. The film was "lopsided entertainment that is wonderfully flamboyant in its high spots and bordering on tedium elsewhere," according to a writer in the *New York Herald Tribune*. While Archer Winsten loved the movie, he thought it was superficial and had no core, heart-tugging element that would make one care deeply about it—more like a circus than a heart-warming film. "It's the musical of the year," Winsten concluded, "unless a better one comes along."[37]

INITIAL RELEASE

As the critics voiced their opinions, M-G-M eagerly kept track of the box office receipts to see if the film would strike gold. Movie musicals tended to be much more expensive to make than most other genres of film, but *The Pirate* was exceptionally costly, even compared to other musicals. As Stephen Harvey has put it, Minnelli's project "needed to provoke a sensation at the box office to make any money" for M-G-M. Initially, it seemed as if *The Pirate* might fulfill that expectation. Carter T. Barron, the manager of Loew's Capitol Theatre in Washington, D.C., reported that it was "doing a very nice business, . . . audience reaction is splendid." On its opening day at the Radio City Music Hall in New York, *The Pirate* garnered $16,795, which put it in the top tier of high-grossing films shown there in the recent past. After four days at the Music Hall it grossed $85,758, the most that any M-G-M film did in that venue for that length of time. The next highest was *Till the Clouds Roll By* (1947), which garnered $83,166. In its fourth and last week at the Music Hall, *The Pirate* grossed $117,774. Only four other M-G-M films had exceeded that amount in their fourth week, including musicals such as *Till the Clouds Roll By* and *Good News* (1947). In twenty-eight days at the Music Hall, *The Pirate* grossed $513,128, outpaced by only three other M-G-M movies in the previous few years.[38]

Unfortunately for Minnelli, Kelly, and Garland, *The Pirate* did not maintain its early momentum. The income derived by *The Pirate* at Radio City Music Hall indicates that people were eager to see the film, but not so eager to come back for a second viewing, which was a major source of revenue for movie studios at the time. As a result, a general impression developed that *The Pirate* was a commercial failure. It had cost $3,768,496 to make, but the revenue it generated during its release amounted to only $2,956,000. That represented a shortfall of $812,496, something Freed was not used to seeing for his musicals. *The Pirate* was widely noted as the only Judy Garland film at M-G-M that lost money for the studio.[39]

Technically, *The Pirate* did lose money in its initial release, but it actually made a profit over time. Therefore, condemnations that it was a commercial failure need to be taken with a large grain of salt. Moreover, the Freed musicals were the most expensive films M-G-M made, which meant that audience interest had to be intense for the studio to make a quick profit. For some products of the Freed Unit, such as the classic *Singin' in the Rain,* the profit was enormous. The movie cost $2,540,800 to make and grossed $7,665,000 in its initial run. By that standard, *The Pirate* could be viewed as a failure but so could every other musical. Besides, *The Pirate* was to a degree an experimental film in which Minnelli had pushed the envelope in terms of acting style, décor, color, and props. With ticket sales as low as thirty-three cents for late-morning showings in Pittsburgh, millions of people would have had to see the film for the studio to quickly recoup its investment. In fact, despite such low prices, *The Pirate* generated nearly three million dollars and came close to breaking even during its initial run. It was not at all "a resounding failure commercially and critically," as one commentator put it a few years after its release. Not only were many critics charmed by the film, the studio actually recovered its investment through re-releases and in the long run made what Minnelli called "a modest profit."[40]

Album Releases

The studio was keen on releasing recordings of Porter's songs as soon as possible but that process ran into some trouble. Porter "was very much disturbed" by the plan to release a long-playing album featuring the songs he had written specifically for *The Pirate.* Apparently, he was not enthusiastic about a movie company producing an album, and would have preferred that a "major phonograph company" do it, but the studio insisted. "The 'Good News' album, I understand, is selling very well," wrote Larry Spier of M-G-M's marketing staff, "and surely, 'The Pirate' should do as well, if not better." When Jesse Kaye, the newly appointed head of M-G-M Records, transferred the prerecordings of these songs to the proper staff at M-G-M, he suggested that disc jockeys raise interest in the album by asking radio listeners to count how many times Kelly says Niña. Kaye reported that "the girls in the office listened to it several times and they caught between thirty-one and thirty-three." The album that M-G-M Records produced included "Love of My Life,"

"You Can Do No Wrong," "Be a Clown" (the version recorded by Kelly and Garland), "Niña," "Mack the Black," and the orchestral music for the "Pirate Ballet."[41]

M-G-M Records and the Mutual Broadcasting System cooperated in the debut of *The Pirate* album by featuring it on the *Jim Backus Program* on May 2 and 9, 1948. Backus was carried by 250 Mutual Broadcasting System stations, so the exposure was wide and deep. Even so, Porter was not satisfied with "the exploitation" of one of his songs, "Love of My Life," when he spoke with Larry Spier in early June. Spier tried to prove that M-G-M Records was doing all it could. He sent Porter a list of more than seventy programs the song had been played on and the more "important commercials" that were scheduled. Spier admitted that the results of six weeks of work on the marketing of that song failed to meet his own expectations, but he hoped for a better response in the near future.[42]

M-G-M also released the same six songs from *The Pirate* on separate albums in 1948, presumably to spur sales. M-G-M 30097 included the orchestral music for the "Pirate Ballet" and the Kelly-Garland version of "Be a Clown." M-G-M 30098 had Garland's "Love of My Life" and "You Can Do No Wrong." Kelly sang "Niña" and Garland sang "Mack the Black" on M-G-M 30099. In 1955, all of these songs were once again put together on a single album, M-G-M E3234, along with selected songs from *Summer Stock* (1950). Rhino released a reissue of *The Pirate* album in 2004 and this time included unused songs, outtakes, and interviews that Kelly and Garland did to promote the film.[43]

NATIONAL AND INTERNATIONAL RELEASES

Although the Breen office had approved *The Pirate*, Minnelli's film still had to be reviewed by state-level censor offices. The movie breezed through that process. State offices in Ohio, Maryland, New York, Massachusetts, Kansas, and Pennsylvania approved *The Pirate* in March and April 1948.[44]

Kelly recalled Louis B. Mayer's prediction that some southern theater managers would be upset by the inclusion of the Nicholas Brothers in "Be a Clown" and would request that number be excised from the release prints sent to them. Mayer was right. Theater managers in Memphis and a few other southern cities called for the deletion of that number, but it remained in the release prints sent to the rest of the segregated South.[45]

Illustration 5.4. Irish censors objected to what they called a passionate embrace in the "Niña" number. It was the only cut M-G-M had to make to satisfy the international market.

M-G-M's international releases of *The Pirate* began on August 30, 1948, with Sweden, where it was called *Piraten*. The film opened in France on September 28, 1949, as *Le Pirate*; in Finland on April 7, 1950, as *Paula kaulassa*; in Portugal on July 12, 1950, as *Pirata dos Meus Sonhos*; in Japan on June 29, 1951; in the Philippines on January 17, 1952; and in Denmark on December 11, 1966, as *Soroveren*. Apparently, the title was not changed in Japan or the Philippines. The movie was released as *O Pirata* in Brazil, *Il Pirata* in Italy, *A kaloz* in Hungary, *Korsan aski* in Turkey, *Pirat* in Poland, and *Pieratis* in Greece, but the release dates for these countries are not available. The film was re-released in Spain as *El Pirata* on December 5, 1973; in France on February 9, 2000, and again on April 14, 2004; and in West Germany as *Der Pirat* on April 20, 1981.[46] It is interesting that Fulda's stage play, representing the origin of the movie plot, had been written and staged many years earlier in Germany as *Der Seerauber*.

Minnelli's film ran afoul of censors only when it hit Ireland around January 1949. The Irish insisted that M-G-M delete the "Shot of girl hanging out of window with Serafin embracing her. Reason given: Passionate embrace," according to a report filed by the Motion Picture Association of America.[47]

The Irish referred to a few seconds in the "Niña" number, and M-G-M would have had no problem with making this editing change. The studio executives often had to make such changes in response to censorship requests or demands by foreign governments, and it was in their interest to do so to ensure international sales.[48] Compared to what M-G-M had to do for other films, it got off very easily for *The Pirate,* which ironically has many sensual and sensuous moments that moral authorities around the world ignored.

CHAPTER SIX

Legacy of *The Pirate*

More than sixty-five years after its release, *The Pirate* has garnered a great deal of attention from fans, critics, and film scholars who have rediscovered its treasures. Or, in some cases, they have held it up to a critical light, much as the critics of 1948 had done. As a result, *The Pirate* has a mixed legacy that tends to mirror the mostly enthusiastic, yet somewhat ambivalent, reception accorded the film when it was released. Nevertheless, *The Pirate* is universally considered a major film in the careers of Gene Kelly, Vincente Minnelli, and Judy Garland. The most favorable evaluation accords it something akin to masterpiece status, while even those who criticize the motion picture acknowledge its brilliant aspects.

THE PLAYERS LOOK BACK

Kelly and Minnelli continued to turn out superb movies and collaborated again on two films—*An American in Paris* (1951) and *Brigadoon* (1954). Both men witnessed the initial reception for *The Pirate* and lived long enough to see the growing respect for their first collaborative project. Both mentioned their view of the film in interviews given late in their lives.

"After the previews," Kelly said in 1973, "Vincente and I honestly believed we were being so dazzlingly brilliant and clever that everybody would fall at our feet and swoon clear away in delight and ecstasy—as they kissed each of our toes in appreciation for this wondrous new musical we'd given them. Well, we were wrong. About five and a half people seemed to get the gist of what we set out to do. And in retrospect, you couldn't really blame them. We just didn't pull it off. Not completely. Whatever I did looked like fake Barrymore and fake Fairbanks." Kelly thought *The Pirate* played well in New York and other urban areas, but it failed to connect with small-town audiences.[1]

Kelly blamed the trick of trying to imitate Barrymore and Fair-banks as the chief cause of the movie's "failure." Most people did not seem to understand, Kelly thought, that the imitation was sincere, flattering, and tongue-in-cheek; instead, they seemed to think it was forgery. During a radio interview at Columbia University in 1958, Kelly blamed himself: "Often I didn't have enough skill or experience to bring the tongue-in-cheek aspects off." Kelly was referring not only to *The Pirate* but another film he did immediately afterward, *The Three Musketeers* (1948). He recalled that his performance looked perfect in rehearsals, but failed to take hold on the screen. It was "the result of the damned elusive camera I'd been trying so hard to tame." For a long time Kelly regretted that he had attempted the clever joke he and Minnelli had cooked up for the part of Serafin. But in fact he took too much blame upon himself. Small-town audiences of the 1940s lacked the sophistication to grasp the tongue-in-cheek aspects and were guided by local critics who saw Kelly merely as a "second-class Barrymore." Kelly realized this in the 1980s when new audiences of college students readily got the joke and were enchanted by the film.[2]

Kelly loved other aspects of *The Pirate* a great deal. He thought Garland "was superb" in the film, and Minnelli's work with color and décor was "as fine as anything that has ever been done." In fact, other than the audience's missing the satirical aspect, Kelly thought *The Pirate* was a nearly perfect product in the long list of films churned out by the Freed Unit at M-G-M. Minnelli, in his memoirs and in interviews throughout his life, acknowledged Kelly's contributions to the film with awe and gratitude.[3] Recall that Kelly not only had to act, dance, and sing in the movie, which he did with consummate skill, but that he contributed significantly to preproduction and postproduction, very much as a co-director would. In fact, the extent of collaboration between these two talented men is the best argument against calling Minnelli or anyone else the auteur of this film.

In recollecting or reporting the names of musical numbers in *The Pirate*, however, much confusion developed over the years among the players as well as among historians. The correct name of the magnificent extended dance sequence by Kelly, representing Manuela's fantasy, was the "Pirate Ballet." But Kelly and others tended in later years to call it the "Mack the Black" number, possibly because much the same music is used for the "Pirate Ballet" and Garland's "Mack the Black" song under hypnosis. Minnelli talked of the "Fire Dance" in 1975, which from his description also seems to be the "Pirate Ballet." And Hugh Fordin, who wrote a history of the Freed Unit, incorrectly referred to the denouement of the film, with its pending execution, hypnosis, and so on, as the "Pirate Ballet."[4]

Another element in the confusion is related to which musical number was found to be too erotic. Kelly mentioned in 1975 that the studio wanted to cut some scenes with him and Garland that were deemed too erotic from the "ballet." Of course, such scenes were never part of the "Pirate Ballet" because Garland is not in it. Based on Kelly's descriptions in his interviews, it is clear that he was referring instead to "Love of My Life." Nevertheless, film historians Joel Siegel and Tony Thomas wrote that Mayer wanted the "Pirate Ballet" to be reshot because it was too erotic. The Internet Movie Data Base, John Fricke's comments on the DVD version of *The Pirate,* and Mark Griffith's book on Minnelli carry this confusion further by erroneously stating that it was the "Voodoo" number that Mayer found erotic and that he demanded the negative be burned.[5]

There is no archival evidence anywhere that such was the case. Moreover, the "Voodoo" number was dropped because the preview audiences found it boring. As mentioned earlier, even the audio outtakes for this number sound very dull. It is highly unlikely that this number could have been deemed erotic. Moreover, the very idea of an erotic number at this point does not fit with the plot or with censorship issues. "Voodoo" was performed when Manuela was under hypnosis, and making it erotic would not play well with Serafin's essentially innocent character, nor would such a scenario have been approved by the Breen office. In contrast, Manuela is only pretending to be hypnotized in "Love of My Life" and she is deliberately goading Don Pedro into a fit of jealousy by displaying her love for Serafin. The eroticism fits nicely into this number, therefore, both in terms of plot and likely approval by Breen. It also clearly matches the specifics that Kelly referred to in his interviews (as discussed in Chapter 4). He talked about the number in question being at a late stage in the film, his and Garland's going a bit too far, and having to re-shoot a segment to tone it down.

In addition to general confusion about the names of musical numbers, Minnelli became confused about some other aspects of *The Pirate* as he grew older. By his later years, the director was afflicted with Alzheimer's disease and the onset of that condition probably accounts for his mistaken memories. In the mid-1970s, he confused S. N. Behrman with the author of the original story of

Illustration 6.1. Serafin and Manuela interact with passion in "Love of My Life." It is likely that the filming of erotic scenes that Kelly mentioned in interviews was done for this segment and later deleted.

Yolanda and the Thief, Ludwig Bemelmans. Minnelli thought the audience enjoyed Kelly's "rakish" performance as Serafin, but did not take well to Garland's "adult role of farceuse," which is not entirely accurate. But Minnelli's comments on *The Pirate* mainly centered on the setting and the décor, which he remembered for the rest of his life as an exciting venue for color and costume. In a sense, this was at the heart of Minnelli's intense, creative spirit, so it is not surprising he would hold on to memories of that aspect of his work. He did remember that *The Pirate* had "wonderful ideas" and recalled Arthur Freed's comment that the motion picture was "twenty years ahead of its time."[6]

Other players had their own memories of the film years later. In an interview conducted in 1990, Lela Simone, who had worked on troubleshooting the vocal aspects of the film, said she thought that parts of *The Pirate* were "*very* good," while other parts "lay flat." She particularly liked the musical score, which she called "very interesting." Many years after the filming of the first "Be a Clown," Fayard

Nicholas believed that public reaction had vindicated his worth as an entertainer. "'When people saw the film,'" he told his biographer, "'some of them didn't know they were looking at the Nicholas Brothers. They thought they were looking at somebody else. They weren't thinking about two black guys dancing with this white man.'"[7]

CRITICAL AND SCHOLARLY ASSESSMENT OVER THE YEARS

Praise and Recognition (1948–1957)

Soon after its release, *The Pirate* began to garner continued interest from writers and critics who recognized bits of genius within the film. These early commentators tended to write very positively about the movie for a decade after its creation, echoing the best newspaper response upon the motion picture's release.

Less than a year after the film was out, film critic Peter Ericsson noted its "deliberate artificiality" but also thought Minnelli had the foresight to "stick to the convention—Technicolor, stars, sentimental numbers—sufficiently to get by at the box-office." Ericsson thought *The Pirate* established Minnelli as the best director of film musicals in the country, and he disagreed with earlier critics who thought the production values turned the movie into a bloated or vulgar exercise in excess. Even a second viewing by Ericsson reinforced his initial impression that it was one of "the most exciting musicals for a long time."[8]

In 1949, barely a year after M-G-M released the film, British dance historian David Vaughan wondered why any critics managed to find fault with *The Pirate*. Himself a dancer, actor, and choreographer, Vaughan thought the film was "far superior" to *The Red Shoes*, a British production also released in 1948—that involved a great deal of ballet dancing, presented one of the best extended dance sequences to be called a film ballet, and was enormously popular with audiences and critics. Calling Kelly's performance "a *tour de force*," Vaughan praised his command of Spanish dance and ballet. He surmised that "with a dancer like Kelly to work with, Minnelli has come very near to achieving one's ideal of a dance film—that is, a film which dances *all* the time, and not merely in its spectacular set-pieces." He also praised Minnelli's "bold use of stylized movement, which perfectly matches the delicious fantasy of plot and setting," and his command of crowd scenes, color, and lighting in *The Pirate*.[9]

Three years later, film critic Lindsay Anderson, who later became a prominent film and theatrical director, called *The Pirate* Minnelli's "most daring experiment in artifice." It was "a film of unrivalled *chic:* an urbane fairy tale dressed and set with exuberant flair, and studded with numbers of the most polished brilliance." Anderson particularly liked the "Pirate Ballet" for its dramatic color, "sweeping crane shots," and "bold and brassy orchestration." While Anderson enjoyed and praised Kelly's performance, the critic also noted that the actor's persona could never really be submerged in the characters he portrayed either in dance or dialogue. "It has been said that Kelly 'dances people,'" Anderson mused. "Perhaps it would be truer to say that he dances 'a person'—himself." The only real criticism Anderson voiced about *The Pirate* was that Kelly and Garland did not have a light enough comedic touch to pull off the tongue-in-check aspects of the film as well as the material deserved.[10] This is probably true where a sophisticated audience is involved. However, for the majority of moviegoers of that era, even Kelly and Garland's overplaying did not convey that the film was meant to be a parody.

Mixed Viewpoints (1958–1967)

The second decade of *The Pirate*'s life saw several critics add more negative comments to the steady stream of published viewpoints about the Minnelli-Kelly-Garland creation. The critical views voiced upon its release seemed to resurface as time passed by, creating an interesting mix in the flow of analysis.

In 1958, film critic Albert Johnson expressed disappointment that Kelly and Garland never danced together in *The Pirate* as they had done so charmingly in *For Me and My Gal.* Although he liked "Niña" very much, Johnson thought the "Pirate Ballet" was overdone and amounted to "nothing of consequence." "It is a piece of cinema trickery that attempts to build the gymnastics into a big ballet," he wrote, "yet there is an inescapable feeling of torpor overhanging the entire business."[11]

Johnson's negative commentary was not shared by film historian Douglas McVay, whose 1959 article showcased the "magic of Minnelli." McVay thought *The Pirate* possessed a degree of "panache" that set it apart from Minnelli's other films. Kelly did a great deal to make the picture what it was, McVay believed. He was particularly taken by the dancer's performance in "Niña," and thought Kelly was "at his most breathtakingly agile" in the "Pirate Ballet." McVay was the first commentator to note the underlying camaraderie between Kelly and Garland in the final shot of their reprise of "Be a Clown." He wrote that the two "dissolve into (one feels quite genuine) laughter" to end the riotous entertainment presented by the film.[12]

In 1964, British commentator John Cutts evaluated Minnelli's product as an extraordinary attempt to do something never done before in a film musical. "Everything here is bold and brazen surface action," Cutts wrote. "The mood is grandiose; its execution likewise." Cutts admired Minnelli's fluid camera action in "Niña," and viewed the film as a watershed in the development of Kelly's skills as both a dancer and a choreographer. In the critic's view, Kelly migrated from tap toward a mix of ballet and gymnastic moves to create in *The Pirate* a style that "was astonishingly flamboyant, most exciting, beautiful to watch, and extremely difficult to describe." Cutts thought that Kelly's ability to dance a character was limited, but he noted the star's supreme ability to express moods, attitudes, and situations through dance. He wrote that Kelly handled even the most difficult movements in his numbers "with a true poet's grace."[13]

Cutts did not so highly praise Kelly's acting, however, concluding that the dancer lacked the "keen edge of sophisticated subtlety" that was needed to bring off Serafin to a fine pitch. "Kelly bulldozed his way through the part," Cutts remarked, "attacking the role rather than assuming it." Kelly tended "to play entirely in *italics*, hitting every line with an exaggerated emphasis. In this respect, the film does suffer." But this did not suppress Cutts's enthusiasm for *The Pirate*. It was "a masterpiece of extravagant entertainment, a boisterous rococo romp" that continued to grow in stature as "a rich and rare musical experiment."[14]

A Turning Point (1968–1978)

It took twenty years, as Freed had predicted, for audiences to understand and appreciate *The Pirate* more fully than had been the case in 1948. The passage of nearly a generation and the cultural changes of the 1960s helped to pave the way for a heightened awareness of its tongue-in-cheek style and its progressive attitudes toward race and gender.

Many people considered film critic Joel Siegel's article, published in 1971, to be the turning point in public awareness of the *The Pirate* as an underappreciated masterpiece of the Freed Unit. Writing for *Film Heritage*, Siegel seemed to criticize the film as often as he praised it, echoing the sometimes negative comments of those who had written of *The Pirate* before him. For the most part, his praise also echoed comments by his predecessors; but it caught the eye of Minnelli, who quoted from the article in his memoirs.[15] Siegel's article also was noticed by many of the newer as well as older film buffs of the 1970s, who now rediscovered *The Pirate*.

Film scholar John Russell Taylor and co-author Arthur Jackson, whose book *The Hollywood Musical* appeared in the same year as Siegel's article, provided readers another opportunity to rediscover *The Pirate*. The two argued that the film "has never really had its due." They particularly liked the Cole Porter songs, the entire musical score, Minnelli's magnificent crane shots, and Kelly's superb acrobatic dancing. The only negative aspect Taylor and Jackson saw in *The Pirate* was that neither Kelly nor Garland was capable of projecting the kind of ultra-sophistication that Minnelli, Porter, or even Behrman were capable of employing in their respective work. "There is . . . something slightly coarse and obvious about Kelly's personality, his approach, his choreography . . . which is at odds with Minnelli's extreme refinement and fastidiousness," the pair wrote. They thought "true sophistication is beyond the range of" both Kelly and Garland. The result, in their opinion, was a film that came close as a hair's breadth to being a true masterpiece.[16]

The Pirate drew even more public and critical attention in 1974 because of the release of a retrospective film, combining segments of many different M-G-M musicals with commentary by well-known actors, entitled *That's Entertainment*. Fred Astaire hosted a segment on Gene Kelly that included excerpts of the "Pirate Ballet" as well as Kelly's "Be a Clown" number with the Nicholas Brothers. This was followed by *That's Entertainment II*, released in 1976, which helped maintain the public's interest in *The Pirate* by including excerpts of Gene's "Be a Clown" with Judy and by playing the music of that piece over the end credits.

The first *That's Entertainment* coincided with the publication of the first major book about Gene Kelly, which also sparked a surge of public interest in the dancer's career. British journalist Clive Hirschhorn, the first major biographer of the star, proclaimed that *The Pirate* was "being 'rediscovered' by cineastes, and is now a cult film its adherents are hailing as a masterpiece." Hirschhorn especially pinpointed "Niña" as the ultimate dance of the film, a number that represented a level of achievement in the development of Kelly's personal dance style. The star danced with "the seductive grace of a panther" to create a "routine of sustained inventive brilliance" that was "mesmeric," in Hirschhorn's estimation. He admired Kelly's blending of ballet with his athletic approach and concluded that in *The Pirate* he "became a master of the genre."[17]

The "Pirate Ballet" did not fare so well in Hirschhorn's view. It was "visually quite exciting, but in the end, more orgiastic than artistic. Nor is it of much consequence choreographically and, if anything, adds to the overall staginess of the film. It is also excruciatingly noisy." The noisiness Hirschhorn refers to in the "Pirate Ballet" is not present in the DVD or videotape versions of the film and must have been caused by the theater's sound system. Hirschhorn also did not seem to understand the import of this number in plot development. He refers to it as Serafin's fantasy (imagining himself as a pirate) and misses the point that it is Manuela's fantasy of Serafin as Macoco. Kelly's biographer echoes an assessment by John Cutts that Kelly and Garland played "all their scenes in capital letters and punctuate every gesture with an exclamation mark." And unlike critics who raved about Minnelli's sense of color, he thought the colors and costumes were too exaggerated and "dizzied the public." Yet, Hirschhorn liked the film as a whole and thought *The Pirate* proved Kelly's ability to dance any possible mood on the screen. He believed Kelly "had come of age" in *The Pirate* as a "dancer, choreographer and innovator."[18]

In 1974, the same year that Hirschhorn's landmark biography appeared, author Tony Thomas published the only book that highlights Kelly's films in coffee-table format, replete with many illustrations, a brief running commentary, and copious quotations from Kelly interviews. Thomas found little to criticize in the film, except to note that the "inside joke" involving the parody of Fairbanks and Barrymore was a mistake. He praised Kelly's and Garland's acting, as well as Kelly's dancing and Harry Stradling's photography. Thomas thought Porter's songs were "top-notch" and found Minnelli's direction, décor, and costumes tuned to a fine pitch of excellence. Thomas loved the "Don Juan treatment" of "Niña" and described Kelly's "Be a Clown" number with the Nicholas Brothers as classic yet zesty. He found the "Pirate Ballet" astonishing in terms of Kelly's athletic dancing and yet thought it "an exhaustingly acrobatic, lurid abstract" of a pirate's life. Thomas would have preferred a cozy, romantic piece to demonstrate Manuela's love rather than an erotic fantasy. Actually, there *is* a cozy, romantic piece that demonstrates Manuela's love—later in the film where it fits with the plot—it is the "You Can Do No Wrong" number. Nevertheless, Thomas concluded that *The Pirate* was "a sumptuous, highly imaginative and sophisticated movie musical."[19]

Minnelli was pleased that commentators were taking *The Pirate* seriously with the passage of time. In 1974, the same year that Hirschhorn and Thomas came out with their books, the director published his memoirs, noting that he liked "to think that they [the critics] just might have grown up to it." Richard Schickel screened *The Pirate* just before interviewing Minnelli for a book he published in 1975, and was captivated by its brilliance in terms of Minnelli's direction as well as the talents of Kelly and Garland. "To miss it is to miss one of the authentic glories of our cinema," he concluded.[20]

Film professor Jeanine Basinger published a short but pungent book on Kelly in 1976 that highly praised his work in *The Pirate*, adding to a growing public awareness of the film's stature within the history of the Freed Unit. She enjoyed every aspect of the film, from Minnelli's direction to the set design, the costumes, and Garland's singing and acting. Kelly was at his career peak to date, in Basinger's view. His portrayal of Serafin as a "beloved rogue" was deft and effective. "Kelly swaggers, he struts, and he swashbuckles. Through it all, he manages to convey to the audience the most complicated of character communications." He "creates a satirical character and manages to carry the satire into his dance." She found Kelly's dancing and choreography in this film to be remarkable and among his best. In the "Pirate Ballet," which Basinger calls "a virgin's magnificent dream of a bad man who sweeps into her life and gets ready to do heaven knows what," Kelly "does some of his strongest, most totally masculine dancing." Basinger thought commentators still had not come to fully appreciate the value of *The Pirate*, and that the single most important roadblock was a persistent inability among some to recognize that the film was a parody of many artistic conventions.[21]

Public reaction to *The Pirate* was further improved with a retrospective viewing at the University of Texas in 1977. The same year, in a book about Minnelli's work, film studies scholar Joseph Casper proclaimed that "critical reaction to *The Pirate* has undergone a *volte-face*, undoubtedly due in part to the distance from the Lunt-Fontanne original." Whether memories of the stage play had anything to do with criticism of the film is difficult to prove, but Casper liked every aspect of the production, including the clever lines, the exotic setting, and the robust characters that audiences could connect with and care about. Casper admired the balanced way in which Minnelli put everything together in the film, and he noted that the director's penchant for surrealism is always grounded in some sort of reality to make it more comprehensible for mass audiences.[22]

Casper thought Garland did very well in playing the comedic role of Manuela, and he admired Kelly's performance in *The Pirate* very much. "Gene Kelly transforms Serafin into a magnificent jack-in-the-box. It is his greatest screen feat." Casper saw the "Niña" number as "Kelly at his dazzling best." Building on McVay, Casper observed that *The Pirate* ends with a classic bit of *"cinema-verite"* as Kelly and Garland seemingly drop the masks of Serafin and Manuela for a second, and look at each other as friends and colleagues.[23]

Casper was the first to use an analytical lens to examine the "Pirate Ballet" from Manuela's viewpoint, which is the key to the

Illustration 6.2. Serafin dances around the white mule as Manuela watches from her window. The mule in the scene is actually a stuffed representation because the real mule refused to sit down.

Illustration 6.3. Manuela imagines Serafin as the pirate Macoco dancing around a woman who seems identified with the mule. Scholars have commented extensively on the underlying meaning of this imagery.

Illustration 6.4. Manuela looks flustered and agitated at her own fantasy of Serafin as the pirate. It is to Garland's acting credit that these reaction shots, which were filmed even before the ballet was fully planned, came out so perfectly.

spectacle. As Manuela imagines herself to be the white mule, "sensuality plays with virginity," he wrote. She is horrified and fascinated by what she imagines to be the life of a bloodthirsty pirate. "Eventually, the pirate lops off her ears with his machete, a phallic gesture at once indicative of his machismo, her masochism, and penetration." But Casper appears to have misread the end of the number. He noted that, "Manuela, with a look of post-coital satisfaction on her face, slowly closes the shutters. She is no longer agitated."[24] In fact, Manuela looks like a young woman alarmed by her own fantasy, far from satisfied or satiated. She looks flustered and agitated as she quickly closes the shutters to shut both her fantasy and Serafin out of her life.

The Pirate had reached such a plateau of acceptance among commentators that Douglas McVay, writing again about the film in 1978, thirty years after its release and nearly twenty years after his first article on it in 1959, called it Minnelli's greatest film, Kelly's finest performance, and Garland's as well. He claimed that *The Pirate* was his own favorite Hollywood musical and could be viewed "as the masterpiece of Hollywood musical comedy," even though a musical drama like George Cukor's *A Star Is Born* was, in McVay's view, a better film overall. Bringing all the elements together accounted for Minnelli's success in *The Pirate*: "If one is going to try to blend words, music, movement, dance sets, costumes, props, color photography and camera fluency into a total, effortless harmony, then this, surely, is the way to do it."[25]

Theoretical Analysis Deepens (1980–1987)

The growth of film studies as an academic discipline created a new stream in the published commentary about *The Pirate* by the 1980s. Rich in sophisticated imagery and style, the film became a prime object of analysis at the hands of film scholars. Joseph Casper had already demonstrated the film's potential in this regard, and other film scholars now stepped up to offer deeper theoretical interpretations of the film.

In 1980, D. N. Rodowick offered the most in-depth evaluation of *The Pirate* yet written. Using psychoanalytic theory to examine the characters and situations of the film, Rodowick became the first of several scholars to plumb the deep recesses of the movie and compile a literature of film criticism that elevated *The Pirate* to the status of an academic icon. As an example of Rodowick's insights, he notes that all three major characters look into a mirror at some point in the film. Representing "doubling or splitting," the act of gazing into the mirror indicates duplicity in all three characters. Don Pedro misrepresents who he really is, Serafin pretends to be Macoco, and Manuela acts as if it is a sacrifice for her to obey Macoco's demand that she be delivered to him unmarried.[26]

Although it is true that all three characters exhibit some level of duplicity, in the case of Don Pedro, it is duplicity of an insidious kind, whereas for Serafin and Manuela, it is closer to the idea that all is fair in love and war. Serafin claims to be Macoco simply to win over Manuela. In fact, he shows little regard for his own safety as a result of his claim. As for Manuela, her duplicity involves giving in to her attraction to Serafin (as Macoco) without admitting to the townspeople that this is her dream; instead she puts on a show of being a martyr who saves the town. Also, it is worth noting that looking into a mirror fits the plot very well in each case, and no further implication may have been planned by the filmmakers. Don Pedro is the nervous bridegroom-to-be, checking his appearance before meeting his intended; Serafin is preening before the "Niña" number in which he has to attract a large crowd for his performance; and Manuela is primping before her "sacrifice."

In any case, extending Rodowick's analysis on this issue, looking into a mirror could also represent an acknowledgment of the hidden self. Recall that Don Pedro and Manuela feel compelled to gaze into Serafin's revolving mirror when it is near them, suggesting that both are hiding something. In the case of Don Pedro, it is his criminal background, but for Manuela it is simply that she is living a life of pretense up to that point.

Rodowick also writes that the very beginning of *The Pirate*, with the reading of Macoco's story in Garland's rich voice, is immersed in desire. In the scenes that follow, the viewer learns that it is not just desire but the "prohibition of desire" in the family context that drives the story. Moreover, Manuela's fascination with the sea and Don Pedro's aversion to it reinforce the notion that he could not possibly be the object of her passion. In contrast, Serafin's having come "from the sea" to perform in Port Sebastian reinforces the viewer's expectation that he will be the object of Manuela's longing. In the "Pirate Ballet," Manuela can barely control the fantasy arising from that longing, and it puts her into a state of turmoil. The only way she can restore order is through castration, presumably of her desire. This repressed sexual energy finally finds an outlet when Manuela discovers that she has been tricked by Serafin.[27]

Whereas Rodowick correctly observes that desire and its prohibition play a huge part in shaping the story, it is not unbridled desire that eventually brings the two lovers together. Instead, it is Manuela's contrition about her uncontrolled anger and how it hurt Serafin. Nevertheless, Rodowick's analysis of this issue could be extended as follows: Manuela finally breaks out of the "prohibition of desire" mode when she stops separating the "practical world" and the "dream world." She does this by recognizing that she loves Serafin and wants to be with him rather than in a loveless marriage to Don Pedro.

Rodowick concludes that Serafin is not only playing Macoco but he is "playing Gene Kelly" as the "ideal masculine object of desire" for Manuela.[28] As most film analysis is done without reference to primary material, it seems that Rodowick was unaware that Kelly was modeling Serafin's portrayal of Macoco on Douglas Fairbanks. But apparently Rodowick could tell from watching the film that Serafin was aping someone when posing as the pirate, and he assumed that it must be Kelly himself, given that Kelly was in superb athletic form.

In the same year that Rodowick published his article, Bernard Timberg also applied psychoanalytic theory to *The Pirate* by examining what he referred to as Minnelli's tendency to incorporate nightmares into the structure of his films. Timberg identified two types of nightmare sequences, one of which was "generated directly out of the psychic experience of one of the characters in the narrative," such as Manuela's imagining the "Pirate Ballet." According to Timberg, the Minnellian nightmare portrays a character who feels trapped and fights his or her way to freedom through the symbolic destruction "of a woman-in-white figure," in this case, the image of a white mule. Timberg believes Minnelli deliberately coded his "nightmares" as a struggle between reds and whites in the color scheme of the film. He notes that in *Yolanda and the Thief*, the reds stood for "innocence, spontaneity, passion, and exuberant fantasy" and the whites for "norms, conventions, and stable forms of a conventional social order." He sees a battle between red and white throughout the "Pirate Ballet," starting with white dominating the color scheme and red symbolizing Macoco and all he represents, and achieving a kind of balance by the end of the dance drama.[29]

Extending Casper's commentary on the "Pirate Ballet," Timberg notes that *The Pirate* has "one of the heaviest doses of phallic imagery in the history of musical comedy." Casper had seen phallic imagery in the symbolic lopping off the mule's ears and wrote that Manuela imagines herself to be the white mule. Timberg believes that Minnelli often portrayed the image of "the aggressive woman, the woman-become-man" and that Manuela is "a spirited woman . . . and she has to be reckoned with." He sees the mule (which he refers to as a horse) as representing Manuela under restraint, an "immobilized horse-woman," and notes that the horse is a widely recognized "phallic image of male sexuality in dream symbolism." He asks: "What better image to portray a fear of feminine aggressiveness? And what better way to negate that fear than to symbolically castrate this immobilized image?" Timberg reminds the reader of the severe marital problems Minnelli and Garland were having at the time of filming as a way to reinforce his interpretation of the "Pirate Ballet."[30]

Whereas this may be an interesting application of psychoanalytical theory, it implies that the ballet is Minnelli's fantasy rather than Manuela's, which is unfair to the director. Some gay studies scholars have drawn similar inferences without any basis in fact, as discussed later in this chapter.

Not all the scholarly comments during this period involved theoretical analysis. Some were simply clever observations about a particular aspect of the film. For example, Jerome Delamater wrote in 1981 that Manuela's yelling, "Aunt Inez, Aunt Inez" sounds very much like Dorothy's "Aunty Em, Aunty Em" from *The Wizard of Oz* (1939).[31] In fact, Inez's line to Manuela, "You can make anything come true by wishing for it"; Manuela's childlike reply, "Anything?"; and Inez's confident "Anything!" are also reminiscent of the spirit of the *Oz* film. As no previous scripts have these lines, Minnelli seems to have added them to create a nostalgic touch for Garland as well as for her many fans.

J. P. Telotte, in an article published in 1982, studied *The Pirate* with an academic interest in what the film reveals about the individual and society. Telotte believes that "both individuation and acculturation, is a key concern of the film" and that the major characters masquerade to fit into society. Pedro pretends to be respectable, Serafin changes like a chameleon, and Manuela fantasizes about a more "romantic" world to live in.[32] The idea of a masquerade by the three major characters fits with Rodowick's earlier thesis about their duplicity.

Technical Aspects and Songs (1977–1986)

Much of the scholarly commentary focused on the technical aspects of making *The Pirate* and on the effectiveness of Cole Porter's songs. This rich literature redirected readers away from cultural analysis and toward the art and craft of moviemaking in its various forms, with opinions usually praising Minnelli's direction.

Not surprisingly, the daring way that Minnelli handled the transition into the reprise of "Be a Clown" to end the film has generated intense interest. Right after Macoco is captured, Kelly, in a huge close-up, tells the audience to wait as the show is not over yet. In 1980, D. N. Rodowick wrote that filling the screen with Serafin's face has "mythic signification"—it suggests that at this point in the film Serafin has triumphed and his identity is merged with the entire production. He also says that Serafin is suddenly the narrator of the story.[33]

Illustration 6.5. Kelly in the much-discussed enormous close-up that abruptly takes the viewer from Macoco's capture to the reprise of "Be a Clown." When Kelly says, "Ladies and Gentlemen," one is not quite sure whether he is addressing the audience assembled for Serafin's hanging or the film audience. It is neither. In a moment it becomes clear that he is addressing an audience in another town where he and his troupe (including Manuela) are entertaining.

It is true that Serafin plays the role of narrator at this point, but it is done to speed up the transition to the final number and the end of the film. Moreover, it is hard to believe that Minnelli intended the close-up of Kelly's face to suggest that Serafin has become one with the film itself. It was mainly a technical issue because it was easier to focus on Serafin's face to provide the transition; had he been shown full figure on stage, he could not have emerged the next moment dressed as a clown.

In 1982, film professor Jane Feuer referred to this close-up of Kelly as an "extremely abrupt and disorienting transition." Feuer points out that the transition is jarring for a number of technical reasons. It is not a smooth shift from the previous scene, such as a dissolve would have provided. The background is a neutral black that fails to connect visually to the scene that precedes it and the scene that follows. And the change in the size of Kelly's face is extreme. In addition, Feuer asks if Kelly is speaking to the audience who saw the performance before the cut, to the audience seeing him perform with Manuela now, or to the film audience. She argues that "when we are encouraged to ask such questions, we are called away from our immersion in the fiction, distanced in that we are asked to reflect upon the spectacle itself."[34]

Feuer's arguments are valid, and the issue is one that was raised by the preview audience in Los Angeles. One reason for the abrupt transition may be that Minnelli wanted to arrest the film audience's attention so he could move on to the finale with bounce and energy. He probably assumed that seeing the different venue and audience would make it clear to the film audience that Serafin and Manuela are now performing together in a different town. In addition, Kelly tells the audience in his close-up shot, "We have a new star in our brilliant galaxy of players—the beautiful, the beguiling, the divine Manuela." The film audience does get it, of course, but not without thought or reflection, and that process snaps viewers out of the reverie they were enjoying to that point. This may be another reason one views Kelly and Garland as themselves in the final number rather than as Serafin and Manuela. The finale begins to enter upon the arena of surrealism because of the abrupt transition and the unusual final segment of the film.

Addressing other technical issues, dance historian Beth Genné closely examined the camera work of *The Pirate* in 1984 and concluded that it is "one of the most beautiful movies of the era." Genné was especially taken by Minnelli's varied and fluid camera setups, and saw his exploration of space—up, down, and laterally—as the key to his genius as a director. She noted the influence of the Minnelli-Kelly collaboration in *The Pirate* on Kelly's later success as a director of classic film musicals such as *On the Town* and *Singin' in the Rain*, projects in which he collaborated with Stanley Donen. Genné also pointed out that both Minnelli and Kelly sought to integrate dance numbers into the overall effect of a film musical more closely than was common in Hollywood, and both learned a good deal from each other about how to do that while working on *The Pirate*. She was also impressed that Minnelli framed Kelly's dancing in this film with the most interesting and effective décor, street scenes, crowds of extras, and color arrangements that the star had ever received, and she called it "one of the most distinguished in the Freed Unit series" of musicals.[35]

The songs were a key element of *The Pirate* for illustrating character, storyline, and overall mood. They obviously were a key foundation of all dances as well. Yet Cole Porter's efforts in *The Pirate* have garnered widely diverse evaluations.

Writing in 1977, Porter's biographer Charles Schwartz saw *The Pirate* as a low point in his subject's career. Schwartz dismissed the film as "little more than a make-believe period piece with colorful costumes and derring-do substituted for plausibility." He wrote that it was "a cloddish affair, . . . ponderous and leaden," so that "Cole's score for *The Pirate* never had a chance."[36]

Schwartz's view is extreme, to say the least, and out of tune with most critical and scholarly assessments of *The Pirate* as well as its hit songs, such as "Be a Clown" and "Mack the Black." He overemphasized early box office results for *The Pirate* in order to cast blame for the supposed failure of Porter's contribution to the film, probably influenced by Porter's own dissatisfaction with the M-G-M marketing program for his songs.

Film critic and music scholar Roy Hemming offered a more positive view of *The Pirate* and its song list than Schwartz, one that is more consistent with critical and audience views. He praised "imaginative dance routines" like "Mack the Black" in 1986, in addition to "the satirical aspect of the movie and the remarkable color and designs" of *The Pirate*. Hemming thought Kelly was at his best in "deliberately caricaturing the flamboyance of . . . Douglas Fairbanks and John Barrymore without ever making his character ridiculous or unbelievable." In sharp contrast to Schwartz, Hemming evaluated

Porter's work on the songs in the film as very good, especially in "Niña" and "Be a Clown."[37]

A New Generation's Appreciation (1987–2009)

By the late 1980s, the work of many people—critics, film scholars, historians, and the new generation of viewers who were interested in older films—had created a whole new life for *The Pirate*. Its slant on fantasy-reality, male-female roles, and reflexive imitation of older cinema styles were readily understood and appreciated nearly half a century after its release.

In 1987, film studies scholar Rick Altman highlighted *The Pirate* in his landmark study of the film musical in America. He called the movie "clearly a morality tale in the medieval style. Never was the desire to extol entertainment and denigrate everything else so clear as in *The Pirate*." Altman considered the picture a good example of the film musical's tendency to mix fantasy with reality. He thought "Niña" the best dance number Kelly ever performed on screen and Garland's performance in "Mack the Black" one of her best as well.[38]

A second retrospective viewing of *The Pirate* in 1987 (following the first one ten years earlier) took place at the Los Angeles County Museum of Art. This public viewing contributed greatly to the new generation's appreciation for the film. Terry Press's program commentary for this event noted that *The Pirate* "was both grossly ignored and generally misunderstood" upon its release, but lately it had been undergoing a reevaluation that placed the picture in "a high standing in the realm of motion picture musical history."[39]

Seeing a broadcast of the film on French television in 1988 prompted film critic Serge Daney to argue that *The Pirate* worked on the small screen as well as it did in the larger format. He countered those commentators who found it difficult to appreciate the décor and costumes on television, stating that the key to the movie was not its visual appeal but its character development and plot.[40]

A major study of Minnelli's directorial career by film curator Stephen Harvey gave much weight to *The Pirate* when the book was published in 1989. Harvey thought it was "the studio's liveliest achievement to date," and he noted the similarities between *The Pirate* and Minnelli's earlier *Yolanda and the Thief*. Like other commentators, Harvey was impressed by Kelly's "athletic sexuality." But he also saw meaning in how Serafin is introduced on screen—jumping on the box from Paris that contains Manuela's trousseau—because it "establishes the free-spirited hero's supremacy over the seductive trappings which are the sum total of Don Pedro's appeal to Manuela." Harvey praised the camera work in "Niña" and saw it as foreshadowing Minnelli's camera work in the famous ballet that was the climax of *An American in Paris* (1951).[41]

But Harvey's view of *The Pirate* was not unalloyed. He thought Garland's performance was less than one would have expected. She made of the tantrum sequence an exhibition of "dogged energy" rather than "hilarity." The actress seemed to lack inspiration. As Harvey put it, "We watch as Garland goes through the requisite motions, her Manuela lurches between hauteur and antic apprehension. Yet the spirit is missing; her puppetlike animation is betrayed by the hollow cast of her eyes in many scenes." This contributed, in Harvey's view, to a lack of chemistry between Garland and Kelly, "which makes the movie's central theme of mutual longing and fulfillment seem theoretical at best." Harvey also complained that the pair does not dance together until the reprise of "Be a Clown," and then it is in a comic rather than romantic dance number: "In the end, its [sic] teamwork, not passion, which is celebrated in *The Pirate's* upbeat fadeout."[42] Actually, Garland and Kelly express passion and longing most convincingly in the "Love of My Life" sequence. That number, and the earlier "You Can Do No Wrong," show the romantic angle sufficiently so that ending the film on the comic, upbeat number works very well.

Overall, Harvey believed the Minnelli-Kelly-Garland film holds a special place in the director's work. "There's an innocence to *The Pirate's* artifice that Minnelli never quite summoned up again." Harvey ascribed it to the breakup of his marriage to Garland. When Minnelli was later assigned to direct musicals that involved fantasy, such as *Brigadoon* (1954) and *Kismet* (1955), "the strain was evident." Harvey concluded that *The Pirate* "represented Minnelli's last moment as a freewheeling fabulist, and for all the backstage angst and turmoil, it was a lovely time while it lasted."[43]

Writers who commented on *The Pirate* well into the 1990s continued to note that the film was increasingly viewed as a classic among certain segments of the movie-viewing public. They also recognized the important role that Kelly's participation in the film played in its enduring appeal. In 1993, James Naremore, who wrote a book about Minnelli's films, said that "Gene Kelly was crucial to *The Pirate*." In 1996, Sheridan Morley and Ruth Leon wrote about the sophistication of the film, while Alvin Yudkoff, writing in 1999, called it Kelly's "masterpiece."[44]

Only Gerald Clarke, who wrote a biography of Garland published in 2000, viewed Minnelli's and Kelly's contributions to the film in a jaundiced way. Clarke criticized Minnelli for focusing more on sets than on the story and for dropping two of Garland's numbers. He castigated Kelly for stealing the show from Garland, and wrote that his "voracious scene-grabbing, threw the entire movie off-balance."[45]

Clarke's criticisms are not at all convincing. Minnelli's focus on sets did not mean he shortchanged the story. Instead, Minnelli's papers clearly show how carefully he attended to plot and dialogue revisions (see Chapters 2 and 3). Secondly, *three* of Garland's numbers were dropped, not two, based on negative audience reaction at the previews, as explained in Chapter 5. In fact, the new "Mack the Black" number by Garland showed her to much greater advantage than the old "Mack the Black" that started the film. Singing "Love of My Life" to a hat, and the troublesome "Voodoo," would have damaged her career rather than enhanced it. As to the charges against Kelly, not only did Garland stand out in all her scenes, Kelly always supported his co-stars and made them look their best because his own vision was that of a director—he wanted what was good for the movie. As discussed in Chapters 3 and 4, Kelly was involved in all facets of production in *The Pirate*, and Minnelli saw him as an amazing collaborator working for the good of the film.

Also in 2000, the biographer of the Nicholas Brothers, Constance Hill, forgot the fact that Kelly took a significant risk in including the men in the film and criticized him for not allowing Fayard and Harold to collaborate on the choreography of "Be a Clown." As discussed in Chapter 4, however, Kelly worked with the Nicholas Brothers in developing the choreography for the number and kept their style in mind. For example, he incorporated the spread-eagled jump the brothers had performed in *Orchestra Wives* (1942). Hill also complained that the brothers did not have an opportunity to develop their characters or even to speak a line. She overlooked the fact that, as part of Serafin's troupe, the brothers were in scenes throughout the film (in non-stereotypical roles), integrated into the story as blacks seldom were in that era. Hill groused that, because the brothers dropped out of film work for a long while after 1947, the last image moviegoers had of them for twenty-two years was lying with Kelly "in a colorful heap at the end of 'Be a Clown.'" She did not seem to recognize the irony in what she bemoaned, given that this image of a white man comfortably touching two black cohorts was most unusual and it seriously challenged racial conventions of the time. Finally, Hill criticized the choreography of this number as boring and unchallenging, and yet, without any sense of contradiction, she noted that discos often projected this number "on their ceilings to excite their young patrons" well into the late 1980s.[46]

In 2004, film professor Douglas Pye authored the last major evaluation of *The Pirate* to date, expressing his admiration for Kelly's performance even as he noted that Kelly could, in some ways, be too much for some audience members. Serafin was "one of Kelly's most extraordinary creations, pushing the confidence and irrepressible energy that are central to his star persona into hyperbolic regions of sexual arrogance, exhibitionism and narcissism." Pye also was impressed by the portrayal of Manuela as an active agent of her destiny. He thought "Mack the Black," which was added after the previews, was the key to understanding that Manuela did not really want to be swept away by a pirate but to become a pirate herself so she could "exercise the freedom and power that she can only consciously imagine as the preserve of the male buccaneer."[47] More than half a century earlier, in 1939, Kurt Weill had half-facetiously suggested a similar scenario in planning the stage version of Behrman's *The Pirate* (see Chapter 1).

Pye argued that Manuela's taunting of Serafin after discovering that he has tricked her, and the resulting tantrum sequence, are key points in her development as an assertive, "modern" woman because she puts him in his place, exacts some revenge, and then makes up with him on her own terms.[48] Actually, Manuela's taunting of Serafin and her subsequent tantrum are hardly aspects of her development and growth. Instead, she comes across first as conniving and then as an out-of-control brat, unable to see reason, who realizes what she has done only when Serafin is hurt by her vengeful behavior. That is when she finally seems to grow up and admit to herself and to Serafin that she loves him.

The "Pirate Ballet" continued to impress viewers, including Pye, who praised Minnelli and Kelly for crafting it so that the number was "more firmly rooted in the surrounding narrative than many MGM ballets by [being] overtly presented as Manuela's fantasy of Serafin as Macoco." In line with Casper's analysis in 1977, Pye writes that, because of the fantasy connection with Manuela, the ballet also became "the most outrageously phallic sequence in Hollywood cinema." Similar to Rodowick's and Telotte's analysis in 1980 and 1982 respectively, Pye notes that all three major players continued to pretend, or put on roles, following the ballet—Pedro as a respectable citizen, Serafin as the pirate, and Manuela as a willing sacrificial lamb for the safety of Calvados—but all three pretenses break down dramatically by the end of the narrative. And just as Harvey complained in 1989, Pye writes that because Manuela's and Serafin's only dance together is performed in unisex clown suits, it tends to give one the impression they are good friends and great performers but not necessarily great lovers.[49] Like Harvey, Pye also seems to have forgotten the passionate "Love of My Life" which is aimed not merely to goad Don Pedro into revealing his identity, but which portrays the true longing that Serafin and Manuela feel for each other at this point.

"There is no denying that this is a weird movie," film critic Victoria Large wrote in 2006, nearly sixty years after its release, "one that comes by its status as a cult classic honestly. It's loopy, knowingly camp, brightly colored, ambitious, and absolutely unique." The studied, elaborate, and self-consciously created setting, décor, and costumes added an insistent air of artificiality to the film that Large thought took "a bit of getting used to." Nevertheless, she thought that the film is "so smart and self-reflexive that it becomes a delight for those who get the joke." More than twenty years earlier, film commentator Pauline Kael had voiced a similar assessment of *The Pirate*, writing that it was "flamboyant in an innocent and lively way. Though it doesn't quite work, and it's all a bit broad, it doesn't sour in the memory." Large liked the film more than did Kael, citing Kelly's "unflagging energy," which charges up the film; Garland's "ardor" and "passion" not found in her other movies; and Porter's "riotous" lyrics. She found it "an oddly addicting charmer, perhaps the most lovable of all the films Garland and Kelly made together."[50]

The commentaries over time, as recorded in this chapter, show that there were enough elements in *The Pirate* to give modern audiences and scholars an opportunity to put whatever spin they wanted on the film. In contrast, recall that in 1942, a newspaper critic had written that Behrman's play contained no hidden meanings and that it was simply a wonderful comedy. This critic's perspective may explain why many people had difficulty understanding the nuances of the movie version of *The Pirate* when it was released in 1948. Audiences at that time were used to a standard cinema product that spoke clearly and directly to different segments of the public. They could easily plug in to whatever genre was presented to them. In that sense, Freed's famous comment that twenty years of cultural change would give *The Pirate* its due appears to have been right on the mark.

GAY SCHOLARS ON *THE PIRATE*

It is also noteworthy that Freed's prediction about *The Pirate* being way ahead of its time was never more correct than in the area of gender studies. Gay theory and history did not become openly acceptable topics in academic circles until the 1980s, and *The Pirate* became a major subject of discussion within that developing literature, especially after the turn of the new century.

Actually, *The Pirate* had caught the attention of gay men very early in its history, creating a cult success among what Brett Farmer, a student of gay theory, calls "urban, Anglo-American gay subcultures." The film was highlighted in publications directed at a gay readership as early as the late 1940s and 1950s.[51]

The Pirate has retained its high degree of interest for this audience ever since. At the same time, in the analysis that follows, one can see how using a different scholarly lens can create varied interpretations of the same product.

Garland's Role

Much of the gay interest in the film centered on the presence of Judy Garland. She was becoming an icon for gay men in the late 1940s because they saw her as someone different from the mainstream Hollywood image of women and also because they empathized with her personal problems. When news of her apparent suicide attempt became known in 1950, Garland's stature among gays soared, and she became a hero to the gay community for many years to come. Her "camp" performance in *The Pirate* seems to have intensified the interest gay men felt in her career. Manuela was very obviously playing roles throughout the film that were at variance with her meek, submissive persona, and doing so with a tongue-in-cheek attitude that was appealing. A definition of camp is difficult to pin down, but it can be considered a self-conscious approach to dealing with issues related to artifice and role playing. While camp approaches to film work are not exclusively gay, students of gender studies have recognized the strong attraction that camp holds for gay audiences. The strong element of camp in *The Pirate*, combined with Garland's throaty performance, made the picture "particularly readable within the gay male subcultural discourse of camp," according to Richard Dyer.[52]

Dyer has also pointed out that Garland's fetching camp portrayal worked only because the entire setting of *The Pirate* supported it. Camp, in short, suffused Minnelli's production by focusing on a "play with sex roles and spectacular illusion." Dyer believes the film is specifically about male sex roles and Manuela's ability to deflate masculine ego, not only Serafin's but also Don Pedro's. At the same time, Dyer writes about Kelly's effective portrayal of Serafin as a "send-up," meaning a parody, which of course is what it was meant to be.[53]

Minnelli's Expressions

Minnelli played a large role in making *The Pirate* into a salient example of camp. Recall that this was Minnelli's intention ever since he began planning the film. According to some scholars, however, the film became associated with camp because of Minnelli's work with décor and setting. Matthew Tinkcom has argued that camp elements exist in the production side of moviemaking, as well as in the acting, and David Gerstner has pointed out that Minnelli's aesthetic was geared toward that of a decorative modernist. The director liked to pile on props to create a cluttered and colorful background to frame his actors on screen. In contrast, Cedric Gibbons and most designers at M-G-M were streamlined modernists who believed a spare and efficient background was not only more stylish but served as a buffer against those observers who tended to think that design was effeminate and that designers were gay. Minnelli had developed his ideas about décor in the 1930s while working on stage productions, and brought those ideas with him to Hollywood. Perhaps the reason he had such battles with the M-G-M art department was because he had "an extravagant and flamboyant eye for excessive detail."[54]

Some scholars suggest that Minnelli was subtly expressing his homosexuality through his work with décor. Gerstner has pointed out that the director never was openly gay—he had married four times and fathered two children. Nevertheless, Gerstner argues that Minnelli "certainly partook of a cultural milieu that was made up of a significant coterie of artists and critics whose aesthetic interests came to be marked as queer." He also writes: "Declared or not, Minnelli participated in and visibly presented a homosexual aesthetic." Lela Simone tried to put this idea across when she told an interviewer many years later that Minnelli "worked like a homosexual," referring to his manner of work rather than to any idea that he was gay. Questions of Minnelli's sexual orientation aside, students of gender studies seem to agree that *The Pirate* "is by any measure a vivid example of camp tastes" that appealed to a select segment of the movie-going audience of 1948 as well as to the same segment of subsequent generations who lived in times more conducive to open discussion of camp and homosexuality.[55]

Kelly's Image

Kelly plays a role in a discussion of *The Pirate* as an element in gay studies. His intense concern about proving that dance was not a reserve of effeminate men has marked the star for examination at the hands of scholars, for gay studies tends also to incorporate discussion of masculinity and images of the body. Gerstner has rightly pointed out that Kelly had no trouble with the concept of gayness, only with the notion that many people of his era automatically categorized creative dance as "sissy." But, in Gerstner's view, Kelly worked excessively hard to counter that viewpoint and to show that "the male body, Kelly's body, was a body projected both to the spectator and to *himself* as an ideal specimen of masculine creativity."[56]

The harder he tried to project masculinity, Gerstner believes, the more Kelly revealed other elements as well. Although virile and energetic, the "Pirate Ballet" shows Kelly in the most revealing costume he ever wore on the screen, designed by Minnelli and approved by Kelly. Also, many scenes were captured at low angles, which further emphasized Kelly's body image. According to Gerstner, the costume and the camera "emphasized Kelly's well-defined thighs, pumped biceps, and well-announced manly bulge." Referring to the "queer mise-en-scene of Minnelli and Jack Martin Smith," Gerstner wondered if the entire thing was meant to entice Manuela's desire or that of someone else. Gerstner also wrote of Kelly as an exhibitionist, referring to "Kelly's hyper-energetic projection of self." He noted that the ballet's point of view may start with Manuela's perspective, but it is so dominated by Kelly's performance that the perspective shifts to a narcissistic indulgence by a supremely gifted performer who cannot help but love himself.[57]

Although Kelly's costume does reveal his muscular thighs and arms, there is no evidence of the "bulge" in the "Pirate Ballet." Also, it is unfair of Gerstner to suggest that Minnelli planned the costume or the camera angles for his personal pleasure. Besides, Minnelli and Kelly were very open about their intentions to portray Serafin (especially in Manuela's fantasy) as virile and strong in contrast to Lunt's portrayal in the stage play. As to Gerstner's final point, the ballet—depicted as Manuela's fantasy—rightly shows the bloodthirsty pirate as self-absorbed. Serafin, however, is very much aware of Manuela watching him, both *before* and *after* the fantasy, which ends with Manuela nervously closing the bamboo shutters on her window as Serafin is looking up at her.

Writing of "homoeroticism" in *The Pirate*, Matthew Tinkcom states that Kelly's bravura performance dominates the picture so that it "resists the expected union of the male and female leads." *The Pirate*, in Tinkcom's words, is concerned "with self-pleasure, and particularly the pleasure of Serafin with the spectacle of his own movement." Brett Farmer's writing may shed some light on this type of reasoning. He declares that "narcissistic displays of male solo dances" and the "insistent eroticization of the male body in the musical" put the male in the "traditionally feminine role of sex object" and create a "strong potential for emphatic identification" by gay audiences. In line with this idea, Richard Dyer writes of Kelly as a sex object in *The Pirate*. He refers to the "low-angle, crotch centered positioning" of the ballet, and to "Niña," in which Kelly, costumed in form-fitting tights, wiggles his rear at the women who gather to watch his performance. As Dyer puts it, *The Pirate* "fully allows Kelly as sex object, to a more sustained degree than any male star between Rudolph Valentino and John Travolta; and at the same time plays around with him as spectacle, so that he is both turn-on and send-up."[58]

Film critic Dan Callahan writes that the film is "all about the promise of sex, . . . tapping into a nervous, adolescent sort of fear and desire." He sees Garland in "Mack the Black" as "obviously fueled by drugs" and refers to her "sexual frustration and blind, undirected anger." Regarding the "Pirate Ballet," Callahan says that Minnelli effectively asks his wife "to pretend to conjure and then witness his own carnal longings." To Callahan, it seems "as if Garland and Minnelli are sharing a kind of erotic meltdown together, creatively, with Kelly in the middle crowing, 'Get a load of my body . . . you'll never have it, but you can look all you like!'" He views

The Pirate as "so off-beat and subterranean that it will always be of interest as a cult film."[59]

Without basing his writing on primary material related to the two dances, Callahan unfairly presumes that Garland's energetic performance in "Mack the Black" was drug related or that she was sexually frustrated. His assertion that Minnelli and Garland hankered for Kelly's body and that Kelly enjoyed such a situation not only is groundless but serves as an example of the overblown rhetorical flourishing that often crops up in literature on controversial movies, and his view of the film as "subterranean" is colored entirely by his own lens.

Brett Farmer has authored the most comprehensive study of gay viewership of films. He argues that the narrative and characters of *The Pirate* constitute a text "driven by contradictory impulses, both toward and against heteronormative idealization, toward and against socially sanctioned desire." For example, he writes that Manuela longs for romance but is doomed to disappointment in her marriage to Don Pedro. Such a scenario makes the film a prime target of gay interest, or, to use Farmer's jargon, for "queer spectatorial investment." Social norms before the 1970s pressured gay men into leading dual lives themselves, and they could readily identify with the characters in this movie, especially Manuela. Farmer also writes that gay viewers could identify with the women in the second half of "Niña," who were "scrutinizing and objectifying Serafin," and they could view the "Mack the Black" number as expressing the "coming out" of Manuela.[60]

Whereas the above explanations provide a good understanding of why the film draws gay interest, Farmer also suggests that the musical numbers in *The Pirate*, instead of being based in "the relatively stable space of heterosexual union," allow desire "to move with relative freedom into various interchangeable configurations," thus making the film appealing to gay audiences.[61]

But more than half the songs and dances in *The Pirate* do not fit Farmer's concept. Out of the seven musical numbers in the film, four are either love songs ("You Can Do No Wrong" and "Love of My Life") or clown songs ("Be a Clown" and its reprise), and three of these four fit the "stable space of heterosexual union" very well. Therefore, Farmer's idea is relevant to only three numbers. Serafin is certainly self-absorbed in "Niña" and the "Pirate Ballet," and Garland also is self-absorbed in "Mack the Black." However, even these three numbers fit the plot and characterizations perfectly, so there is no need to attribute hidden nuances to them. In "Niña," Serafin is deliberately dancing in a way to attract attention and draw people to his performance that evening. The "Pirate Ballet" is Manuela's fantasy, and it is appropriate for the pirate of her wild imagination to be self-absorbed. As for "Mack the Black," Manuela is hypnotized and singing in a trance, so her "self-absorption" is expected and natural.

In any case, despite the varied perspectives even among gender studies scholars, there seems to be strong agreement that many elements in *The Pirate* are particularly attractive to gay audiences. Whether the interest originates in Garland, Minnelli, or Kelly, or whether it is created by the characterizations, the story, or the virile dancing is almost secondary; the different elements seem to work together so that the film has retained its strong appeal for gay audiences in enduring ways.

GOOFS AND GAFFES

Repeated viewings of *The Pirate* on videotape, and after 2007 on DVD, reveal that a number of mistakes occurred in the production and postproduction phases of the film. All of them are small goofs and gaffes probably not noticeable on first viewing, and many of them undoubtedly stemmed from the hurried pace of filmmaking at M-G-M, which produced up to sixty films every year at the height of its output. Teams of crewmembers worked on each project with limited time to spend on any one of them. Rather than embarrassments, these goofs and gaffes provide entertainment for modern audiences and bring the process of moviemaking in the studio system down to an earthly, human level. For a similar discussion of goofs and gaffes in the classic film musical *Singin' in the Rain*, see Hess and Dabholkar.[62]

An artist traces Manuela's bridal silhouette on a screen with a pen, but when Manuela moves her head to thank the artist for a compliment *and* when the artist picks up the blank screen and walks away, there is no outline of her silhouette on the screen. It is obvious why no tracing was done on the screen in the film. The man playing an artist was not a real artist and could not be counted on to make a good tracing. Given the dim lighting in the scene, the absence of a tracing was unlikely to be noticed.

When Serafin is walking across the tightrope to Manuela's bedroom, there is a moment when one sees a gap between Kelly's feet and the tightrope. The reason for this is that although Kelly actually performed this stunt, there is a moment when he is supposed to almost lose his balance and Minnelli did not want to take the chance of hurting his star. So only this brief portion of the ropewalking had to be put together through editing, as explained in Chapter 4, and apparently the editing was slightly less than perfect. If one is focusing on the action, this flaw is easy to miss.

Soon after Serafin enters Manuela's bedroom, Don Pedro comes quickly to deal with the interloper. Yet the voice that yells "Manuela!" just before he arrives is not that of Walter Slezak. Also, this voice pronounces her name *Man-u-e-la,* as an American would. Slezak, being European, pronounces it correctly as *Munwela* in the very next scene. Apparently the crew forgot to schedule Slezak to do this voiceover while he was still available and had to substitute someone else's voice in this scene.

Shortly afterward, Serafin yells "Macoco!" when he realizes who Don Pedro really is and wants to let him know of his discovery. Even though the audience hears the full name, Kelly's mouth clearly enunciates only the first two syllables *Ma-co—* on the screen. Still later, Kelly begins to yell the name a second time to force Pedro to reckon with him. This time, one hears only the first two syllables and sees Kelly mouthing them too. Apparently, Minnelli had intended for Kelly only to begin yelling the name, as *Ma-co—,* both times, before he is stopped by Don Pedro. But later he thought it necessary for the audience to hear the full name the first time. Indeed, this seems a good idea because Kelly yells "Macoco!" and follows up with the pirate's piercing trademark scream very effectively. Yet, even though Minnelli had Kelly re-record the first yell for great effect, he did not reshoot that scene to coordinate sight and sound.

In the same scene, when Serafin yells "Macoco!" for Pedro's benefit, Manuela, Inez, and Capucho are standing right outside the door, which has slats for ventilation. Yet none of them seems to hear Serafin's loud yell, followed by his piercing scream. Obviously this was done in the interest of the storyline, but it does make the situation somewhat unreal.

There is a discrepancy in the script when Serafin "reveals" to the family that he is Macoco. Manuela is shocked and says, "But you can't be. You're a—" and Serafin interrupts, "Strolling player?" As she nods speechlessly, Serafin tells her that even though he is "desperately in love," he has to hide from the law, implying that he took on the guise of a strolling player after falling in love with her. As mentioned in Chapter 2, this contradicts the film's own plotline because Serafin is in Port Sebastian as a strolling player getting ready for his performance *before* he meets Manuela.

Of course, even without this discrepancy, Serafin's story that he is Macoco is unbelievable. A pirate would be unlikely to become a good performer and, as a person wanted by the law, it would not be in his self-interest to draw attention to himself. This unbelievable aspect of Serafin's story is present even in Behrman's stage play, although it works better there because neither Behrman's Manuela nor his Viceroy fully believes Serafin's claim to be the pirate.

In the tantrum sequence, Manuela throws an ax toward Serafin, inadvertently cutting the wire holding a picture, which falls on the distraught actor's head and knocks him out. Serafin is lying quite close to the wall when he passes out. But, in the next scene, he is lying much farther from the wall as the shocked Manuela approaches him gingerly. Although today this would be classified as a problem with continuity, it is understandable that it was done to allow Manuela enough room to crouch behind Serafin and face the camera so she could sing "You Can Do No Wrong" to the prone actor.

Another instance of lack of continuity results from the placement of props. When Serafin is led down the staircase from the church to the plaza for his execution, the steps of the gallows are very close to the bottom of the staircase, and a large group of rocks frames the bottom step of the staircase. Yet later, when everything is cleared away for the first performance of "Be a Clown," the gallows are magically much farther away from the staircase, and there are no rocks to be seen anywhere near its bottom step. Obviously this was done to focus first on the gallows and later to allow enough room for the performance. One can overlook the lack of continuity for the two excellent scenes that were created.

In another continuity issue, Don Pedro's eyes change color from one scene to another. Throughout the film his eyes are brown, seen clearly in close-up shots, but in two close-ups during Serafin's second performance, they are blue. The first instance is when Pedro stares at the revolving mirror, almost in a trance. After this his eyes are brown again while Manuela and Serafin are talking on stage, right up to Manuela's singing "Love of My Life." When she starts to sing this song to Serafin, the camera moves in for a close-up of Don Pedro's face, and his eyes are clearly blue. Later when Don Pedro jumps on the stage and declares he is the real Macoco, his eyes are brown again. A similar pattern is noticeable in *State Fair* (1945), where Percy Kilbride and Dick Haymes have blue eyes in some close-ups but brown eyes in the rest of the film. It is possible filmmakers thought that blue eyes were more expressive in close-up shots and did this for effect in certain shots where expression was crucial. Indeed, Slezak's face is very expressive as he becomes tortured while watching Manuela profess her love for Serafin. It is not clear whether the actors actually wore blue contact lenses for these scenes. It seems more likely that the colors were changed through the Technicolor process described at the beginning of Chapter 5.

When Pedro stands up, seemingly in a trance, Serafin holds the revolving mirror far too much out of the way as he tries to entice Pedro to come forward. It is clear that Kelly does this to allow Gladys Cooper ample opportunity to whack the mirror out of his hand with her umbrella, but he leans so far that it looks unnatural.

Earlier in the film, an important plot discrepancy arises when Manuela tells the Viceroy, who has just entered Don Pedro's salon with his militia, that Serafin pretended to be Macoco only because he knew that she was fascinated with the pirate. Astonishingly, Don Pedro is in the room, standing only a few feet from Manuela, yet apparently does not hear this important bit of information. Later, he seems most surprised when Manuela declares her admiration for Macoco just before singing "Love of My Life" to Serafin (as Macoco) on stage.

One wonders, also, how Don Pedro managed to secure Serafin's prop box and fill it with the stolen jewels when it was guarded by Serafin's troupe. Also, when did he have the time to do this? After all, he rushed away to the capital to fetch the Viceroy when the citizens came to his house for Manuela, and he had no henchman who could have helped him arrange this. And why do the troupe members fail to intervene to save their leader and, conversely, why does the Viceroy not arrest them as Macoco's accomplices? In Behrman's play, they were all to be arrested after the performance. It is also perplexing why Manuela does not show the Viceroy the ring Don Pedro has given her. It perfectly matches the bracelet in the prop box right in front of them and would prove beyond a doubt that the mayor is the real pirate. And why does Pedro so readily succumb to Serafin's attempt to hypnotize him? There is no motive for him to pretend and actually he does not even seem to be pretending. He looks dazed and under Serafin's spell, which is decidedly uncharacteristic for a man who has cagily lived a double life in Calvados for a couple of years. The only answer to all these questions is that the rational alternatives would detract from the dramatic aspects of the story. The moviemakers sacrificed credibility to create drama and excitement, and one can certainly understand and appreciate that. After all, the main reason to watch a movie is to enjoy it, and this film achieves that goal superbly.

Perhaps the worst error in the film is that O. Z. Whitehead, the actor who played Coutat, never received credit for his work, despite his significant role in the film, while many who spoke only one line or less are listed in the credits. In fact, it is Coutat who inadvertently tells Manuela that Serafin is not really the pirate Macoco, which is one of the turning points of the film's plot. Neither on screen, nor in any list of cast and crew members, is the character of Coutat even indicated, nor does this character appear in any of the many scripts written by various screenwriters before production began. In fact, most of Coutat's lines in the film are spoken by Trillo in the scripts as well as in the stage plays, and most of Trillo's lines in the film are spoken by Esteban in the scripts and stage plays. In the film, Esteban is the juggler and has no lines. Apparently, Minnelli added a new character (Coutat) while filming and changed the names of some troupe members, which may have led to this oversight.

In addition to these errors that we observed, the Internet Movie Data Base (IMDB) has posted a list of its own. It mentions wires attached to Manuela's hat in the scene where she meets Serafin, support wires for Kelly in the ropewalking sequence, and a guiding wire for the white "donkey." The list also refers to a continuity issue when a flower falls from a dancer's hair in the "Niña" number and reappears in her hair later on. Another error listed on the website mentions that showing Maison Worth on Manuela's trousseau box is an anachronism because the company was formed circa 1860, and the movie was set in 1830.[63]

If one looks intently for them, it is possible to see the wires mentioned in the three instances. But it is so easy to miss these contrivances that viewing pleasure is not interrupted. It is true that the flower reappears in the dancer's hair in "Niña" but after all, these complex numbers were shot in many segments and with a huge number of retakes. So the "reappearance" of the flower occurred in the interest of splicing together the best possible number as a whole. This type of "discontinuity" issue is present in most dance numbers in the classic musicals of the 1940s and 1950s. And finally, although Minnelli did say in his interviews years later that he was inspired by

Martinique in the 1830s while conceiving the setting for *The Pirate*, nowhere in the film is it mentioned that the time period is 1830. The director deliberately leaves the time and place vague as discussed in Chapters 1 and 3. So the inclusion of Maison Worth is not really an anachronism.

If one wants to look for an anachronism, it is the idea of a ruthless, legendary pirate in the nineteenth century. Fulda had placed his story in the seventeenth century to properly tie in to the pirates who plagued ships in the sixteenth and seventeenth centuries. When Behrman changed the setting to the early 1800s, the story became somewhat anachronistic. However, this is a minor issue and certainly does not detract from the stage play or the film.

CONNECTIONS

The Pirate has interesting connections to many films. Some of them are stylistic and others are thematic, while still others are choreographic or technical in nature. All the connections are personal, with links to the cast or the director, and several cases involve multiple connections to a given film.[64]

The stylistic similarity of *The Pirate* to *Yolanda and the Thief* (1945) has already been mentioned in Chapter 3. Both films have vibrant colors, a Latin American setting, and a surrealistic dream ballet. Moreover, a personal connection is that both films were directed by Minnelli.

There is also stylistic similarity and a personal connection between *The Pirate* and *The Three Musketeers* (1948). Both were originally set in the seventeenth century by Ludwig Fulda and Alexander Dumas, respectively. In addition, Kelly played his starring role as D'Artagnan with much the same tongue-in-cheek gusto with which he created Serafin.

For Me and My Gal (1942) and *Summer Stock* (1950) have multiple personal connections with *The Pirate*. Both film musicals starred Kelly and Garland, as did *The Pirate*. Other films with multiple personal connections include *An American in Paris* (1951) and *Brigadoon* (1954). Kelly and Minnelli collaborated very closely on both of those projects much as they had done on the set of *The Pirate*.

Three films connect with *The Pirate* choreographically and personally through a dance step that Kelly performed. One of Kelly's signature routines was to bounce on the palms of his hands with his legs stretched out behind him. He did this in *For Me and My Gal, Du*

Barry Was a Lady (1943), and *Invitation to the Dance* (1956), as well as in *The Pirate*, with the Nicholas Brothers in "Be a Clown."

Technical and personal connections to *The Pirate* exist in two other Kelly films. In *Words and Music* (1948), the Ubangi, which had been devised for the "Pirate Ballet," was used to film Kelly's dance with Vera Ellen. In the "Circus" segment of *Invitation to the Dance*, Kelly once again demonstrated his ability to walk on a tightrope as he had done when playing Serafin.

The Pirate also has a thematic connection to *Invitation to the Dance*, where Kelly created a mostly sad figure of a clown in the "Circus" segment. In contrast, his upbeat clown persona in "Be a Clown" supported a number that has become an icon of the entertainment creed.

Similarly, there is a personal and thematic connection between *The Pirate* and Garland's *Wizard of Oz* (1939). Both are fantasies and, as mentioned earlier in this chapter, some of Garland's lines and scenes in *The Pirate* evoke the spirit of the *Oz* film.

The Pirate has close thematic and stylistic connections with *The Black Pirate* (1926), discussed in Chapter 3. Serafin's costume in the "Pirate Ballet" and Kelly's athletic antics are closely tied to those of Douglas Fairbanks Sr. in the earlier movie. In fact, much of Serafin's character development was based on the style and bravado of Fairbanks.

Walter Slezak could count several thematic connections between his role in *The Pirate* and other projects in his career. In fact, this was his fourth film about pirates, but he had not portrayed a pirate in the previous films. Slezak played a corrupt governor in *The Princess and the Pirate* (1944), a comedy starring Bob Hope. In *The Spanish Main* (1945), a swashbuckler starring Paul Henreid, Slezak was a villainous Spanish ruler. And in *Sindbad the Sailor* (1947), a comedy starring Douglas Fairbanks Jr., Slezak portrayed an evil barber.

"Be a Clown" became very popular and created thematic connections with two subsequent movies, *Easter Parade* (1948) and *Singin' in the Rain* (1952). Even before filming had ended, Arthur Freed planned to re-create the magic of *The Pirate* through a second vehicle, *Easter Parade*, for his two stars Kelly and Garland. Minnelli again was slated to direct the picture, and Freed assigned the same team of scriptwriters (Goodrich and Hackett) to write the screenplay for it.[65]

But Freed's plans had to be changed along the way. Garland initially seemed happy with the new project. She had spent some time at the Las Campanas Sanatorium at Compton, outside Los Angeles, after principal filming had ended for *The Pirate*. It was her first visit to such a facility. She was later transferred to another institute, the Austen Riggs Foundation in Stockbridge, Massachusetts. Garland spent only a short time there until checking herself out and returning home.[66]

Minnelli remembered that his wife returned in seemingly good health and spirits. She did not seem to mind the enormous amount of time that Minnelli and Kelly spent preparing for *Easter Parade*. The director thought that Irving Berlin's music "suited the talents of Gene and Judy exceedingly well," and "'A Couple of Swells' was to be the spiritual successor to 'Be a Clown.'" Then one day Freed told Minnelli that Judy's psychiatrist had advised her not to work with her husband anymore, and that Charles Walters would direct *Easter Parade*. The news stunned Minnelli, and he obviously was not happy with the psychiatrist's view that he symbolized Judy's problems with the studio.[67]

Moreover, Kelly broke his ankle six weeks into rehearsals while playing volleyball. His recovery time would cost the studio money, so Kelly insisted that Mayer call Fred Astaire out of retirement to replace him. Astaire checked with Kelly if this was okay before he signed on. He also expressed concern that the choreography might not suit him, but Kelly convinced him that the arrangements were flexible. *Easter Parade* was a big success when it was released in late 1948. Kelly always watched "A Couple of Swells," as Astaire and Garland created it, with much regret that he had lost this wonderful opportunity to dance a second comic routine with his friend. The fact that the number originated with his own "Be a Clown" hit sharpened the irony.[68]

A few years later, while planning a solo for Cosmo, Donald O'Connor's character in *Singin' in the Rain*, Kelly and his co-director, Stanley Donen, thought it would be a good idea to have a peppy number like "Be a Clown" from *The Pirate*. Donen went to Freed with this idea, given that the film was to catalogue Freed's previous songs written with composer Nacio Herb Brown. But Freed's quickly written "Make 'Em Laugh" number turned out to be much too similar to "Be a Clown" for comfort. Fortunately, Porter did not take issue with this, and the visual success of the number compensated for any embarrassing associations.[69]

The other connection—thematic, stylistic, and personal—between *The Pirate* and *Singin' in the Rain* is that Kelly played an actor in both films, and moreover, one who was supposed to deliberately overact at times. In *The Pirate*, the overplaying was done as a parody when Serafin pretended to be Macoco or when he promoted his performance. *Singin' in the Rain* also parodied silent film stars and their tendency to overact. Consequently, Kelly overplayed when his character, Don Lockwood, acted in "The Royal Rascal" and "The Dueling Cavalier," which were fictitious silent films depicted in *Singin' in the Rain*. Kelly also embellished the style of his character whenever Don Lockwood spoke to his fans.

Concluding Thoughts

It is interesting that although *The Pirate* is not really a movie about pirates, and in fact, the only scenes about pirates are part of a fantasy, the film has fared strongly among movies about pirates. A total of 323 feature films, as well as 183 shorts, television movies, and television series, have been made about pirates. Twenty-two of these were silent films, the earliest of which was *The Pirate's Gold* by D. W. Griffith in 1908. Recent attempts to evaluate the hundreds of pirate films ever made have included the Kelly-Minnelli-Garland vehicle near the top of their lists. For example, in 2007, Helen Geib placed it in the number five slot, with *Peter Pan* (1924) at the top, and a 2011 "25 best pirate movies list" (which did not rank these 25 films) included *The Pirate*. Even in terms of viewer ratings, the film has done pretty well. For example, in 2013, *The Pirate* tied with Douglas Fairbanks's *The Black Pirate* (1926) and *Peter Pan* (1924) for a viewer rating of 7.0 on the Internet Movie Data Base, exceeded by only a handful of pirate films such as *Captain Blood* (1935) with a rating of 7.7 and *The Crimson Pirate* (1952) with a rating of 7.3.[70]

It is amazing how much is being written about this movie even sixty-five years after its release. Despite the problems associated with its production and the mixed response by some critics and viewers upon its release, *The Pirate* has demonstrated that it has staying power. The interesting elements in the film, and they are legion, have sustained and enhanced its reputation with the passage of time. Some see the movie as a cult classic, and it certainly can be viewed in that way. For instance, the film has a huge appeal for gay audiences and gay study scholars as discussed in this chapter. But the Kelly-Minnelli-Garland film is much more than a cult classic. It was the first film musical in which a white man danced with black men as equals in an era when the races were strictly segregated on film in terms of social class and with separate dance segments. It was not a financial loss for M-G-M as scholars have claimed, but in fact recouped its investment and made a modest profit over its run. Nor is it an example of an auteur in action, as scholars have argued, but involved intense collaboration between Minnelli and Kelly as well as the contributions of many talented people from its inception to its release.

Over the years, many people began to view the film as a classic movie musical and a landmark accomplishment for its director and its two stars. Indeed, the film was Minnelli's best—particularly in his use of vivid color; high, low, and wide camera angles; multiethnic crowd scenes; and imaginative sets. The movie spurred Kelly's most successful phase as star, dancer, and choreographer, and his collaboration with Minnelli helped him greatly in his own directorial work to follow. Despite all her personal problems, Garland is at her best in a role that was very different for her, and her brilliant camp performance helped trigger the film's cult following. It is time that *The Pirate* received its long-awaited due; we hope this unique film will continue to garner more attention and accolades with each passing generation.

APPENDIX A

Discarded Screenplays for *The Pirate*

Given the overlap between the discarded screenplays and the two stage plays in terms of the basic story, it would be repetitive to lay out each version fully. Instead, this Appendix focuses on the major changes in each version and analyzes their merits or weaknesses to make this discussion more informative.

Synopsis and Analysis of the Mankiewicz Screenplay

Joseph Mankiewicz included no specific place or time period for the venue, other than referring to an unnamed island in the Caribbean.[1] (This change is retained in subsequent revisions by a string of writers to come, but, in the final, filmed version, the fictitious towns of Port Sebastian and Calvados are mentioned.)

As in the stage versions, Pedro and Manuela are married, Isabella is Manuela's friend, and Lizarda is her "colored" maid. As in Behrman's play, Pedro is the mayor, but Manuela's parents are dead.

Several scenes slow the story down. For example, in a long sequence, Manuela fantasizes about a pirate ship that is sailing the sea with a dashing Estramudo walking about, picking Manuela out of many women on board, and ultimately taking her to his cabin and kissing her.

Other sequences seem disjointed. For example, Serafin bounces on Manuela's bed and says, "So this is where you toss at night and dream of me," which so excites Manuela that they almost kiss. Yet, when Serafin suggests they run away together, Manuela replies sarcastically, as she did in Behrman's stage play, but this is inconsistent with her ardor a moment earlier. A close reading of both scripts shows that Mankiewicz changed some sections from Behrman's version but left others untouched, creating discrepancies in character and situation.

Certain aspects of the main characters are taken to an extreme. When Pedro realizes that Manuela loves Serafin, he tells his wife that he could kill her for adultery and get away with it. Then Pedro suggests sadistically that instead of killing her, they could sit together and watch Serafin hang. But Mankiewicz also makes Manuela goad Pedro into behaving in this extreme way. She taunts her husband, telling him that she loves Estramudo (Serafin), and throws the rabbit's foot at him.

Serafin is also portrayed differently than in Behrman's play. Instead of the noble swain who is willing to stake all for his love, Mankiewicz's Serafin tells his men to be packed and ready to escape at the end of the performance, and to keep two fast horses ready. This is a throwback to Fulda's play. The denouement is also somewhat different because Serafin chants, "Mene, Mene, Tekel, Upharsin" (the phrase taken from Behrman) during his performance. This so worries Pedro that the disguised pirate crosses himself and strokes all his good luck charms, giving himself away to the alert Viceroy.

The ending is somewhat similar to Behrman's except that Mankiewicz tried to make it more flippant than romantic in an attempt to revert to Fulda's style. For example, Manuela winks elaborately at the Viceroy, and the Viceroy jokes crudely as Serafin carries Manuela into the house.

Synopsis and Analysis of the Connolly-Koster Screenplay

Myles Connolly had written an outline, but it was director Henry Koster who developed the entire screenplay.[2] Koster brought Manuela's parents back to life and dropped Lizarda. He made Isabella black, along with troupe members Trillo, Bolo, and Gumbo. But rather insensitively, he made the black characters ignorant and buffoonish. He also produced a script filled with details tangential to the thrust of the story and offered unbelievable plot twists and characterizations.

This version has one improvement over Mankiewicz's script. To address the issue of a married woman's falling in love with the actor, which would undoubtedly have caused trouble with the censors, Koster had Pedro and Manuela marry on the day that Serafin arrives in town. In fact, all the action takes place that day, so the marriage is never consummated.

However, Koster had great difficulty making this plot change work. Having just arrived in town, Serafin and his troupe head for the wedding, where Serafin flirts with the bride, who he met only a few minutes after she took her vows. He then tries to kiss her with Pedro and all the wedding guests watching. Serafin pretends to know Pedro, who initially denies acquaintance with him. Then, inexplicably, Pedro becomes nervous when Serafin mumbles something incoherently and he begs Serafin not to tell anyone who he is. Further straining audience belief, Pedro reveals to Serafin that he is Estramudo and that Manuela would faint if she knew who he really is. Why he has to reveal this, if he thinks Serafin already knows it, is a mystery. Serafin promises to keep Pedro's identity a secret if he will allow the actor to give a performance. The twists and turns become torturous when it is revealed that Serafin has never heard the name Estramudo and only learns later from his troupe that it is the name of a villainous pirate.

Next, instead of setting up for his performance as he does in the stage plays, Serafin goes to the wedding reception, where he dances and continues to flirt with Manuela. It seems out of character for Serafin to so ignore his upcoming performance, especially when Koster includes a lengthy sequence at the beginning of the script to demonstrate how desperately hungry the troupe is.

Pedro orders his black henchman named Sampson to kill Serafin. The would-be killer throws a knife at Serafin several times and misses. In a scene attempting to be humorous, Serafin notices what is going on and gives the man a lesson in knife throwing.

The script continues to strain credulity in many of the scenes that follow. Pedro tells Manuela that Serafin is a killer, but does not explain why he, the mayor, has given Serafin a permit to perform instead of arresting him. The actor then walks the tightrope to Manuela's bedroom and is surprised that he has walked into her house. In fact, Koster does not explain why Serafin walked the rope, which has no connection with his performance as it does in Behrman's stage play.

Manuela thinks Serafin is Estramudo and questions him about his background. He pretends to be Estramudo even though he has no indication that Manuela is enamored of the pirate. When Pedro walks in and hears this, he leaves to fetch the Viceroy. Yet, Manuela and Serafin seem unconcerned about the dire consequences of the

Viceroy's arrival. They talk at length about irrelevant things as they walk through the large house and garden. For unexplained reasons, Serafin drops hints now and then that Pedro is really Estramudo but Manuela misses all the hints.

In a sequence that would have vaulted the censors through the ceiling, Manuela asks Serafin to tie her to a bedpost so she will not be implicated in his piracy when the Viceroy arrives, but she makes it obvious that this is her sexual fantasy. Serafin ties her and she begs him to whip her until she bleeds. This the actor does not do, but he musses her hair while she is tied to the post, loosens her dress, and kisses her passionately.

The Viceroy in this script is also unbelievable. When Serafin escapes from his handcuffs, this so fascinates the Viceroy that he goes to the prison with him to learn magic tricks. Manuela arrives at the prison and begs the Viceroy to pardon Serafin. Then Pedro arrives and yells at Manuela, but the Viceroy only wants to learn more tricks. In fact, Serafin makes a bargain that he will teach the Viceroy magic if he is allowed to give a performance. In contrast, the Viceroy in Behrman's play is described as "shrewd, sardonic, and distinguished" in the stage directions, and he orders the guards to watch Serafin closely when he slips out of his handcuffs.

Over dinner at their home, Manuela admits to Pedro that she is in love with Estramudo. This leads Pedro to reveal that *he* is Estramudo. When Manuela does not believe him, Pedro orders Sampson to take the terrified Manuela to the vault, which is filled with his treasure. Pedro then covers Manuela with jewels despite her protests.

Later, at the performance, Serafin pretends to hypnotize Manuela and asks if she has a wish, but Manuela sees that Pedro has a gun pointed at her through the draperies and she stalls. She cannot, however, resist Serafin's mirror and under hypnosis, reveals to the audience that Pedro is Estramudo. Pedro fires his gun but is blinded by the mirror, and the bullet misses its mark. Pedro runs away with the crowd running after him, soon joined by the Viceroy's soldiers.

The ending emphasizes several of the script's weaker elements. For example, after trying unsuccessfully to "awaken" Manuela, Serafin succeeds only when he threatens to flog her. Even after Pedro is caught, the Viceroy for some unknown reason orders Serafin to spend a few months in jail. Serafin then pretends to know something about the Viceroy's past, and this makes the public official so nervous that he slips Serafin a bag of gold and sets him free.

Finally, as the wedding march plays, Serafin's troupe gathers near the steps of a palace. Serafin and Manuela appear, and "among the darkies stands Sampson," now a member of the troupe. The screenplay ends as Serafin and Manuela "drive off in the general direction of paradise."

Synopsis and Analysis of the Blum Screenplay

Edwin Blum made some minor, inoffensive changes in the relationships between characters.[3] Capucho and Trina (not Inez) are Manuela's uncle and aunt, but they are also brother and sister in his version. Also, Lizarda is part of Serafin's troupe.

The one improvement Blum made was in deference to Breen—Pedro and Manuela were not yet married but about to be, so there could be no question of adultery to run afoul of the moral code of the censors. Unfortunately, the rest of Blum's changes were poorly conceived. For example, the script begins with Pedro telling Manuela stories about Estramudo that are voiced over scenes of pirates looting ships. Pedro continues to tell her these stories until she is in love with Estramudo, although he has no intention of revealing his identity and he hopes to marry Manuela.

Overall, Blum wrote the worst screenplay for *The Pirate*. He included a number of strange twists and turns that made his script completely unacceptable. For example, when Serafin learns that Manuela loves Estramudo, he claims to be the pirate and announces this to the village. He even creates a stage show about pirates, which draws *real* pirates to see the performance, something that is hard to swallow. In a private conversation with Serafin, Pedro says, "*You posing as an actor!*" which makes little sense as the two men know who the real pirate is.

During the performance, Serafin, pretending to be Estramudo, goes into the audience, pulls Manuela on stage, and throws her over his shoulder as she screams for help. Only later is it revealed that she was merely acting. Pedro jumps on stage and fights with Serafin, and they struggle on the floor as Trina and others join the fight. This supposedly is real as opposed to Manuela's acting. Serafin acts wild and bawdy like a pirate, and several men jump on stage with knives to kill him.

Serafin escapes and catches up with Manuela, who has already walked away from the fray. He praises her acting talent but she says she does not love him. Moreover, she calls him a "cheap actor." The gist of the conversation is one of the few elements retained in the movie, but in a different setting—in Manuela's room before her impending marriage to Pedro—where it works much better.

The story then takes more unnecessary twists as Serafin frees Pedro's prisoners and returns to townsfolk possessions that had been stolen from them. It is not at all clear how Serafin has access to the prisoners or to the stolen possessions, or how the pirate stole anything from the townspeople to begin with.

Pedro is furious and stabs Serafin but happens to use a prop knife so that Serafin is safe. Manuela now regrets that she treated Serafin badly. He asks her how she would feel if he really was an actor but still does not reveal that he really is a strolling player. It is strange that she does not know this already as she had already scorned him for being a cheap actor.

The third act of the screenplay descends to the level of the bizarre. Serafin disguises himself as Pedro and goes to Pedro's home, where he blubbers to the Viceroy and others that Serafin is innocent. He also suggests they open Pedro's vault. As the crowd goes to do so, the real Pedro joins them and Serafin drops off in the shadows. On reaching the vault, Pedro refuses to open it, confusing everyone. Then Serafin comes back, still disguised as Pedro, and the people are further puzzled. As Serafin is trying to tell everyone that Pedro is Estramudo, Pedro pulls off Serafin's disguise and the people "recognize" *him* as Estramudo.

Serafin is arrested and Manuela faints. The Viceroy later allows her to visit Serafin in prison, where he admits to her that he is not Estramudo and that he played the part only to win her love. Manuela is touched. She calls Serafin a great actor, and they kiss. She then asks him if Pedro is really Estramudo, and, for reasons that are entirely unclear to the audience, Serafin says he does not know.

The story ends on a horrible note. As the guards come to take Serafin to be shot, he embraces the crying Manuela and they kiss for the last time. He then walks away with the guards to face his execution.

Synopsis and Analysis of the Loos-Than Screenplay

By the time Anita Loos and Joseph Than worked on their version of *The Pirate,* Cole Porter was on board and "Estramudo" was changed to "Macoco" to please the songwriter.[4] The story starts with a handsome and athletic Macoco ordering passengers captured from a ship to walk the plank one by one, except that he holds the rich for

ransom and the pretty women for "recreation." After some gratu-
itous violence, Serafin appears and is ordered to walk the plank. He
begs for his life, promising to write a ballad to immortalize Macoco.
The song "Mack the Black" is born, followed by scenes of different
people singing it across the islands. Including this song was a clever
way to satisfy Porter's request to use this title as well as to establish
the pirate's legend.

Several characters are changed. Lizarda is now Manuela's
thirteen-year-old sister, Capucho is part of Serafin's troupe, and
Manuela has an aunt named Lucia. As in some previous scripts,
Serafin recognizes Pedro as the pirate but promises not to reveal his
identity if he can give a performance. Manuela goes to the show,
but in the very next scene, Serafin is chatting with her as the crowd
leaves; it appears the performance is over without ever having started. Serafin tries to tell Manuela that marrying Pedro would be like
falling into the clutches of the Black Macoco, but she tells him *that*
is her fantasy.

Some changes follow Minnelli and Than's notes, at least to an extent. For example, the two suggested that Don Pedro should be the
governor of the island, not the mayor, and that he should send an
assassin named Pancho to kill Serafin. Loos and Than created a new
character, an obsequious Governor, whom Pedro bribes and bullies
to get him to release Pedro's henchman Sanchez from prison so he
can kill Serafin.

Minnelli and Than suggested that Serafin leap over soldiers to
retrieve a rabbit his starving troupe had caught on its way to the
town. Manuela sees him leap and fantasizes that he is Estramudo.
(The pirate is named Estramudo in the notes, which predated Porter's association with the film.) Loos and Than follow this basic idea.
As Sanchez hurls knives at them, Serafin puts Manuela in a buggy
and leaps over an enormous vase and onto the roof. Watching him
leap excites Manuela, and she imagines him cavorting about a pirate
ship, giving up shades of the "Pirate Ballet" to come in the movie.

Similar to a comical sequence in Koster's version, a knife magically circles Serafin's throat and boomerangs to hit Sanchez in the
rear. Then, Serafin goes to Manuela and kisses her. She is sure he is
Macoco, even though he halfheartedly denies it, and she invites him
to her balcony. Serafin appears to walk a tightrope to her balcony,
but really Trillo and Capucho help him with a moving platform that
Manuela cannot see but the audience can. Loos and Than borrowed
this device from stage directions in Behrman's play, where it helped

Lunt (as Serafin) to create the illusion of tightrope walking for the audience.

Later, Manuela tells Pedro she loves Serafin but refers to him as Macoco in the conversation. Pedro is furious. He says, "I'll wrench his tongue out, I'll make him walk the plank," but apparently Manuela misses these clues.

Minnelli and Than had envisioned the townspeople as more active than in earlier versions; they hear of the approach of the pirate and encourage the authorities to arrest Serafin and his troupe when they arrive in town. Loos and Than have the people shout "kill Macoco" as Pedro spreads the word that the pirate is in town.

Serafin runs away but as Manuela tries to follow, Sanchez carries her off to a room and locks her up. Serafin grabs a gun from Sanchez and forces him to reveal where Macoco's treasure is hidden. Sanchez takes Serafin to a dungeon under Pedro's house, locks the door, and attacks him. Serafin fights him off, but they end up dueling and Serafin kills Sanchez in self-defense.

Manuela arrives at the dungeon and picks the lock with a hairpin. When she takes in the scene, she misunderstands what happened and starts to hit Serafin. She then grabs a sword, apparently wounding him, and becomes distraught. Serafin finally convinces her that he is not Macoco and that Pedro is the real pirate. The movie retains Manuela's attack on Serafin but with a different setting and details. In the film, Manuela is angry when she finds out that Serafin is *not* the pirate and that he tricked her to come to him.

They hear footsteps and Serafin jumps to his feet, explaining to Manuela's relief that his "wound" was just greasepaint. Pedro and the Governor arrive, accompanied by a mob, and the Governor congratulates Manuela for capturing Macoco. Manuela tries to tell him that Serafin is not the pirate, but Serafin gives her a warning glance. Manuela leaves and the Governor orders Serafin to be put into chains and announces that he will be hanged. The movie also retains this sequence for the most part.

The third act in the Loos-Than version starts out rather dull, but the ending competes with Koster's script for outlandishness. At first, the Viceroy, his wife, the Governor, and Pedro arrive for the hanging. There is much irrelevant and boring conversation. Then Serafin begs to give a performance and flirts with the Viceroy's wife, who grants his request. Manuela tells Pedro that she knows he is Macoco, holds him close, and starts singing "Mack the Black." It is not clear why she does any of this.

The performance starts with Serafin's hypnosis act. As Pedro is watching from the audience, Manuela suddenly appears on the scene in a trance. Pedro objects, as he does in the movie, but the segment is brief. Then "Love of My Life" is sung (presumably by Manuela, but this is not indicated in the script) and then Manuela does "all sorts of magical things." Serafin pulls out two guns, but the guards are relieved to see that these are only props. He fires them anyway and unrolls a net that engulfs Manuela. It is "glittering like a Christmas tree with the jewels of the Infanta" as the crowd gasps. The Viceroy's wife recognizes the jewels, and Pedro tries to run but is surrounded by a "menacing ring of actors, and has to sit down again." It is not clear why Pedro starts to run, because up to this point, only Serafin and Manuela know he is Macoco.

But that is about to change. Serafin asks Manuela to tell everyone who gave her the jewels. After some stalling, Manuela says it is Pedro. The crowd rushes to kill Pedro but he is gone. It is not clear what happened to the menacing actors who were watching him.

Pedro then reappears, grabs Manuela, and threatens to jump off the cliff's edge if the crowd follows him. This is the first indication that the town is atop a cliff near the sea.

Serafin tries to hold back the "snarling, angry mob" but fails. Pedro throws Manuela over the cliff and jumps off himself. Serafin follows them, also leaping off the cliff. Pedro drowns, but Manuela is caught in a fisherman's net. Serafin lands in it too, making her bounce up. As the crowd cheers, Serafin tells Manuela, "We'll include this in our act." The script ends with Manuela pledging her love for Serafin and singing "Mack the Black" as Pedro's body is seen underwater with fishes circling him.

This last sequence involving the sea may have been somewhat influenced by Minnelli and Than's suggestions for a comic sequence early on. The notes mention that soon after they meet, Manuela arranges a rendezvous with Serafin. They row out to sea, and the actor pretends to be Estramudo to win her affection. But he becomes seasick and Manuela has to row them back to shore.

Behrman's Lines in the Goodrich-Hackett Screenplay and the Film

The following is a comprehensive discussion of the overlap be-tween the Goodrich-Hackett screenplay and Behrman's stage play.[1] Goodrich and Hackett used many lines from S. N. Behrman's stage play in their screenplay and these lines were retained in the film. The overlap between the two is classified into four categories: (1) verbatim incorporation of Behrman's lines in critical scenes, (2) other direct use of Behrman's lines throughout the film, (3) using Behrman's lines in different contexts, and (4) Behrman's lines spo-ken by other characters.

Verbatim Incorporation of Behrman's Lines in Critical Scenes

Frances Goodrich and Albert Hackett incorporated Behrman's lines extensively in critical scenes in the film, such as when Serafin meets Manuela, when he recognizes Pedro as Macoco, and when he talks the Viceroy into allowing him to perform before his impending ex-ecution. The writers also borrowed liberally from Behrman in other important scenes, namely, when Serafin actually hypnotizes Manu-ela (at his first performance) and when Manuela pretends to be hyp-notized (at his second performance). Most of these incorporations are verbatim.

When Manuela and Serafin meet, their conversation in Behrman's play is kept almost entirely in the Goodrich-Hackett screen-play. For example, Manuela says, "In Madrid, I hear, the ladies do not walk without their duennas. . . . Here at least I should have thought bodyguards were unnecessary." Serafin replies, "Were you to walk the lonely spaces of the Sahara . . . You, gracious lady, will always need a bodyguard." When Manuela informs Serafin that she already is married (in the play) or about to be (in the film), Serafin tells her, "Then you should never step into the sight of other men. It is a provocation not to be endured." Manuela wittily replies, "I shall remove the provocation." Serafin tells her that her husband (or fi-ancé) should "have stood aside," and Manuela sarcastically replies, "For you I suppose." When Serafin walks around her, obviously fas-cinated, Manuela complains, "I do wish you'd stop circling around me like that—it's like talking to a top," and Serafin replies, "You be-wilder me." Even the rest of their conversation, as Manuela tries to get away from Serafin, is taken directly from Behrman.

Goodrich and Hackett also kept (or closely matched) most of Behrman's lines associated with the moment when Serafin recog-nizes Pedro as the pirate. For example, Serafin says, "Speak more, master, speak more," and "When we last met—you were lithe—you were strong." Pedro calls Serafin a "mountebank" and says, "This is a respectable community. We do not entertain the scum of the cit-ies." Goodrich and Hackett also used Pedro's lines about "malodor-ous riffraff" and giving the players "ten minutes to get out of town," except that they changed it to five minutes. Just as Behrman's Ser-afin repeats the phrase "Mene, Mene, Tekel, Upharsin" to frighten Pedro into allowing him to give a performance, Goodrich and Hack-ett have Serafin start to yell "Macoco!" a second time to achieve the same end. Where Behrman's Pedro says, "Merciful Mother of God!" on realizing that his secret identity has been discovered, Goodrich and Hackett have Pedro say, "Merciful Saints in Heaven." In both the play and the film, when Serafin calls the pirate by his name (Es-tramudo or Macoco), a frightened Pedro pleads, "Don't say that name."

The conversation between Serafin and the Viceroy before Sera-fin's impending execution is also taken verbatim from Behrman's play. When Serafin asks to give a performance, the Viceroy replies, "You must see that the procedure would be irregular. . . . If you es-caped, I should have to consider myself a fool. I do not care to un-dervalue myself." When Serafin persists, the Viceroy muses, "It is always helpful politically, you know, to capture an important criminal," and Serafin replies, "I shall be only too happy, Excellency, to further your career." The Viceroy then calls out, "Stand back, men, give the impresario a little room." He adds, "There's something rather perverse about this. I feel like a Roman Emperor of the decadence. Rather agreeable." Serafin continues the repartee, saying, "It will be a pleasure to be executed by a man of such charm!" Goodrich and Hackett kept all of these lines, including the stage direction of the two bowing to each other.

When Serafin actually hypnotizes Manuela (during his first performance in the film), Goodrich and Hackett took Behrman's lines directly from the hypnotism scene at the end of Behrman's stage version, which is Serafin's *only* performance in the play. Serafin first explains to the audience that hypnotism is "the new and sensational science of animal magnetism . . . taught me by the great Mesmer himself. You know, of course, the principles enunciated by the great Mesmer. . . . Hypnosis—hypnosis . . . And now, Ladies and Gentlemen, before your very eyes I shall perform this experiment!" Serafin also explains (in *both* performances in the film) that, "Control cannot be exercised over everyone. I have failed with the recalcitrant, with the confused, with the rebellious. . . . I need a pure person."

In hypnotizing Manuela, Serafin says, "Nymph, in thy orisons, be all my sins remembered. Purity at last—purity! Gracious lady— that you should be here, at my farewell, makes it a blessing indeed. . . . Come, come . . . I Serafin ask it." He also tells her, "You know whatever I ask of you—whatever power I have over you—is for your happiness. . . . Sit, gracious lady. . . . pure spirit, rest." These exact lines (except for the phrase "at my farewell") are used in the film.

Manuela's petulant response to Serafin, "Don't call me pure soul—it irritates me," is used by Goodrich and Hackett during Serafin's first performance to suggest that Manuela wants to appear worldly. In Behrman's play, Manuela is irritated because she had already explained to Serafin that she was "an unhappy, love-starved woman" and that "you can't be pure when you're frustrated."

Even for Serafin's second performance in the film, Goodrich and Hackett used Behrman's lines verbatim. Serafin says, "This is apt to be my farewell performance. Not that this is my first farewell performance . . . but this time I think I can rely on our honored guest to make it a genuine farewell. . . . Usually at this time I perform a rope trick—but under the circumstances I thought it might be in questionable taste. . . and so I skip the rope." When he starts the hypnosis, Serafin repeats the lines about "control" and needing a "pure person" from Behrman's play.

Behrman's play also contributed the lines spoken after Manuela comes forward while pretending to be hypnotized. Pedro says, "I forbid this! This is a disgrace!" and Serafin appeals to the Viceroy, "Will you please explain to him, Excellency, that this is not passion it is science." In a minor change, "passion" is replaced with "flirtation" in the film. The Viceroy's reply, "It's science," and Pedro's retort, "Whatever you call it, I don't like it," are also retained in the film.

Serafin then says to Manuela, "Speak freely to me who am your friend," and Manuela replies, "I have only one wish. . . . I wish, I wish—" Pedro yells, "Black magic! I won't have him practice black magic on my wife!" The Viceroy admonishes him, "This promises to be an amusing experiment. I will not have it spoiled by your bourgeois possessiveness." He tells Serafin, "Proceed, Mesmer, with your mesmerism." All of these lines are kept in the film with one minor change where "my wife" is changed to "my future wife."

The troupe members in Behrman's play offer Serafin fantastic advice, such as, "Use voodoo, get her out of it with voodoo," "Try rattlesnakes' skins and vinegar," and "They say lizard's milk and chili." Goodrich and Hackett have the troupe offer exactly this advice after the first performance, when Manuela is truly in a trance. But Serafin awakens Manuela with a kiss in the movie, while in the play he merely passes his hands over her face and speaks of their love for each other.

OTHER DIRECT USE OF BEHRMAN'S LINES THROUGHOUT THE FILM

A close comparison of the two versions shows that even in smaller scenes sprinkled throughout the film, Goodrich and Hackett did not hesitate to use Behrman's lines directly. For example, Behrman's Ines tells her daughter, "Morning and night you should burn incense; you should offer prayers and thanks" for being married to Don Pedro. Aunt Inez in the movie offers the same advice to her niece about her being engaged to Don Pedro. (Recall that Behrman spelled Manuela's mother's name as "Ines" whereas Goodrich and Hackett made her Manuela's aunt and, following Fulda, they spelled her name as "Inez.")

Behrman was responsible for creating "the revolving mirror" as well as Serafin's lines, "Is it wound? Is it oiled? Is it true?" Behrman's Trillo warns Serafin, "The man you persuaded to concentrate on that mirror in Valencia ain't waked up yet," to which Serafin replies, "That was a mistake. I had the misfortune to practice on a victim of chronic sleeping-sickness." The movie essentially retains these lines but in conversations with Coutat instead of Trillo because Minnelli changed the names of the characters at a late stage.

When Serafin claims to be Macoco, the critical lines in the film come directly from Behrman. Pedro says, "What has he told you? What has he said to you?" and when Serafin replies that he has told the truth, Pedro blurts, "The truth? What truth?" Serafin asks Pedro, "Is it warm? You are sweating," and Pedro says to Manuela, "Whatever he's told you is a lie." When Serafin tries to entice Manuela into going away with him, he says, "I have engagements on the seven seas. Will you keep them with me?" Manuela replies, "With a man I hardly know?" Serafin replies, "I hardly know you either. We'll have the excitement of discovery. . . . We'll have a glorious life." This conversation in Behrman's play takes place when Pedro is out of the room, but he is present to hear it in the movie. Behrman has Pedro return to discover the two deeply engaged in conversation, and he whines, "Do you two realize that I am in the room?" which is also used in the film at this point.

USING BEHRMAN'S LINES IN DIFFERENT CONTEXTS

Comparing the two scripts also shows some creative adaptations by Goodrich and Hackett in using Behrman's dialogue in new contexts. For example, in the film, Manuela's line, "Where you are, is it sunset or is it daybreak?" is placed during the sequence in which she fantasizes about the pirate while her friends are visiting. In the play it is a soliloquy. The short discussion that follows between Manuela and her friends in the film, about "being more spiritual," takes place between Manuela and Pedro in Behrman's play. "I do wish you'd change a little to the spiritual side," she tells her husband when he discovers that she is reading a book about Estramudo and criticizes her for romanticizing a pirate.

Pedro retorts that he attends Mass and distributes prayer books to the poor and that he restored the church belfry. Behrman's Manuela then admits, "Perhaps spiritual is not the word. Perhaps I should have said imaginative." Goodrich and Hackett should have had Manuela clarify her meaning as well, because considering the worship of a bloodthirsty pirate to be spiritual is difficult to swallow. Pedro's making a big deal of restoring the church belfry is also taken by Goodrich and Hackett but for a different scene where Pedro is trying to convince Serafin that he is a changed man. It works well here because Kelly almost laughs at this ludicrous suggestion in the film.

Behrman's Manuela tells Serafin of her fascination with Estramudo: "On the moving waters he darts about, this dragon-fly of the seas, glittering and uncapturable" and "he has slashed across the world the great pattern of his imagination." Goodrich and Hackett have Manuela say the first line to her friends near the start of the film and a modification of the second line to Serafin on stage near the end of the film before he is to be hanged as Macoco. She also tells Serafin: "There is the practical world and the world of the imagination. I know which is which. I don't mix them." Goodrich and Hackett have Manuela use these lines with minor changes to assure Aunt Inez that she will be a good wife to Pedro despite her romantic daydreaming.

In Behrman's play, Serafin says, "We shall galvanize it!" when Trillo quips that the heart of the little town where Manuela lives has stopped. Goodrich and Hackett have Serafin use the line (changing "it" to "them") in referring to the dull audience before the troupe's first show in Port Sebastian. When Behrman's Trillo asks Serafin how he can be so optimistic about their upcoming performance, Serafin replies, "Don't ask me to explain the mystery of genius." Goodrich and Hackett add a funny twist to the line when Serafin says it in response to his men's complaint that he always manages to avoid doing any work when they have to set up the stage and props.

When Behrman's Serafin walks the tightrope into Manuela's bedroom and sees her parents, Capucho and Ines, gambling, he says, "I sense in this room an atmosphere of strangulated discomfort. These must be relatives. Won't you introduce me?" Goodrich and Hackett use the first two lines as Serafin, after claiming to be Macoco, tells Pedro to dismiss Aunt Inez and Uncle Capucho.

Behrman's Manuela tells Serafin, "I shall despise you—I shall hate you" when he tries to persuade her to run away with him. She also says, "We're not for each other" in this scene. Later, she says, "You fool!" when Serafin refuses to escape after she tells him that Pedro has gone to get the Viceroy. In the Goodrich-Hackett script, Manuela says the first and third lines to Serafin when she thinks he is a mere strolling player and she is trying to get him to leave before Pedro finds him. She says the second line to Serafin in Pedro's presence when she thinks Serafin is the pirate, and he asks her to join him in his adventures on the sea.

Behrman's Serafin says, "You do love me then," to Manuela when she wants him to escape and be safe before Pedro returns. In the Goodrich-Hackett script, Serafin says the line when Manuela tries to stop him from going across the tightrope out of concern for his safety (which, incidentally, she also does in Behrman's play).

On hearing that the Viceroy is arriving, Behrman's Serafin naïvely assumes it is for the performance and assures Trillo, "I have played before the King of Spain. I have appeared before the Khedive of Egypt," to show he is not nervous about performing for a mere government official. In the movie, he says this to the Viceroy to plead for one last performance before he is hanged.

Behrman's Lines Spoken by Other Characters

The last part of this comparative analysis reveals that Goodrich and Hackett demonstrated a higher level of creativity in using some of Behrman's gems for characters other than those for whom they were written. For example, in Behrman's play, Isabella calls Pedro a pumpkin and Ines calls him a lump. Goodrich and Hackett had Serafin use both epithets for Pedro to playfully annoy Manuela. Behrman's Ines calls Serafin "Reverend Pirate," but it is the advocate who uses that show of respect in the film. It is funny in both instances.

When he refuses to escape, Behrman's Manuela tells Serafin, "You have the manners of a spoiled brat, and the effrontery of an unbridled egotist. Because I succumbed to your charm . . . don't think I'll endure your temperament." In the film, it is Serafin who says these lines to Manuela when she throws things at him in rage after discovering that he tricked her about being Macoco.

Behrman depicted Serafin as having difficulty bringing Manuela out of her trance and warning the audience, "Don't come near her— don't touch her, she may die." In the film, it is the Viceroy who offers a similar warning to Manuela's friends when she pretends to be hypnotized.

In Behrman's play Serafin says to Manuela, "You are a glorious prism that dazzles me with all its facets," and "I cannot believe destiny would be so perverse—to give me the vision and then to snatch it away." Goodrich and Hackett have Manuela say the exact first line and a slight modification of the second line to Serafin (as Macoco) near the end of the film, on stage and supposedly in a trance.

APPENDIX C

Cast and Crew List with Mini-Biographies

The following list is compiled from several sources, including the Internet Movie Database and the assistant director's reports.[1] Putting all sources together, it appears that a total of 109 people were noted as having worked on making *The Pirate*, not counting extras who played the roles of soldiers, audience members, or citizens in "crowd" scenes.

Four of the people on this compiled list were principal actors, including Gene Kelly, Judy Garland, Gladys Cooper, and Walter Slezak, who constituted only 3.7 percent of the total. Another group of thirteen supporting actors represented 11.9 percent. The bit players and dancers who had a line to speak amounted to eleven people, or 10.1 percent, while bit players and dancers with no lines totaled thirty-one people, or 28.4 percent. Finally, fifty backstage people, including crew members, writers, the producer and director, as well as the various departmental directors, constituted 45.9 percent of the people who brought *The Pirate* to life.

A number of people involved in the making of this movie remain obscure, with very little information about their lives available today. For eight of them, or 7.3 percent of the list, literally no information was found. In contrast, there are several people on the following list whose contributions to *The Pirate* wound up on the cutting room floor; therefore, they do not appear in the release print of the film, but they do get some credit in this Appendix.

The Cast and Crew of The Pirate

Lola Albright (friend of Manuela): Born July 20, 1925, in Akron, Ohio. Albright worked as a model and in a radio station in Akron before moving to California in the mid-1940s. She appeared in *Champion* (1949) with Kirk Douglas and, after a few more movie roles through 1951, went on to a successful career in television, becoming a regular in series such as *Peter Gunn* (1958–1961) and *Peyton Place* (1964). *The Pirate* was only her second film, and it appears she was added late in the production as one of Manuela's friends because, unlike the rest of the friends, she has no on-screen credit.

Lester Allen (Uncle Capucho): Born November 17, 1891, in Utica, New York, and died November 6, 1949, in Hollywood. He performed in vaudeville, in the circus, and in burlesque theaters before appearing in his first film, *Pusher-in-the-Face,* in 1929. As mentioned in Chapter 4, Garland wore Allen's clown costume from a Broadway show for the "Be a Clown" reprise. The show, *Rufus LeMaire's Affairs,* played at the Majestic Theatre in New York for fifty-six performances from March 28 to sometime in May 1927, and Allen performed in five different roles in this revue. Soon after *The Pirate* was released, Minnelli and Garland attended a costume party hosted by Groucho Marx and dressed in replicas of the clown suits worn in the reprise of "Be a Clown." Garland, of course, wore the replica of Allen's clown suit that she had performed in, while Minnelli wore a replica of Kelly's suit.[2] Allen was killed when hit by a car driven by a twenty-five-year-old driver while crossing Ventura Boulevard, only a year after the release of *The Pirate.* His last film, *Love That Brute,* was released the next year, 1950.

Marie Allison ("Niña" girl): Allison appeared in only four films; *The Pirate* was her first and *Two Tickets to Broadway* (1951) was her last.

Robert Alton (co-director for dance): Born Robert Alton Hart, January 28, 1906, in Bennington, Vermont, and died June 12, 1957, in Los Angeles. Alton studied ballet in New York and worked as a choreographer on Broadway before choreographing his first film in 1936. He directed films and stage shows throughout a long career, winning a Tony Award for Best Choreography for his work on the 1952 production of *Pal Joey.* His credits list twenty-three movies as choreographer (from 1933 to 1955, including some of the most important film musicals of the Freed Unit), two as producer (1955–1956), two as director (1947 and 1950), and one as actor (in an adaptation of Fulda's original play *Two-Faced Woman,* 1941).

Anne Beck ("Niña" girl and dancer): Beck began her seven-film career as a dancer in *Living in a Big Way* (1947), starring Gene Kelly. *The Pirate* was her third movie and her last was *Here Comes the Groom* (1951).

Sally Benson (writer, assistant to Freed): Born September 3, 1897, in St. Louis and died July 19, 1972, in Woodland Hills, California. Benson was a novelist and script writer whose semi-autobiographical stories for *The New Yorker* became the basis for Freed and Minnelli's film *Meet Me in St. Louis* in 1944. Her first screenplay became a movie in 1943, and she racked up twenty-one projects as a writer for the silver screen and for television.

Jerry Bergen (Bolo, Serafin's troupe member): Born January 4, 1899, in Russia and died January, 1986, in Yonkers, New York. His first film was *Arabian Tights* (1933) and his last appearance was on *The Jackie Gleason Show* in 1969.

Oliver Blake (baker, a citizen of Calvados): Born Oliver Prickett, April 4, 1905, in Centralia, Illinois, and died February 12, 1992, in Los Angeles. Starting with *New York Town* in 1941, Blake appeared in a total of 111 films and television shows by 1960. His character roles graced eleven films, including *The Pirate,* in 1948 alone. After the advocate pleads (through the closed door) with Manuela to "sacrifice" herself, the baker reminds her that Macoco will level Calvados "with not one stone left upon another" — and Manuela promptly steps out of her room.

Edwin Blum (writer, an earlier screenplay): Born August 2, 1906, in Atlantic City, New Jersey, and died May 2, 1995, in Santa Monica, California. He was involved in twenty-five projects from *The New Adventures of Tarzan* (1935) until the 1980s. His most famous writing was for *Stalag 17* (1953).

Richard Borland (grip): Involved in nineteen projects as a grip. *The Pirate* was his first project, and an episode of *Eight Is Enough* on television in 1977 was his last.

Jack Bruce (dance assistant): Appeared on screen in only two films: a baseball player on the Wolves team in *Take Me Out to the Ball Game* (1949), starring Gene Kelly, and a barker in *Slightly French,* also in 1949.

Florence Brundage ("Niña" girl): No information available.

Wheaton Chambers (plays an artist): Born James Wheaton Chambers, on October 13, 1887, in Philadelphia, and died January 31, 1958, in Hollywood. Chambers appeared in 189 projects, from *The Florentine Dagger* (1935) to a movie in 1958, with a lot of television appearances in between. In *The Pirate,* Chambers is the silhouette artist supposedly tracing Manuela's profile just before her planned wedding.

George Chandler (carriage driver): Born June 30, 1898, in Waukegan, Illinois, and died June 10, 1985, in Panorama City, California. Chandler's first movie appearance was in *Speed and Spurs* (1928). He served as president of the Screen Actors Guild from 1960 to 1963, and his last appearance was in a television episode in 1979. Along the way, Chandler accumulated a total of 444 on-screen and television appearances.

Myles Connolly (writer, an earlier screenplay): Born October 7, 1897, in Boston, and died July 15, 1964, in Santa Monica, California. He is credited with twenty-three projects as writer and contributor, from *Face in the Sky* (1933) to several television episodes in the 1950s. Connolly also worked as a producer on fifteen projects from 1929 to 1937, and on three as miscellaneous crew in the 1920s.

Gladys Cooper (Aunt Inez): Born December 18, 1888, in Lewisham, a suburb of London, and died November 17, 1971, in Henley-on-Thames, Oxfordshire. Cooper became a model at age six, an actor by 1905, and a postcard beauty at the time of World War I. She co-managed the Playhouse Theater from 1917 to 1927 and was the sole manager from then until 1933. Her first sound movie was released in Britain in 1934. Her first American film was *Rebecca* (1940) with British director Alfred Hitchcock and starring another countryman, Laurence Olivier. Cooper was nominated for best supporting actress, the first of three Oscar nominations, for her role as Bette Davis's mother in *Now, Voyager* (1942). Her varied career took her to the American stage, back to the London stage in 1947, and then to British television. She returned to the United States to perform on American television in the early 1950s. She was the mother of Henry Higgins in the film *My Fair Lady* (1964), and was made Dame Commander of the Order of the British Empire three years later. Cooper was married three times, first to Captain Herbert Buckmaster in 1908, then to Sir Neville Pearson in 1928, and then to Philip Merivale in 1937. She remained single after Merivale's death in 1946. Through her children Cooper became the mother-in-law of the well-known English actors Robert Morley and Robert Hardy. Her resume lists sixty-eight projects, from her first silent movie in 1913 through her last television appearance in 1972, which was broadcast after her death at age eighty-two.

Bruce Cowling (guard): Born October 30, 1919, in Coweta, Oklahoma, and died August 22, 1986, in Los Angeles. Cowling's first appearance was as Steve Baker in the *Show Boat* segment of *Till the Clouds Roll By* (1947). His last was on television in 1959, with thirty-three more projects in between.

Jeanne Coyne (dance assistant): Born February 28, 1923, in Pennsylvania and died May 10, 1973, in Los Angeles. Coyne was a student of Gene Kelly's dance school as a child in Pittsburgh and followed him to New York to start a career in the theater when she was older. She also followed him to Hollywood and eventually became his chief dance assistant. Coyne, a talented dancer in her own right, was married briefly to another member of Kelly's trusted inner circle of assistants, Stanley Donen, from 1948 to 1949. She appeared as a dancer in "All I Do Is Dream of You" and the Montage number in *Singin' in the Rain* (1952) and in "From This Moment On" in *Kiss Me Kate* (1953). Coyne married Kelly on August 6, 1960, and they had two children, Tim and Bridget.

Willa Pearl Curtis (black maid): Born March 21, 1896, in Texas and died December 19, 1970, in Los Angeles. Curtis appeared in her first film in 1938 and made her last appearance on television, in an episode of *Wagon Train* in 1964, with thirty more appearances in between. She appears, without speaking any lines, in the sequence wherein Don Pedro enters Inez and Capucho's house to finalize his marriage plans with Manuela, as well as in the background of other scenes.

Peter Cusanelli (jovial citizen): Born April 12, 1898, in New Haven, Connecticut, and died April 10, 1954, in Los Angeles. The rotund Cusanelli first appeared in *Up in Arms* (1944), and his last performance was as the translator in Gene Kelly's drama *The Black Hand* (1950). He appeared in twenty-five other projects. In *The Pirate*, Cusanelli helps Kelly segue into the "Niña" dance number by asking him why he calls all the girls Niña.

Jack Dawn (makeup artist): Born February 10, 1892, in Kentucky and died June 20, 1961, in Glendale, California. All but one of Dawn's career films were with M-G-M Studios, and the list includes doing makeup for *The Wizard of Oz* (1939), *Meet Me in St. Louis* (1944), *Bud Abbott and Lou Costello in Hollywood* (1945), *The Postman Always Rings Twice* (1946), and *Easter Parade* (1948). He is credited with 217 projects in all, the last in 1950.

Jean Dean (friend of Manuela): Born Jeanne Louise Dean, May 30, 1925, in Illinois and died August 20, 1993, in Malibu, California. Dean was a Vargas model in the 1940s and "a former calendar model for *Esquire Magazine*," according to her biography on IMDB. Her first screen appearance took place in *Killer McCoy* (1947), and her last was a television episode in 1959. *The Pirate* was her third movie and although she is given on-screen credit as Casilda, it is clear from her photographs that she is not Casilda, the only friend Manuela refers to by name in the film.

Lola Deem (friend of Manuela): Deem appeared in only two films: *The Unfinished Dance* (1947) as a fashion model and as one of Manuela's friends in *The Pirate*. She is given on-screen credit as Isabella although she is not referred to by name in the film. As a note of interest, Isabella was Manuela's only friend in both stage plays, compared to the five friends shown in the movie.

Howard Dunham ("Pirate Ballet" dancer): No information available.

Roger Edens (musical arrangements): Born November 9, 1905, in Hillsboro, Texas, and died July 13, 1970, in Los Angeles. Edens owed his multilayered career in moviemaking to Arthur Freed, who gave him the opportunity to write music, produce, and direct films. With little fanfare and no on-screen credit, Edens wrote the musical arrangements for *The Pirate* as well as many of the most famous productions of the Freed Unit. He was the recipient of three Oscar awards, was instrumental in launching the career of Judy Garland, and lived a quietly gay life at a time when it was not fashionable to be openly gay in Hollywood.

William Edmunds (town clerk): Born January 1, 1886, in Italy and died December 7, 1981, in Los Angeles County. Typically cast in a Latin role, or as an unspecified but exotic character, Edmunds was Mr. Martini in *It's a Wonderful Life* (1946). His first role was in *Going Spanish* (1934), and his last was on television in 1959. He stacked up a resume of ninety-four projects in the meantime. No town clerk is identified in *The Pirate,* but Edmunds is one of the few prominent citizens of Calvados.

Mary Jo Ellis (friend of Manuela): Born May 31, 1899, in New York City and died November 19, 1998, in Barnstable County, Massachusetts. The first of her twenty-five projects was *Forbidden* (1932), in which she played a twelve-year-old girl, according to IMDB. If so, she would have been thirty-three when she played that part. Nevertheless it may be so, because Ellis played one of Manuela's friends, even though at age forty-eight, she was more than twice as old as the others. If one looks closely at the group, she is easy to spot. She receives on-screen credit as Lizarda, although she is not referred to by name in the movie. As a note of interest, Lizarda was Manuela's black maid in Behrman's stage play. The last film Ellis appeared in was released only three years later, in 1951.

George Emerson (boatswain with parrot): As an actor, Emerson's only appearance was slated to be in *The Pirate*. But there is no sailor with a parrot to be seen in the release print of the movie, so one has to assume his scenes were deleted. Emerson worked as an animal trainer or supervisor for four films, most of them Tarzan movies in the 1930s and 1940s.

Sally Feeney ("Niña" girl and dancer): Born May 28, 1928, in San Diego. M-G-M hired her as a dancer after she graduated from high school, and Feeney performed in several dance films, starting with *Till the Clouds Roll By* (1947). Her best success was as the lead actress in *Not Wanted* (1949), and her last appearance was in an episode of *Family Affair* in 1967.

Norwood A. Fenton (sound): Fenton's first work was *Presenting Lily Mars* (1943), and his last was a television episode of *The Munsters* in 1965.

Arthur Freed (producer): Born Arthur Grossman, September 9, 1894, in Charleston, South Carolina, and died April 12, 1973, in Los Angeles. Freed's long career in show business included writing some of the most popular songs in the movies in partnership with Nacio Herb Brown, especially during the advent of sound pictures in the late 1920s and early 1930s. He joined the staff at M-G-M and worked his way up to being the most important producer of film musicals at the studio, managing the famous Freed Unit from the early 1940s until the late 1950s. His lyrics were used in the music of at least 144 movies between 1929 and 2005. He produced or co-produced fifty-one films from 1939 to 1962.

Judy Garland (Manuela): Born Frances Ethel Gumm on June 10, 1922, in Grand Rapids, Minnesota, and died June 22, 1969, in Chelsea, London. At four feet eleven inches tall, she was one of the towering figures in film musicals of the twentieth century. Garland already had legendary success by the time she created the role of Manuela on screen in *The Pirate*. Married five times, she was directed by then-husband Vincente Minnelli during the production of *The Pirate*. As an actress, Garland appeared in thirty-two projects from 1936 to 1963, as herself on fifty-one projects on the silver screen and television, and has eighty-eight projects to her credit as a contributor to the sound tracks of films and television shows.

Gaudsmith Brothers (as themselves, part of Serafin's troupe): These Dutch-born brothers appeared in *The Pirate* and in two episodes of Ed Sullivan's *The Toast of the Town* in 1954–1955, also as themselves. (IMDB incorrectly reports that their "poodle act" was deleted from the movie.)

Cedric Gibbons (art direction): Born Austin Cedric Gibbons, March 23, 1893, in Dublin, Ireland and died July 26, 1960, in Hollywood. Gibbons worked with M-G-M for thirty-two years, supervising the art direction for 1,050 movies and designing sets for seventy-two films. He was production designer on five films and directed one movie in 1934. Gibbons's name was put on nearly every film that M-G-M made because of his executive control of the art department's activities.

Fred Gilman (coachman): Born November 24, 1902, in Virginia and died March 30, 1988, in Capistrano Beach, California. His first film was *The Shoot 'Em Up Kid* (1926) and his final movie was *Last Across the Wide Missouri* (1951). Gilman appeared in fifty-seven films, forty-eight of them before 1935.

Frances Goodrich (writer, final screenplay): Born December 21, 1890, in Belleville, New Jersey, and died January 29, 1984, in New York. Goodrich married Robert Ames and then Henrik Van Loon before pairing professionally and conjugally with writer Albert Hackett in 1931. The couple was married until her death. They won two Tony awards in 1956 for Best Author (Dramatic) and Best Play, for *The Diary of Anne Frank,* as well as a Pulitzer Prize for Drama for the same production. Goodrich is credited with forty-five projects as a writer.

Sydney Guilaroff (hairstyle designer): Born November 2, 1907, in London and died May 28, 1997, in Beverly Hills. Guilaroff's name appeared in the credits of many M-G-M films because of his dominant role in designing the hair of most of its top female stars. He is credited with 390 projects on the big and small screens from 1938 to 1989.

Albert Hackett (writer, final screenplay): Born February 16, 1900, in New York, and died March 16, 1995, in New York. Hackett shared the credit for writing the screenplay for *The Pirate* with his writing partner and wife, Frances Goodrich. He worked as a writer on forty-four projects from 1931 to 1996, and acted in twenty-three films from 1912 to 1930.

Suzette Harbin (black maid): Born July 4, 1911, in Ledbetter, Texas, and died September 5, 1994, in Texas. Harbin's first performance was in *Up Jumped Devil* (1941), and her last was an episode of *Wagon Train* in 1958, with a resume of fifteen performances in all. The assistant director's report of February 17, 1947, for *The Pirate* indicates Harbin participated in filming that was taking place on Manuela's patio, but these scenes appear to have been cut. It is possible that Harbin is in the scene where Manuela's bridal portrait is being traced. The maid is in the background very briefly and she is in the shadows, so it is not clear whether it is Harbin or Willa Pearl Curtis.

Lennie Hayton (musical director): Born February 13, 1908, in New York and died April 24, 1971, in Palm Springs, California. Music director at M-G-M from 1940 to 1953, jazz pianist, composer, conductor, and arranger, Hayton played a quietly important role in the musical department of the studio for many years. He was perhaps better known as the husband of Lena Horne from 1947 to 1971, one of the rare interracial public marriages of the era. Hayton is listed as a composer for sixty film projects from 1941 to 1969, and as a member of the music department for fifty-four other projects from 1933 to 1969.

Wally Heglin (orchestrator): Born September 20, 1904, in South Dakota and died November 3, 1992, in Los Angeles. Heglin worked as orchestrator on 191 films from 1939 to 1957.

Jerry Hester (still photographer): Hester's job was to take photographs of the production for publicity purposes. He worked as a still photographer on only four movies, all of them in 1948, and *The Pirate* was his first work.

Jane Howard ("Niña" girl and dancer): Also known as Betty Jane Howarth, her first performance was in *The Pirate* and her last was *Straight Time* (1978). She danced or acted in twenty-four films.

Charolette Hunter ("Niña" girl): No information available.

Irene (costume supervisor): Born December 8, 1900, in Baker, Montana, and died November 15, 1962, in Los Angeles. Irene, who went by only one name, worked on the costumes of 101 movies, from gowns for Ginger Rogers in *Shall We Dance* (1937) to the end of her life in 1962. She is credited with 195 films. Moreover, she acted in eight silent movies during the early 1920s. Irene was married to the brother of Cedric Gibbons from 1936 to 1962.

Patricia Jackson ("Niña" girl and dancer): Jackson performed as a dancer in only five films from 1945 to 1955 and in a television episode of *Coronado 9* in 1961.

Henri Jaffa (associate color director, Technicolor): Born April 13, 1905, in California and died August 14, 1988, in Los Angeles. The Technicolor Corporation sent its own technicians to the set to advise on the process of shooting films for the application of color in the lab, and Jaffa worked on 137 movie productions in this capacity from 1937 to 1959. He also worked in the editorial department on fifteen movies from 1958 to 1976, and on five in the art department.

Van Allen James (sound editor): Born June 23, 1904, in Oakland, California, and died February 27, 1985, in Los Angeles. James is credited with work on sixty-two projects, most of them movies, from *The Wizard of Oz* (1939) to *That's Entertainment* (1974). *The Pirate* was only his second film.

Ellis Jenkinson ("Pirate Ballet" dancer): No information available.

Fred Jenkinson ("Pirate Ballet" dancer): No information available.

Natalie Kalmus (color director, Technicolor): Born Natalie Dunfee in 1878 in Boston and died there November 15, 1965. Kalmus worked as a catalog model before marrying Herbert T. Kalmus, the inventor of the Technicolor process, in 1902. They divorced in 1922 but continued to live together for twenty-two years. Theirs was a working relationship, for Natalie was the Technicolor color director on 354 projects from 1933 to 1956, fifty-one films in 1948 alone. She is listed as a member of the art department for fifteen additional projects.

Barbara Karinska (costume execution): Born Varvara Zhmoudsky, October 3, 1886, in Kharkov, Russia, and died October 19, 1983, in New York. She designed costumes for the New York City Ballet and went on to do the same work for twenty film projects, winning an Oscar for costumes in *Joan of Arc* (1948).

Gene Kelly (Serafin and co-director for dance): Born August 23, 1912, in Pittsburgh and died February 2, 1996, in Los Angeles. Along with Fred Astaire, Kelly was the most important film dancer of the twentieth century. *The Pirate* represents the true start of his post-World War II career, a movie that gave him the opportunity to flower as a dancer and actor. It was soon followed by a series of musicals in which Kelly not only starred and danced, but directed and choreographed as well. Kelly's best films are the Freed Unit's best as well.

Tom Keogh (costume design): Worked in costume and wardrobe on two projects in 1955–1956, as miscellaneous crew on one in 1960, and as costume designer only for *The Pirate*. All of Keogh's credits are film musicals.

Henry Koster (writer, an earlier screenplay): Born Hermann Kosterlitz, May 1, 1905, in Berlin and died September 21, 1988, in Camarillo, California. He began to write scenarios for silent films at age seventeen and became a director by 1932. Reportedly, Koster fled Nazi Germany after he hit a Nazi officer in a scuffle at a bank during his lunch break and left the country immediately. He is credited with forty-nine movies as director from 1932 to

1966, forty-eight as writer from 1925 to 1967, and five as producer from 1938 to 1965.

Arthur Krams (associate set decorator): Born July 15, 1912, in New York and died September 29, 1985, in Woodland Hills, California. He worked as a set decorator on fifty-one projects from 1946 to 1968, and in the art department on eleven projects from 1948 to 1951.

Sam Leavitt (camera operator): Born February 6, 1904, in New York and died March 21, 1984, in Woodland Hills, California. He is listed as a cinematographer on sixty-six projects from 1932 to 1977, on the big screen and on television. He also worked in the camera and electrical departments on nineteen projects from 1934 to 1978, including many of the best Hollywood musicals.

Bera Lee ("Niña" girl): No information available.

Doris Lee (paintings): Born May 15, 1926, in Harrow, England and died in 1992. Lee worked in the costume and wardrobe department on eleven films from 1944 to 1954 and in costume design for six projects from 1944 to 1955. She made the paintings that accompanied Manuela's narration of Macoco's exploits at the beginning of *The Pirate*.

Ben Lessy (Gumbo, Serafin's troupe member): Born April 29, 1902, in New York and died October 30, 1992, in Beverly Hills. Lessy first appeared in *Café Rendezvous* (1938), and his last performance was in *Buddy Buddy* (1981). He was on a number of television shows in bit parts as well.

Anita Loos (writer, an earlier screenplay): Born April 26, 1888, in Sisson, California, and died August 18, 1981, in New York. Her career as a writer began with screenplays for silent movies. Loos wrote *The New York Hat*, which was directed by D. W. Griffith and starred Mary Pickford when released in 1912. Loos wrote the card titles for Griffith's *Intolerance* (1916) and became most famous for her novel *Gentlemen Prefer Blondes*, published in 1925. Her credits include 136 projects as a writer, from *The Musketeers of Pig Alley* (1912) to a film released in 1956, more than thirty of which were silent movies. She also produced seven films from 1918 to 1922, and acted in one silent film and in two television episodes.

Wilkie C. Mahoney (writer, revisions): Born June 25, 1897, in San Miguel, California, and died July 30, 1976, in Los Gatos, Calfornia. Mahoney worked on a dozen projects as a writer, from *Some Like It Hot* (1939) to *Three on a Spree* (1961).

Joseph L. Mankiewicz (writer, the first screenplay): Born February 11, 1909, in Wilkes-Barre, Pennsylvania, and died February 5, 1993, in Bedford, New York. Mankiewicz is credited with forty-nine films as a writer from 1929 to 1985, twenty-three as director from 1946 to 1972, twenty-three as producer from 1936 to 1970, and one as an actor in 1929. He won Oscars for writing and directing two films, *A Letter to Three Wives* (1949) and *All About Eve* (1950). His older brother, Herman J. Mankiewicz, won the Best screenplay Oscar for *Citizen Kane* (1941).

Frances Marion (writer, treatment): Born Marion Benson Owens, November 18, 1888, in San Francisco and died May 12, 1973, in Los Angeles. Marion did some acting and modeling before traveling to Los Angeles, where she became an assistant to the director Lois Weber and wrote films for Mary Pickford. Marion received Oscars for *The Big House* (1930) and *The Champ* (1931), but left Hollywood in 1946 and wrote novels and plays. She was married to the movie cowboy Fred Thomson in the 1920s.

Leslie H. Martinson (script supervisor): Born January 16, 1915, in Boston. Martinson worked as part of the miscellaneous crew for sixteen projects, mostly films, from 1946 to 1953, and as second unit or assistant director on three movies, including the Gene Kelly musicals *Take Me Out to the Ball Game* (1949) and *Summer Stock* (1950). He also directed 105 films and television episodes from 1952 to 1989.

Paul Maxey (hotel manager): Born March 15, 1907, in Wheaton, Illinois, and died June 3, 1963, in Pasadena, California. The heavyset Maxey appeared in 141 projects, from a film in 1937 to his last performance in an episode of the television series *Perry Mason* in 1963.

Jill Meredith ("Niña" girl): Meredith appeared in only three films. *The Pirate* was her second.

Ruth Merman ("Niña" girl): No information available.

Vincente Minnelli (director): Born February 28, 1903, in Chicago and died July 25, 1986, in Beverly Hills. Minnelli ranks as one of the most important Hollywood directors of the mid-twentieth century, especially for his film musicals. Married four times, Minnelli directed his then-wife Judy Garland in *The Pirate*. He worked on thirty-eight films as director from 1942 to 1976, and five as part of the miscellaneous crew from 1937 to 1952.

Marion Murray (Eloise): Born about 1885 and died November 11, 1951, in New York. Murray appeared in only four films from 1941 to 1948. *The Pirate* was her last movie, but it is not clear what role she played in it because at sixty-three, she was too old to be one of Manuela's friends. Also, the character Eloise is not in any of the stage plays or screenplays.

Robert Nathan (writer, revisions): Born January 2, 1894, in New York and died May 25, 1985, in Los Angeles. Nathan's uncle founded Barnard College, but Nathan attended Harvard University, where he wrote poetry and short stories. However, he dropped out during his junior year after getting married, and worked in the advertising business for a few years before resuming his writing career. He produced several successful novels in the 1920s and 1930s, including *The Bishop's Wife*, published in 1928, which was made into an M-G-M movie in 1947. He also co-wrote *The Clock*, a 1945 M-G-M film starring Judy Garland and directed by Vincente Minnelli. Nathan worked on a total of fourteen projects as screenwriter.

Aurora Navarro (duenna): Navarro appeared in five films, from *Drums of Destiny* (1937) to *Around the World in Eighty Days* (1956). Navarro acted as the duenna for one of the "Niña" girls. She takes a swipe at Serafin with her fan when he gets too close to her charge and later watches him dance from the balcony.

Fayard Nicholas (specialty dancer): Born October 20, 1914, in Mobile, Alabama, and died January 24, 2006, in Los Angeles. Nicholas paired with his younger brother Harold to form the Nicholas Brothers, a spectacular dance team that performed mostly in movies for black audiences but also crossed over into films designed primarily for white audiences. The brothers received the Kennedy Center honors in 1991. Fayard is credited with eighteen projects as actor and forty-four as himself. Shortly after the release of *The Pirate*, he and his brother went to Europe for three years. After their return, they conducted a major tour across the southern states with Dizzy Gillespie. Fayard had insisted on a number of things, such as "assurances of personal security, dignified lodging and lots of money," according to an interviewer. "Mr. Nicholas says that the entire company received an exuberant welcome, and that the trip went smoothly without incident."[3]

Harold Nicholas (specialty dancer): Born March 27, 1912, in Winston-Salem, North Carolina, and died July 3, 2000, in New York. The other half of the Nicholas Brothers, Harold received credit in twenty-three projects as actor and thirty-three as himself, mostly on television. Neither brother performed in an American film musical after *The Pirate* partly because they left immediately for Europe and partly because other than Kelly, Minnelli, and Freed, no one in Hollywood was willing to ignore racial barriers and give the Nicholas Brothers the type of exposure they received in *The Pirate.*

Reginald Owen (the advocate): Born August 5, 1887, in Wheathampstead, Hertfordshire and died November 5, 1972, in Boise, Idaho. Owen was one of the stalwarts among the character actors at M-G-M. He first appeared on the stage at age eighteen in England and came to New York early in the 1920s and to California for film work in 1928. After a long career on the big screen, Owen was a principal in the Broadway revival in 1972 of *A Funny Thing Happened on the Way to the Forum* just before passing away of a heart attack. He was writing his autobiography at the time. Owen appeared in 142 films and television episodes from 1911 to 1973, and was credited as a writer on two movie projects in the 1930s.

Jimmy Page (black barber): Page appeared in only two films; *The Pirate* was his first and the other was *Stranger at My Door* (1950).

Dorothy Ponedel (makeup): Born July 2, 1898, in Illinois and died April 30, 1979, in Los Angeles. Ponedel came to Hollywood in 1920 and was an extra and a dancer in silent films. She began working with makeup in 1930 and became a close friend of Judy Garland's in that capacity. Ponedel worked on makeup for many other M-G-M stars but retired after being diagnosed with multiple sclerosis in 1951. She is credited as part of the makeup department in a dozen movies from 1930 until her last, *Singin' in the Rain* (1952).

Cole Porter (song lyrics): Born June 9, 1891, in Peru, Indiana, and died October 16, 1964, in Santa Monica, California. A famed writer of some of Broadway's most successful musicals, Porter won two Tony Awards in 1949 for *Kiss Me Kate.* Porter's beloved mother passed away in August 1952 and his wife, Linda, died in May 1954. In 1958, he underwent thirty-three operations on his leg, which was mangled in a horse-riding accident twenty-one years earlier. Porter's songs were used in 422 films and television shows from 1929 to 2010. He also is credited as composer for a dozen projects, and as a part of the music department for six works.

Harold Ramser ("Pirate Ballet" dancer): No information available.

Elynne Ray ("Niña" girl and dancer): Ray danced in only three films, all of them M-G-M musicals starring either Gene Kelly or Fred Astaire.

Cully Richards (Trillo, one of Serafin's two main assistants): Born October 31, 1908, in Ohio and died June 17, 1978, in Los Angeles. A vaudeville comic during the 1920s, Richards appeared in seventeen films on a sporadic basis from 1935. His last performance was in an episode of "The Honeymooners" on *The Jackie Gleason Show* in 1969.

Howard Emmett Rogers (writer, treatment): Born July 13, 1890, in New York and died August 16, 1971, in Hollywood. Rogers wrote forty-one projects, from *Tin Gods* (1926) to his only television episode in 1955.

Ellen Ross (friend of Manuela): Ross appeared in only five films beginning in 1946. *The Pirate* was her last project. Although she is given on-screen credit as Mercedes, it is clear from her photographs that she is Casilda, the only friend Manuela refers to by name in the movie. As a note of interest, Mercedes was Inez's friend and neighbor in Fulda's original stage play.

Conrad Salinger (instrumental arrangements): Born August 30, 1901, in Massachusetts and died July 6, 1961, in Pacific Palisades, California. Salinger helped Edens with the arrangements for the sound track for *The Pirate*. He is credited with eighty-one film projects from 1931 to 1962.

Russell Saunders (stunts): Born Russell Maurice Saunders, May 21, 1919, in Winnipeg, Manitoba, in Canada, and died May 29, 2001, in West Los Angeles. Saunders doubled and performed stunts during a long career in Hollywood. He is credited as a stunt man in thirty-five films from 1933 to 1988 and played bit parts in twenty-five other movies and television episodes from 1940 to 1981.

Sharon Saunders ("Niña" girl and dancer): Sharon Saunders danced in only three films. *The Pirate* was her first.

Val Setz (Esteban, Serafin's troupe member): Setz was a juggler in one other film (*Mardi Gras* in 1943) besides *The Pirate,* and played the Great Balso in *Powder River* (1953). In *The Pirate,* he is simply given credit as the "juggler."

Blanche Sewell (editor): Born October 27, 1898, in Oklahoma and died February 2, 1949, in Burbank, California. Sewell worked only at M-G-M as editor on sixty-four films from 1925 to 1949. *The Pirate* was her second-last movie. Many of her projects were among the studio's best musicals.

Douglas Shearer (recording director): Born November 17, 1899, in Westmount, an affluent suburb of Montreal and died January 5, 1971, in Culver City, California. As creator and head of the sound department at M-G-M, Shearer's name appears on the credits list of 910 films from 1928 to 1955. He won twelve Oscars during his career, and his sister, Norma Shearer, became one of the studio's most successful actresses.

Al Shenberg (production manager): Born August 3, 1900, and died November 1968 in Los Angeles. He was the nephew of Louis B. Mayer. Shenberg is credited as second unit or assistant director for forty-six movies and television episodes from 1929 to 1968, and fifteen as production manager from 1942 to 1967. He worked on many films directed by Vincente Minnelli.

Dick Simmons (militia captain): Born August 19, 1913, in St. Paul, Minnesota, and died January 11, 2003, in Oceanside, California. Simmons attended the University of Minnesota and traveled the world in the 1930s as a crewman on tankers and freighters before settling in the Los Angeles area. According to folklore, Louis B. Mayer saw him break in an Arabian horse and gave him a screen test that led to a number of bit parts in many films and television shows from 1937 to 1977. Simmons won his greatest popularity as the star of *Sergeant Preston of the Yukon* on television, beginning in 1955.

Walter Slezak (Don Pedro Vargas): Born May 3, 1902, in Vienna and died April 21, 1983, in Flower Hill, New York. Slezak, the son of a popular operatic tenor, had a flourishing career as a leading man in German films and on the European stage before coming to the United States in the 1930s where his career was spent mostly as a character actor. He continued to perform in many movies after *The Pirate* and returned to Broadway, where he won a Tony Award in 1955 as best actor in *Fanny*. Slezak is credited as actor in ninety-two films and television shows from 1922 to 1980. He also appeared in an opera and is credited with appearing in thirty-one projects as himself, all of them on television, some in quiz and game shows. Slezak committed suicide at his home on Long Island after suffering serious illnesses, including heart trouble. His daughter Erika Slezak appeared in 399 episodes of the television soap opera *One Life to Live* from 1971 to 2010.[4]

Jack Martin Smith (art direction): Born January 2, 1911, and died November 7, 1993. Smith was involved in 152 projects as art director, from *Broadway Rhythm* (1944) to an episode of the television series *Dynasty* in 1989. He also worked on six projects as production designer, and on five as a member of the art department. Despite sharing on-screen credit with Cedric Gibbons, Smith was solely in charge of art direction for *The Pirate*. (See explanation under entry for Gibbons.) Smith was nominated for Oscars six times and won three of them.

Melba Snowden ("Niña" girl and dancer): Snowden danced or acted in six films from 1945 to 1953, including *An American in Paris* (1951), starring Gene Kelly.

Wanda Stevenson ("Niña" girl and dancer): Stevenson danced in four films from 1938 to 1951, in addition to her work for *The Pirate.*

Harry Stradling Sr. (cinematography): Born September 1, 1901, in Newark, New Jersey, and died February 14, 1970, in Hollywood. One of the most respected cinematographers in Hollywood, Stradling is credited with 134 projects, from *The Devil's Garden* of 1920 to *The Owl and the Pussycat* in 1970. His list includes at least fourteen silent films and at least twenty-six French and German movies in the 1930s, as well as many of M-G-M's finest musicals. His son and nephew also became cinematographers.

Marvin Stuart (substitute assistant director): Born May 6, 1901, in Seneca, Missouri, and died June 22, 1968, in Los Angeles. Stuart was the second unit or assistant director for fifty-seven titles from 1937 to 1967, and production manager for eight titles from 1958 to 1968. He is best known for his work on *Singin' in the Rain* (1952) and *The Untouchables* (1959).

Bruce Tegner ("Pirate Ballet" dancer): Born October 28, 1929, in California and died August 1985 in Ventura, California. Tegner worked as an actor in four films from 1959 to 1967, and as part of the makeup department on one other.

Joseph Than (writer, earlier screenplay): Born July 26, 1903, in Vienna and died December 2, 1985, in Hollywood. Also known as Pepi Than, he founded ABC-Film in Berlin in 1931 to produce his own screenplays. Than established his company in Austria in 1934 and Taris-Film in Paris in 1938. He emigrated to the United States in 1942 by way of North Africa, reminiscent of *Casablanca,* which came out the same year. He is credited with thirty-one projects as a writer from 1915 to 1971, including three television episodes of *I Spy* (1967) and *Hawaii Five-O* (1971). He also is credited with seven films as a producer, all of them released in Germany from 1931 to 1940.

Kay Thompson (musical arrangements): Born Katherine L. Fink, November 9, 1908, in St. Louis, Missouri, and died July 2, 1998, in New York. Her father was an Austrian immigrant. Thompson played the piano with the St. Louis Symphony by age sixteen and sang with bands on the radio. Arthur Freed hired her as an arranger and vocal coach. Thompson started a popular club act in 1947 that lasted for six years. Later, she wrote children's books, starting with *Eloise* in 1956. She is credited with working on the sound track of thirteen projects, eleven as part of the music department, five as an actress from 1937 to 1970, four as a writer, and fourteen as herself from 1955 to 1972. Thompson made a musical arrangement of

"Mack the Black" for Judy Garland in *The Pirate,* but it was not used. Roger Edens rewrote it to make it work for the film.

Dee Turnell ("Niña" girl named Louisa and dancer): Born November 27, 1925. Her first appearance, as a Copa Girl, was in *Copacabana* (1947). *The Pirate* was Turnell's third film. She danced in an impressive string of M-G-M musicals, several of them starring Gene Kelly or Fred Astaire, until her last performance in *The Opposite Sex* (1956).

Dorothy Tuttle ("Niña" girl and dancer): Born April 21, 1918, and died August 12, 1998, in Encino, California. Tuttle acted or danced in eleven films, many of them major M-G-M musicals, from 1937 until the 1950s.

Irene Vernon ("Niña" girl and dancer): Born Irene Vergauwen, January 16, 1922, in Mishawaka, Indiana, and died April 21, 1998, in South Bend, Indiana. Her first dance appearance was in *Till the Clouds Roll By* (1947), and *The Pirate* was her third film. Vernon mostly performed on television from 1951 on. She was the first Mrs. Larry Tate on *Bewitched,* 1964–1966, her last work on screen.

O. Z. Whitehead (Coutat, one of Serafin's two main assistants): Born Oothout Zabriskie Whitehead, March 1, 1911, in New York and died July 20, 1998, in Dublin, Ireland. Whitehead's banker father provided well for his family, and O. Z. attended Harvard University before he performed on the New York stage. He became a regular in John Ford films, appearing in five of them. His most famous role was as Al Joad in Ford's *The Grapes of Wrath* (1940), which was his second movie. *The Pirate* was his fifth film. Despite his prominent role in *The Pirate,* O. Z. received no onscreen credit, as discussed in Chapters 4 and 6. IMDB and TCM incorrectly credit him as Hurtado. Whitehead moved to Ireland in 1963.

Edwin B. Willis (set decoration): Born January 28, 1893, in Decatur, Illinois, and died November 26, 1963, in Hollywood. Willis worked only at M-G-M studios as a set decorator on 606 projects from 1925 to 1957. Twenty-two of those films were released in 1948. He also worked in the art department on 196 films from 1933 to 1955, and on sixteen as art director from 1925 to 1937. Willis has a total of 818 movies to his credit over the course of thirty-two years, an average of twenty-five films per year.

Marie Windsor (Madame Lucia, alterations lady): Born Emily Marie Bertelson, December 11, 1919, in Marysvale, Utah, and died December 10, 2000, in Beverly Hills. Windsor attended Brigham Young University and trained for the stage, working mostly in B films in the 1940s. She found her niche in film noir by appearing in *The Killing* (1956), and often accepted roles as a gun moll or an adulterous wife. She is credited with 167 projects, from *Weekend for Three* in 1941 to an episode of *Murder, She Wrote* in 1991. Her scenes in *The Pirate* were dropped from the movie.

Wallace Worsley Jr. (assistant director): Born June 27, 1908, in Fort Wayne, Indiana, and died June 18, 1991, in Los Angeles County. He was called Wally, because his father, who had the same name, was also a director with M-G-M. Wally started as a messenger at M-G-M in 1932, and worked as production manager on forty-three projects, many of them for television. He was the second unit or assistant director on twenty-five projects from 1948 to 1971. Worsley also worked as miscellaneous crew on twenty projects, directed seven television episodes, produced a film and two television episodes, and wrote one project in 1979.

Dolph Zimmer (substitute assistant director): Born July 2, 1892, in Queens, NY, and died August 23, 1975, in North Hollywood. His birth name was Adolph, which he changed to Dolph (aka Dolf). Zimmer was the second unit or assistant director for eighty-seven projects from 1931 to 1968. He is best known for his work on *Leave It to Beaver* (1958–1963) and *The Munsters* (1964–1966).

George Zucco (viceroy): Born January 11, 1886, in Manchester, England, and died May 28, 1960, in Hollywood. His father was a merchant of Greek heritage, and his mother had been a lady-in-waiting for Queen Victoria. Zucco entered a serious phase of his acting career by going to Canada and acting on the stage in 1908. He returned to England, served as a lieutenant in a Yorkshire regiment during World War I, and suffered a serious gunshot wound to his right arm. He was back on the stage in the 1920s and in British films the next decade before coming to the United States in 1935. Zucco became a staple among character actors in Hollywood, usually as an authority figure but also as a long string of dark characters. He suffered a stroke on the set of *The Desert Fox: The Story of Rommel* in 1951 and retired, living in a nursing home for the rest of his life. Zucco is credited with ninety-eight projects from *Dreyfus* (1931) to his last, *David and Bathsheba* (1951).

Notes

ABBREVIATIONS

AMPAS	Academy of Motion Picture Arts and Sciences, Margaret Herrick Library, Beverly Hills, California
BU	Boston University, Howard Gottlieb Archival Research Center, Boston, Massachusetts
CU	Columbia University Libraries, Oral History Research Office, Popular Arts Project, New York, New York
MPAA	Motion Picture Association of America
NYPL	New York Public Library, Manuscripts and Archives Division, New York, New York
USC	University of Southern California, Archives of Performing Arts and Warner Bros. Archives, Los Angeles, California
WFTRC-WHS	Wisconsin Center for Film & Theater Research and Wisconsin Historical Society, Madison, Wisconsin
WHS	Wisconsin Historical Society, Madison, Wisconsin

CHAPTER ONE: *THE PIRATE* ON STAGE

1. Ludwig Fulda biography on www.jewishencyclopedia.com, www.imdb.com, and www.wikipedia.org; Behrman, *The Pirate*, vii-ix; *New York Times*, February 8, 1894; "The Emperor's New Clothes" on www.wikipedia.org.

2. Ludwig Fulda biography on www.imdb.com; Behrman, *The Pirate*, vii; *New York Times*, October 29, 1913; Siegel, "The Pirate," 22; Thomas, *Films of Gene Kelly*, 75; Ludwig Fulda filmography on www.imdb.com and www.citwf.com.

3. This and the following synopsis are based on Fulda's original version of *The Pirate*, *Der Seerauber*, Leroy Linick, translator, n.d., copied January 25, 1943, Turner/MGM Script Collection, Herrick Library, AMPAS.

4. "Lunt Salvages Idea From Play Staged in 1917," *New York Herald Tribune*, November 22, 1942; Brown, *Fabulous Lunts*, 76; Peters, *Design for Living*, 36. Some writers have asserted that Lunt played the role of Trillo, not Serafin, in the 1917 stage production of *The Pirate*. See Reed, *S. N. Behrman*, 75, and Peters, *Design for Living*, 36; Alfred Lunt on www.ibdb.com.

5. "Lunt Salvages Idea From Play Staged in 1917," *New York Herald Tribune*, November 22, 1942; Zolotow, *Stagestruck*, 234; Reed, *S. N. Behrman*, 75.

6. Peters, *Design for Living,* 19, 22, 27, 39, 44.

7. Ibid., 5, 14–15, 53, 55, 58, 72–73.

8. Reed, *S. N. Behrman,* 19–20, 24–26, 29–30.

9. Five outlines of *The Pirate,* July-August, 1939, and first draft of Act 1, September 9, 1939, S. N. Behrman Papers, WFTRC-WHS; Kurt Weill to Behrman, September 20, 1939, Folder 13, Box 26, S. N. Behrman Papers, NYPL. There is a rough translation from German to English of Fulda's *The Pirate,* translated by Herbert Zoellner, in Folder 9, Box 10, Alfred Lunt and Lynn Fontanne Papers, WHS. It probably had been done so that Lunt and Fontanne could become familiar with Fulda's creation while Behrman was writing his own version of the play.

10. Drew, "Weill, Kurt (Julian)," 300–310.

11. Kurt Weill to Behrman, September 28, November 22, 29, 1939, Folder 13, Box 26, S. N. Behrman Papers, NYPL.

12. Kurt Weill to Behrman, April 29, 1941, S. N. Behrman Papers, WF-TRC-WHS; Kurt Weill to Behrman, May 9, 1942, Behrman to Kurt Weill, May 12, 1942, Folder 13, Box 26, S. N. Behrman Papers, NYPL.

13. Zolotow, *Stagestruck,* 168; Brown, *Fabulous Lunts,* 297, 305–306; Peters, *Design for Living,* 199, 202; fifth draft of *The Pirate,* June 19, 1942, S. N. Behrman Papers, WFTRC-WHS.

14. Zolotow, *Stagestruck,* 235; en.wikipedia.org/wiki/The_writing_on_the_wall; jewishencyclopedia.com; Reed, *S. N. Behrman,* 20.

15. Zolotow, *Stagestruck,* 234.

16. This and the following synopsis are based on S. N. Behrman, *The Pirate,* New York: Random House, 1943.

17. Brown, *Fabulous Lunts,* 306; Theodore Strauss, "The Lunts—and a Pirate," *New York Times Magazine,* October 4, 1942; clipping of *Variety,* September 16, 1942, MPAA Production Code Administration Records, Herrick Library, AMPAS.

18. Peters, *Design for Living,* 202–203; Terry Helburn to Behrman, n.d., S. N. Behrman Papers, WCFTR-WHS; Gross, *S. N. Behrman,* 130–133; Behrman, *People in a Diary,* 83; Brown, *Fabulous Lunts,* 307; Omar Ranney, "Hanna Play is Gay Escape from War," *Cleveland Press,* September 22, 1942.

19. Behrman, *People in a Diary,* 84; Reed, *S. N. Behrman,* 76.

20. Reed, *S. N. Behrman,* 75–76; Peters, *Design for Living,* 202–203; Brown, *Fabulous Lunts,* 360.

21. Gross, *S. N. Behrman,* 166–167, 130–135; "The New York Play," unidentified clipping, MPAA Production Code Administration Records, Herrick Library, AMPAS; Omar Ranney, "Hanna Play is Gay Escape from War," *Cleveland Press,* September 22, 1942. See Theodore Strauss, "The Lunts—and a Pirate," *New York Times Magazine,* October 4, 1942, for eleven photographs of *The Pirate* on stage to get a sense of the set designs, costumes, and multiracial atmosphere of the Lunt and Fontanne production.

22. Reed, *S. N. Behrman,* 75–76; Harvey, *Directed By Vincente Minnelli,* 87; Peters, *Design for Living,* 204; Brown, *Fabulous Lunts,* 297.

23. Kathryn S. Oswold to Behrman, December 1, 1942, S. N. Behrman Papers, WCFTR-WHS.

24. Brown, *Fabulous Lunts,* 306–307; Peters, *Design for Living,* 204.

25. Helene Fulda to Behrman, January 2, 1944, S. N. Behrman Papers, WCFTR-WHS.

26. Elza Behrman to Lynn Fontanne, October 6, n.d., Folder 4, Box 2 Alfred Lunt and Lynn Fontanne Papers, WHS.

27. Reed, *S. N. Behrman*, 76.

28. Siegel, "The Pirate," 22.

29. Harvey, *Directed By Vincente Minnelli*, 91.

30. Donald E. Musselman to Behrman, October 23, 1962, S. N. Behrman Papers, WCFTR-WHS.

Chapter Two: Creating the Perfect Screenplay

1. Fordin, *M-G-M's Greatest Musicals,* 203; Harvey, *Directed By Vincente Minnelli,* 87. Another report indicated that M-G-M bought the rights to *The Pirate* for $275,000. See Reed, *S. N. Behrman,* 76.

2. This and the following analysis are based on Joseph L. Mankiewicz, *The Pirate,* temporary complete screenplay, August 4–6, 1943, Turner/MGM Script Collection, Margaret Herrick Library, AMPAS.

3. Lower and Palmer, *Joseph L. Mankiewicz,* 6–9; David Shipman interview with Mankiewicz, 1982, in Dauth, ed., *Joseph L. Mankiewicz,* 155.

4. Lower and Palmer, *Joseph L. Mankiewicz,* 11; Schatz, *Genius of the System,* 366–367, 374.

5. Lower and Palmer, *Joseph L. Mankiewicz,* 264; David Shipman interview with Mankiewicz, 1982, in Dauth, ed., *Joseph L. Mankiewicz,* 154–155.

6. This and the following analysis are based on Henry Koster, *The Pirate,* temporary complete screenplay, October 28, 1943. to January 5, 1944, Turner/MGM Script Collection, Margaret Herrick Library, AMPAS.

7. This and the following analysis are based on Myles Connolly, *The Pirate,* temporary complete screenplay, January 18, 1944, Turner/MGM Script Collection, Margaret Herrick Library, AMPAS.

8. R. Monta to Freed, memo, April 9, 1947, Folder 1 (1 of 3), Box 19, Arthur Freed Collection, USC.

9. Harvey, *Directed By Vincente Minnelli,* 87; Myles Connolly and Henry Koster, www.imdb.com.

10. M. Norden to Joseph Breen, January 22, 1944: Breen to Louis B. Mayer, January 26, 1944, MPAA Production Code Administration Records, Herrick Library, AMPAS. A copy of Breen's letter can be found in Folder 1 (1 of 3), Box 19, Arthur Freed Collection, USC.

11. Edwin Blum, www.imdb.com.

12. This and the following analysis are based on Edwin Blum, *The Pirate,* temporary, incomplete, March 30-May 12, 1944, Turner/MGM Script Collection, Herrick Library, AMPAS.

13. Fordin, *M-G-M's Greatest Musicals,* 203.

14. H. E. Rogers and Frances Marion, www.imdb.com; H. E. Rogers and Frances Marion treatment, October 16, 1944, is listed but not included in the Turner/MGM Script Collection, Herrick Library, AMPAS.

15. Harvey, *Directed By Vincente Minnelli,* 88; Freed to Bert Allenberg, July 31, 1945, Folder 1 (2 of 3), Box 19, Arthur Freed Collection, USC. *The*

Rosary was made into a film at least seven times between 1910 and 1931, but not by M-G-M, www.imdb.com.

16. Minnelli interview (1975), in Schickel, *Men Who Made the Movies,* 250; Harvey, *Directed By Vincente Minnelli,* 87; Minnelli, *I Remember It Well,* 164.

17. Fordin, *M-G-M's Greatest Musicals,* 204n; Joseph Than, www.imdb.com; Anita Loos, www.imdb.com.

18. "The Pirate Notes, 11/27/45," and "The Pirate Notes, 12/5/45," Folder 115, Box 7, Vincente Minnelli Collection, Herrick Library, AMPAS.

19. "The Pirate Notes, 12/5/45," Folder 115, Box 7, Vincente Minnelli Collection, Herrick Library, AMPAS.

20. Joseph Breen memo, February 23, 1946, MPAA Production Code Administration Records, Herrick Library, AMPAS.

21. Ibid.

22. Ibid.

23. Hess and Dabholkar, *Singin' in the Rain,* 19, 27–28. There are claims on websites and in books with poorly cited secondary sources that Minnelli always thought of Kelly for the part. This may well be true as mentioned in the chapter but there is no reliable recorded evidence of it.

24. Minnelli, *I Remember It Well,* 179.

25. Ibid., 180; Fordin, *M-G-M's Greatest Musicals,* 204; Minnelli interview with Henry Sheehan, 1978, www.henrysheehan.com; John Fricke's comments in "A Musical Treasure Chest," *The Pirate,* DVD, 2007; Griffith, *Hundred or More Hidden Things,* 114.

26. This and the following analysis are based on Anita Loos and Joseph Than, *The Pirate,* temporary complete screenplay, n.d., copied June 30, 1946, Turner/MGM Script Collection, Herrick Library, AMPAS.

27. Fordin, *M-G-M's Greatest Musicals,* 204; Minnelli, *I Remember It Well,* 180.

28. Goodrich, *Real Nick and Nora,* 7, 12–13, 19, 21, 24, 31, 37–38, 52.

29. Ibid., 169–170, 172–173; Minnelli interview with Henry Sheehan, 1978, www.henrysheehan.com; Frances Goodrich and Albert Hackett, *The Pirate,* complete OK screenplay, September 18, 1946, Turner/MGM Script Collection, Herrick Library, AMPAS.

30. Harvey, *Directed By Vincente Minnelli,* 88; Minnelli, *I Remember It Well,* 180–181; unsigned, undated notes, 18, Folder 117, Box 7, Vincente Minnelli Collection, Herrick Library, AMPAS.

31. Freed and Minnelli, story notes, 1, 6, 7–9, 12–15, Folder 2, Box 19, Arthur Freed Collection, USC; unsigned, undated notes, 5–7, 9, 18, Folder 117, Box 7, Vincente Minnelli Collection, Herrick Library, AMPAS.

32. Unsigned, undated notes, not paginated, Folder 117, Box 7, Vincente Minnelli Collection, Herrick Library, AMPAS; Freed and Minnelli, story notes, 1, 3, Folder 2, Box 19, Arthur Freed Collection, USC.

33. Freed and Minnelli, story notes, 1, 10, Folder 2, Box 19, Arthur Freed Collection, USC; unsigned, undated notes, 10, Folder 117, Box 7, Vincente Minnelli Collection, Herrick Library, AMPAS.

34. Harvey, *Directed By Vincente Minnelli,* 88.

35. Goodrich, *Real Nick and Nora,* 170.

36. The following analysis is based on: Frances Goodrich and Albert

Hackett, *The Pirate*, complete OK screenplay, September 18, 1946 to May 9, 1947, Turner/MGM Script Collection, Herrick Library, AMPAS; S. N. Behrman, *The Pirate*, New York: Random House, 1943; and Fulda's original version of *The Pirate, Der Seerauber,* Leroy Linick, translator, n.d., copied January 25, 1943, Turner/MGM Script Collection, Herrick Library, AMPAS.

37. Clipping of *Variety*, September 16, 1942, MPAA Production Code Administration Records, Herrick Library, AMPAS.

38. Frances Goodrich and Albert Hackett, *The Pirate*, complete OK screenplay, September 18, 1946 to May 9, 1947: Changes by Wilkie Mahoney for Minnelli, June 4, 1947: Incomplete notes by Robert Nathan, December 8, 1947: and Retakes by Arthur Freed, October 21, December 16, 1947, Turner/MGM Script Collection, Herrick Library, AMPAS; Freed and Minnelli, story notes, 3, 14, Folder 2, Box 19, Arthur Freed Collection, USC; the release print of *The Pirate*. Note that although the Goodrich-Hackett script is dated through May 1947, they stopped work on it in December 1946. All subsequent changes were made by Minnelli and others.

39. Siegel, "The Pirate," 23.

40. Harvey, *Directed By Vincente Minnelli*, 91.

41. Hess and Dabholkar, *Singin' in the Rain*, 57–65; Harmetz, *Round Up the Usual Suspects*, 77.

42. Powdermaker, *Hollywood*, 31, 157; Behlmer, *Behind the Scenes*, 25, 33, 119, 124, 132, 155, 158, 164, 165, 176.

CHAPTER THREE: MAJOR PLAYERS AND PREPRODUCTION

1. Minnelli interview, 1975, Schickel, *Men Who Made the Movies*, 245–247; Minnelli interview, 1969, Higham and Greenberg, *Celluloid Muse*, 174; Minnelli, *I Remember It Well*, 28–97.

2. Minnelli interview, 1969, Higham and Greenberg, *Celluloid Muse*, 174; Minnelli interview, 1963, Serebrinsky and Garaycochea, "Vincente Minnelli," 23; McVay, "Minnelli and THE PIRATE," 35; Clarke, *Get Happy*, 208.

3. Minnelli interview, 1969, Higham and Greenberg, *Celluloid Muse*, 174–175; Minnelli interview with Jerome Delamater, 1973, Delamater, *Dance in the Hollywood Musical*, 272–273; Minnelli interview, 1975, Schickel, *Men Who Made the Movies*, 268; Minnelli interview with Joseph Casper, 1973, Casper, *Vincente Minnelli*, 91; Minnelli interview, 1963, Serebrinsky and Garaycochea, "Vincente Minnelli," 24.

4. Fordin, *M-G-M's Greatest Musicals*, 147.

5. Ibid., 167.

6. Minnelli interview with Henry Sheehan, 1978, www.henrysheehan.com; Minnelli interview, 1969, Higham and Greenberg, *Celluloid Muse*, 175; Minnelli interview, 1963, Serebrinsky and Garaycochea, "Vincente Minnelli," 24.

7. Minnelli interview, 1963, Serebrinsky and Garaycochea, "Vincente Minnelli," 24; McVay, "Minnelli and THE PIRATE," 36.

8. Previn, *No Minor Chords*, 68.

9. Johnson, "Films of Vincente Minnelli," Pt. 1, 22; Minnelli interview,

1969, Higham and Greenberg, *Celluloid Muse,* 183; Minnelli interview, 1975, Schickel, *Men Who Made the Movies,* 268.

10. Minnelli, *I Remember It Well,* 178; Fordin, *M-G-M's Greatest Musicals,* 205; Minnelli interview, 1969, Higham and Greenberg, *Celluloid Muse,* 177.

11. Jack Martin Smith interview with Jerome Delamater and Paddy Whannel, 1973, Delamater, *Dance in the Hollywood Musical,* 256.

12. Ibid., 257–258.

13. List of model draftsmen, *The Pirate* Clippings, Core Collection, Herrick Library, AMPAS.

14. Page from exhibitors' campaign book, *The Pirate,* Scrapbook 8, Box 9, Gene Kelly Collection, BU; Fordin, *M-G-M's Greatest Musicals,* 206.

15. Minnelli interview with Jerome Delamater, 1973, Delamater, *Dance in the Hollywood Musical,* 273; *MGM News,* February 28, 1947, in *The Pirate* Clippings, Core Collection, Herrick Library, AMPAS; Fordin, *M-G-M's Greatest Musicals,* 205; Minnelli, *I Remember It Well,* 185.

16. "Hollywood Inside," *Daily Variety,* April 10, 1947.

17. Hirschhorn, *Gene Kelly,* 5–123.

18. Kelly quoted in Morley and Leon, *Gene Kelly,* 76.

19. Fordin, *M-G-M's Greatest Musicals,* 204–205; "Gene Kelly Interview," Marilyn Hunt, 1975, 159–160, Oral History Program, NYPL.

20. Kelly interview, 1979, in Kelly, "Dialogue on Film," 36; "Reminiscences of Gene Curran Kelly—Oral History, 1958," 14, Oral History Research Office, Popular Arts Project, CU; Hirschhorn, *Gene Kelly,* 136; McVay, "Minnelli and THE PIRATE," 38.

21. Gene Kelly interview, 1974, 44, SMU/Ronald L. Davis Oral History Collection, Herrick Library, AMPAS; "Gene Kelly Interview," Marilyn Hunt, 1975, 158, Oral History Program, NYPL.

22. Kelly, "I'll Always Remember," Folder 13, Box 3, Gene Kelly Collection, BU.

23. Herndon, *Mary Pickford and Douglas Fairbanks,* 236–239; Schickel, *His Picture in the Papers,* 111–112; Schickel, *Fairbanks Album,* 152–155.

24. Fordin, *M-G-M's Greatest Musicals,* 206; "Gene Kelly Interview," Marilyn Hunt, 1975, 161, 171, Oral History Program, NYPL.

25. "Gene Kelly Interview," Marilyn Hunt, 1975, 161, 171, Oral History Program, NYPL; Minnelli interview with Henry Sheehan, 1978, www.henrysheehan.com; Minnelli interview, 1975, Schickel, *Men Who Made the Movies,* 260.

26. "An Oral History with Lela Simone," Rudy Behlmer, 1990, 27, Oral History Program, Herrick Library, AMPAS.

27. Gene Kelly interview, 1974, 22, SMU/Ronald L. Davis Oral History Collection, Herrick Library, AMPAS; undated, unsigned note, Folder 1 (1 of 3), Box 19, Arthur Freed Collection, USC.

28. Luft, *Me and My Shadows,* 10, 24–26; Clarke, *Get Happy,* 37–40, 58.

29. Fordin, *M-G-M's Greatest Musicals,* 5; Clarke, *Get Happy,* 54.

30. Clarke, *Get Happy,* 197–198; Fordin, *M-G-M's Greatest Musicals,* 85–86, 107–109, 161–162.

31. Luft, *Me and My Shadows,* 42, 33–34.

32. Hirschhorn, *Gene Kelly,* 162.

33. Clarke, *Get Happy*, 206, 211, 213, 216, 218; Fordin, *M-G-M's Greatest Musicals*, 146–147; Minnelli, *I Remember It Well*, 145, 150, 154. Fordin writes that Minnelli and Garland were married on September 7, 1945, but the correct date was June 15, 1945. See Fordin, *M-G-M's Greatest Musicals*, 177, and Clarke, *Get Happy*, 218.

34. Minnelli, *I Remember It Well*, 157, 164.

35. Clarke, *Get Happy*, 223–225; Minnelli interview, 1975, Schickel, *Men Who Made the Movies*, 251; Fordin, *M-G-M's Greatest Musicals*, 177–178; Minnelli, *I Remember It Well*, 177–178; Frank, *Judy*, 224, 226.

36. Jack Martin Smith interview with Jerome Delamater and Paddy Whannel, 1973, and Minnelli interview with Delamater, 1973, Delamater, *Dance in the Hollywood Musical*, 259, 271; "Gene Kelly Interview," Marilyn Hunt, 1975, 173, Oral History Program, NYPL; Gene Kelly interview with Jerome Delamater and Paddy Whannel, 1973, Delamater, *Dance in the Hollywood Musical*, 209.

37. Gene Kelly interview with Jerome Delamater and Paddy Whannel, 1973, Delamater, *Dance in the Hollywood Musical*, 208–209; Minnelli interview, 1975, Schickel, *Men Who Made the Movies*, 248–249; Freed to Esme Ward, July 3, 1947, Folder 1 (1 of 3), Box 19, Arthur Freed Collection, USC; Genné, "Vincente Minnelli and the Film Ballet," 229–233, 236, 239–241.

38. Jack Martin Smith interview with Jerome Delamater and Paddy Whannel, 1973, Delamater, *Dance in the Hollywood Musical*, 258; Fordin, *M-G-M's Greatest Musicals*, 208.

39. Minnelli interview with Henry Sheehan, 1978, www.henrysheehan.com; Minnelli interview, 1975, Schickel, *Men Who Made the Movies*, 258; Ranciere, "*Ars gratia artis*," 396.

40. Unsigned, undated notes for the Goodrich and Hackett screenplay, 10–11, Folder 117, Box 7, Vincente Minnelli Collection, Herrick Library, AMPAS; story notes, 11, Folder 2, Box 19, Arthur Freed Collection, USC; Frances Goodrich and Albert Hackett, *The Pirate*, complete OK screenplay, September 18, 1946, to May 9, 1947, 62–65, Turner/MGM Script Collection, Herrick Library, AMPAS. Note that although the Goodrich-Hackett script is dated through May 1947, they stopped work on it in December 1946. All subsequent changes were made by Minnelli and his assistants.

41. "*Idea suggested by Robert Alton for Gene Kelly's solo number in 'The Pirate'*", January 24, 1947, File 116, Vincente Minnelli Collection, Herrick Library, AMPAS.

42. Ibid.

43. McBrien, *Cole Porter*, 4–5, 7, 11, 21, 28, 55, 69, 73, 103; Hemming, *Melody Lingers On*, 152.

44. Hemming, *Melody Lingers On*, 153–154; McBrien, *Cole Porter*, 15, 135, 148, 166, 210–212.

45. McBrien, *Cole Porter*, 267.

46. Minnelli, *I Remember It Well*, 179; Minnelli interview, 1969, Higham and Greenberg, *Celluloid Muse*, 174–175; Fordin, *M-G-M's Greatest Musicals*, 204, 302; Eells, *Life That Late He Led*, 225–228.

47. Page from exhibitors' campaign book for *The Pirate*, Scapbook 8, Box 9, Gene Kelly Collection, BU; Fordin, *M-G-M's Greatest Musicals*, 204; Rich-

ard Barrios' comments in "A Musical Treasure Chest," *The Pirate,* DVD, 2007; Griffith, *Hundred or More Hidden Things,* 115.

48. Mack the Black, verses 5 and 9, July 19, 1946, and verse 2, Ship Episode, November 15, 1946, "THE PIRATE—Lyrics from Cole Porter," Turner/MGM Script Collection, Herrick Library, AMPAS.

49. Rudi Monta to Freed, January 2, 1947, Folder 1 (1 of 3), Box 19, Arthur Freed Collection, USC.

50. "Voodoo," August 1, 1946. and "Manuela," August 16, 1946, "THE PIRATE—Lyrics from Cole Porter," Turner/MGM Script Collection, Herrick Library, AMPAS.

51. "You Can Do No Wrong," September 6, 1946, Ibid.

52. Gene Kelly interview, 1974, 3–4, SMU/Ronald L. Davis Oral History Collection, Herrick Library, AMPAS.

53. Kelly quoted in Hirschhorn, *Gene Kelly,* 137–138; Gene Kelly interview, 1974, 44, SMU/Ronald L. Davis Oral History Collection, Herrick Library, AMPAS; "Gene Kelly Interview," Marilyn Hunt, 1975, 170, Oral History Program, NYPL; Vincente Minnelli interview, 1980, 16, SMU/Ronald L. Davis Oral History Collection, Herrick Library, AMPAS; McBrien, *Cole Porter,* 12–13; Fordin, *M-G-M's Greatest Musicals,* 205.

54. "Gene Kelly Interview," Marilyn Hunt, 1975, 172, Oral History Program, NYPL.

55. Al Block to Joseph Breen, July 29, August 9, September 9, October 31, November 4, 1946: Breen to Mayer, July 31, August 12, 21, September 10, October 22, November 6, 1946, MPAA Production Code Administration Records, Herrick Library, AMPAS.

56. Block to Breen, August 19, November 2, 11, 1946: Breen to Mayer, August 21, November 5, 13, 1946, MPAA Production Code Administration Records, Herrick Library, AMPAS.

57. Assistant Director's Reports, December 27–28, 1946, Folder 2, Box 19, Arthur Freed Collection, USC.

58. Al Shenberg to Butcher, Freed, and Datig, November 6, December 5, 7, 17, 1946, January 31, February 14, 1947: Shenberg to Mayer, MacArthur, Craig, and Hendrickson, December 30, 1946, Folder 1 (1 of 3), Box 19, Arthur Freed Collection, USC.

59. F. A. Datig to Freed, August 17, December 30, 1946, January 6, 29, March 7, July 2, 1947, Folder 1 (1 of 3), Box 19, Arthur Freed Collection, USC.

60 Breen to Mayer, November 29, 1946, MPAA Production Code Administration Records, Herrick Library, AMPAS.

61. Ibid.

62. Block to Breen, November 26, 1946, February 7, 17, 1947, and undated: Breen to Mayer, December 23, 1946, February 10, 19, 1947, MPAA Production Code Administration Records, Herrick Library, AMPAS.

63. Peters, *Design for Living,* 202–203; Slezak, *What Time's the Next Swan?,* 1, 14, 27; Peter B. Flint, "Walter Slezak, 80, a Suicide; Character Actor Had Been Ill," *New York Times,* April 22, 1983; Paramount press release for *The Caper of the Golden Bulls* (1967), Walter Slezak Clippings, Core Collection, Herrick Library, AMPAS.

64. Virginia Wright column in *Los Angeles Daily News,* June 29, 1943; 20th

Century-Fox Press Release, [1943], Walter Slezak Clippings, Microfiche, Core Collection, Herrick Library, AMPAS; Walter Slezak, www.imdb.com.

65. 20ᵗʰ Century-Fox Press Release, [1943], and "Walter Slezaks Christen Daughter," unidentified clipping, April 7, 1947, Walter Slezak Clippings Microfiche, and Paramount press release for *The Caper of the Golden Bulls* (1967), Walter Slezak Clippings, Core Collection, Herrick Library, AMPAS; "Walter Slezak Discloses Plan to Marry Dutch Singer," *Los Angeles Times*, September 30, 1943; Dan Smith column in *Los Angeles Daily News*, July 16, 1951; Frank Eng column in *Los Angeles Daily News*, July 8, 1948; Walter Slezak biography on www.imdb.com.

66. Page from exhibitors' campaign book for *The Pirate*, Scrapbook 8, Box 9, Gene Kelly Collection, BU; Charles Stinson, "Walter Slezak: Character Acting Demands Talent," *Los Angeles Times*, October 19, 1958.

67. Parish and Bowers, *MGM Stock Company*, 127–129; Stokes, *Without Veils*, 15, 31–34, 51, 65, 84, 150. Three Cooper postcards of the World War I era are housed in Gladys Cooper Biography Stills, Core Collection, Herrick Library, AMPAS.

68. Stokes, *Without Veils*, 164, 198.

69. Ibid., 180, 206.

70. Unidentified newspaper clippings in Scrapbook 8, Box 9, Gene Kelly Collection, BU; Parish and Bowers, *MGM Stock Company*, 543–544.

71. George Zucco biography on www.imdb.com.

72. Hill, *Brotherhood in Rhythm*, 9, 34, 42, 55, 68, 96, 150; Fayard Nicholas interview, 1998, www.jitterbuzz.com.

73. Fayard Nicholas interview, 1988, Frank, *Tap!*, 72; Hill, *Brotherhood in Rhythm*, 169, 174–176, 178–179, 185, 188, 196.

74. Fayard Nicholas interview, 1998, www.jitterbuzz.com; Hill, *Brotherhood in Rhythm*, 213.

75. Hill, *Brotherhood in Rhythm*, 152, 199; Fayard Nicholas interview, 1988, Frank, *Tap!*, 66–74; Fayard Nicholas' comments in *Anatomy of a Dancer*, DVD, 2002.

76. "Gene Kelly Interview," Marilyn Hunt, 1975, 169, Oral History Program, NYPL; Thomas, *Films of Gene Kelly*, 82; Hirschhorn, *Gene Kelly*, 27.

77. Nicholas Brothers interview, 1999, Fantle and Johnson, *Reel to Real*, 84; Fayard Nicholas quoted in Hill, *Brotherhood in Rhythm*, 229; Harvey, *Directed By Vincente Minnelli*, 91–92; F. L. Hendrickson to L. K. Sidney, January 21, 1947, Folder 1 (1 of 3), Box 19, Arthur Freed Collection, USC.

78. http://black-face.com/blackface-actors.htm; Racism in Early American Film http://en.wikipedia.org/wiki/Racism_in_early_American_film; African-Americans in Motion Pictures http://www.freewebs.com/black-legacy/actorsmovies.htm; Maynard, *The Black Man on Film*, 126–127.

79. Minnelli, *I Remember It Well*, 184.

CHAPTER FOUR: FILMING CHALLENGES

1. Daily Progress Report, February 17, 1947: Assistant Director's Reports, February 17–18, 1947, Folder 2, Box 19, Arthur Freed Collection, USC; Fordin, *M-G-M's Greatest Musicals*, 208.

2. Al Shenberg to Freed, February 19, 1947: F. A. Datig To Freed, February [1947], March [1947], April [1947], May [1947], and May 5, 1947, Folder 1 (1 of 3), Box 19, Arthur Freed Collection, USC.

3. Minnelli, *I Remember It Well,* 186–187.

4. Al Shenberg to Freed, February 22, 27, 28, March 10, April 18, May 6, 19, 1947, Folder 1 (1 of 3), Box 19, Arthur Freed Collection, USC.

5. Ibid.; Assistant Director's Reports, February 22, 27, May 19, 1947, Folder 2, Box 19, Arthur Freed Collection, USC.

6. Assistant Director's Reports, February 22, 27, 28, May 6, 7, 10, 15, 19–26, 1947, Folder 2, Box 19, Arthur Freed Collection, USC.

7. Fordin, *M-G-M's Greatest Musicals,* 208–209; Assistant Director's Reports, June 12–14, 16, 20–21, 1947, Folder 2, Box 19, Arthur Freed Collection, USC; Hess and Dabholkar, *Singin' in the Rain,* 131.

8. Minnelli, *I Remember It Well,* 187; Griffith, *Hundred or More Hidden Things,* 117.

9. Minnelli, *I Remember It Well,* 188.

10. Ibid., 187; Minnelli interview with Beth Genné, 1980, in Genné, "Vincente Minnelli and the Film Ballet," 243.

11. Harvey, *Directed By Vincente Minnelli,* 88–89; Clarke, *Get Happy,* 229–231; Edwards, *Judy Garland,* 106.

12. Frank, *Judy,* 226–227.

13. Clarke, *Get Happy,* 226, 231; Edwards, *Judy Garland,* 107. Garland was too ill to come to work on July 11 and 12, according to Assistant Director's Reports, July 11–12, 1947, Folder 2, Box 19, Arthur Freed Collection, USC.

14. "An Oral History with Lela Simone," Rudy Behlmer, 1990, 57, 256, Oral History Program, Herrick Library, AMPAS.

15. Goodrich, *Real Nick and Nora,* 170; "An Oral History with Lela Simone," Rudy Behlmer, 1990, 54–55, 57, 256, Oral History Program, Herrick Library, AMPAS.

16. Clarke, *Get Happy,* 209–210, 234; Luft, *Me And My Shadows,* 39; Levy, *Vincente Minnelli,* 112.

17. Clarke, *Get Happy,* 233.

18. Pasternak, *Easy the Hard Way,* 230.

19. Minnelli interview (1975), in Schickel, *Men Who Made the Movies,* 251; Harvey, *Directed By Vincente Minnelli,* 88.

20. Jack Martin Smith interview with Jerome Delamater and Paddy Whannel, 1973, Delamater, *Dance in the Hollywood Musical,* 258.

21. Ibid.

22. "Gene Kelly Interview," Marilyn Hunt, 1975, 172, Oral History Program, NYPL; Minnelli interview with Jerome Delamater, 1973, Delamater, *Dance in the Hollywood Musical,* 271; Hirschhorn, *Gene Kelly,* 137; Assistant Director's Reports, February 26–27, March 3, 8, 10–13, 15, 18, 20–22, 24, 26–27, 31, April 1–5, 7–9, 11, 1947, Folder 2, Box 19, Arthur Freed Collection, USC.

23. Dorothy Kilgallen, "Voice of Broadway," undated clipping in Scrapbook 4, Box 7, Gene Kelly Collection, BU.

24. Casper, *Vincente Minnelli,* 132; Taylor and Jackson, *Hollywood Musi-*

cal, 62; Thomas, *Films of Gene Kelly,* 81; Harvey, *Directed By Vincente Minnelli,* 92.

25. Minnelli interview with Jerome Delamater, 1973, Delamater, *Dance in the Hollywood Musical,* 271.

26. Ibid.

27. "An Oral History with Lela Simone," Rudy Behlmer, 1990, 55–56, 255–256, Oral History Program, Herrick Library, AMPAS.

28. Assistant Director's Reports, February 18, 20–22, 25–27, March 3, 10–13, 15, April 10, 12, 14–16, 18, 22, 25, 1947, Folder 2, Box 19, Arthur Freed Collection, USC.

29. Fordin, *M-G-M's Greatest Musicals,* 208–209.

30. McBrien, *Cole Porter,* 302; Eells, *Life That Late He Led,* 235–236; Gene Kelly interview, 1974, 44, SMU/Ronald L. Davis Oral History Collection, Herrick Library, AMPAS; "An Oral History with Lela Simone," Rudy Behlmer, 1990, 230, 260, Oral History Program, Herrick Library, AMPAS; Assistant Director's Reports, May 13, 1947, Folder 2, Box 19, Arthur Freed Collection, USC; Fordin, *M-G-M's Greatest Musicals,* 209; Siegel, "The Pirate," 30.

31. Kelly interview, 1979, in Kelly, "Dialogue on Film," 36; Siegel, "The Pirate," 29; Thomas, *Films of Gene Kelly,* 79; Hemming, *Melody Lingers On,* 171.

32. McVay, "Minnelli and THE PIRATE," 37.

33. Assistant Director's Reports, March 31, April 11, 19, 21, 23, 26, 28, 30, May 1–2, 5, 8, 1947, Folder 2, Box 19, Arthur Freed Collection, USC.

34. Assistant Director's Reports, May 3, 1947, Folder 2, Box 19, Arthur Freed Collection, USC; stills in MGM Photo Collection, *The Pirate* folder, Herrick Library, AMPAS.

35. Minnelli interview with Jerome Delamater, 1973, Delamater, *Dance in the Hollywood Musical,* 271; "Gene Kelly Interview," Marilyn Hunt, 1975, 157, Oral History Program, NYPL; Assistant Director's Reports, May 9, 1947, Folder 2, Box 19, Arthur Freed Collection, USC.

36. Assistant Director's Reports, May 28, 29, 31, June 2, 1947, Folder 2, Box 19, Arthur Freed Collection, USC.

37. Fordin, *M-G-M's Greatest Musicals,* 209.

38. Luft, *Me and My Shadows,* 192.

39. Edwards, *Judy Garland,* 105; page from exhibitors' campaign book for *The Pirate,* Scrapbook 8, Box 9, Gene Kelly Collection, BU; stills in MGM Photo Collection, *The Pirate* folder, Herrick Library, AMPAS.

40. Assistant Director's Reports, June 3–7, 9, 11, July 5, 1947, Folder 2, Box 19, Arthur Freed Collection, USC; page from exhibitors' campaign book for *The Pirate,* Scrapbook 8, Box 9, Gene Kelly Collection, BU; Fordin, *M-G-M's Greatest Musicals,* 210.

41. "THE PIRATE—Sec. of chgs from Wilkie Mahoney," March 25, 1947, Folder 625, Turner/MGM Script Collection, Herrick Library, AMPAS; Al Block to Joseph Breen, April 7, 11, May 14, 1947: Breen to Louis B. Mayer, April 8, 14, May 15, 1947, MPAA Production Code Administration Records, Herrick Library, AMPAS.

42. Untitled list regarding *The Pirate* cast and crew party, Folder 118, Box 7, Vincente Minnelli Collection, Herrick Library, AMPAS.

43. Minnelli interview with Jerome Delamater, 1973, Delamater, *Dance in the Hollywood Musical*, 272; Hill, *Brotherhood in Rhythm*, 230; "THE PIRATE—Sec. of chgs from Wilkie Mahoney," March 25, 1947, Folder 625, Turner/MGM Script Collection, Herrick Library, AMPAS.

44. Fayard Nicholas interview, 1998, www.jitterbuzz.com; Delamater, *Dance in the Hollywood Musical*, 81–82; Harold Nicholas interview, 1999, Fantle and Johnston, *Reel to Real*, 84.

45. Hirschhorn, *Gene Kelly*, 62–63.

46. Harold Nicholas interview, 1999, Fantle and Johnston, *Reel to Real*, 84.

47. Hill, *Brotherhood in Rhythm*, 230; Fayard Nicholas' comments in "A Musical Treasure Chest," *The Pirate*, DVD, 2007.

48. Assistant Director's Reports, June 17–19, 23–28, 30, July 1–3, 8, 9–10, 1947, Folder 2, Box 19, Arthur Freed Collection, USC.

49. Jack Martin Smith interview with Jerome Delamater and Paddy Whannel, 1973, Delamater, *Dance in the Hollywood Musical*, 255.

50. Fordin, *M-G-M's Greatest Musicals*, 205, 206, 210; Clarke, *Get Happy*, 225; Eells, *Life That Late He Led*, 237; Assistant Director's Reports, July 7, 1947, Folder 2, Box 19, Arthur Freed Collection, USC; page from exhibitors' campaign book for *The Pirate*, Scrapbook 8, Box 9, Gene Kelly Collection, BU; Al Shenberg to Freed, May 2, 1947, Folder 1 (1 of 3), Box 19, Arthur Freed Collection, USC; "Hollywood Inside," *Daily Variety*, April 10, 1947.

51. Assistant Director's Reports, July 15–17, 1947, Folder 2, Box 19, Arthur Freed Collection, USC.

52. McVay, "Magic of Minnelli," 31; Siegel, "The Pirate," 31.

53. Minnelli, *I Remember It Well*, 189.

54. Minnelli interview with Jerome Delamater, 1973, Delamater, *Dance in the Hollywood Musical*, 269; Minnelli interview with Henry Sheehan, 1978, www.henrysheehan.com.

55. Fordin, *M-G-M's Greatest Musicals*, 210–211; Assistant Director's Reports, July 18, 21, 23, 25–26, 28–31, August 1–2, 4–8, 1947, Folder 2, Box 19, Arthur Freed Collection, USC; Hemming, *Melody Lingers On*, 172; "An Oral History with Lela Simone," Rudy Behlmer, 1990, 26, Oral History Program, Herrick Library, AMPAS.

56. F. A. Datig to Freed, July [1947], August 14, 1947, Folder 1 (1 of 3), Box 19, Arthur Freed Collection, USC.

57. Thomas, *Films of Gene Kelly*, 24; Basinger, *Gene Kelly*, 123.

58. Hess and Dabholkar, *Singin' in the Rain*, 40–43.

59. Gerstner, "Dancer from the Dance," 55; Carey, *Doug & Mary*, 167; Ernie Schier, "Gene Kelly Performs More Like a Yeoman," *Washington Times Herald*, June 3, 1948.

60. Jack Martin Smith interview with Jerome Delamater and Paddy Whannel, 1973, Delamater, *Dance in the Hollywood Musical*, 259; Assistant Director's Reports, August 9, 11–12, 1947, Folder 2, Box 19, Arthur Freed Collection, USC; Minnelli, *I Remember It Well*, 191.

61. Genné, "Vincente Minnelli and the Film Ballet," 245–246.

62. McVay, "Minnelli and THE PIRATE," 38; Minnelli, *I Remember It Well*, 191; Minnelli interview with Jerome Delamater, 1973, Delamater,

Dance in the Hollywood Musical, 269; Assistant Director's Reports, August 11, 1947, Folder 2, Box 19, Arthur Freed Collection, USC; Genné, "Vincente Minnelli and the Film Ballet," 246; Genné, "Film Musicals," 239, 254; Hirschhorn, *Gene Kelly,* 138; Fordin, *M-G-M's Greatest Musicals,* 552.

63. Assistant Director's Reports, *Words and Music,* April–July, 1948, Folder 2, Box 26: Assistant Director's Reports, *The Pirate,* August 13–14, 1947, Folder 2, Box 19, Arthur Freed Collection, USC.

64. Delamater, *Dance in the Hollywood Musical,* 159, 161; Assistant Director's Reports, August 13–14, 1947, Folder 2, Box 19, Arthur Freed Collection, USC.

65. Jack Martin Smith interview with Jerome Delamater and Paddy Whannel, 1973, Delamater, *Dance in the Hollywood Musical,* 259.

Chapter Five: Postproduction and Reactions to the Film

1. Vincente Minnelli interview, 1980, 14, SMU/Ronald L. Davis Oral History Collection, Herrick Library, AMPAS; Gene Kelly interview, 1974, 34–35, SMU/Ronald L. Davis Oral History Collection, Herrick Library, AMPAS.

2. Lela Simone to Bill Seracino, September 3, 1947, Folder 1 (2 of 3), Box 19, Arthur Freed Collection, USC; "An Oral History with Lela Simone," Rudy Behlmer, 1990, 257–258, Oral History Program, Herrick Library, AMPAS; Assistant Director's Reports, August 15, 18, 27, September 19, 1947, Folder 2, Box 19, Arthur Freed Collection, USC; Hess and Dabholkar, *Singin' in the Rain,* 151, 293.

3. Unsigned, undated notes, Folder 1 (1 of 3), Box 19, Arthur Freed Collection, USC.

4. "*Main Title Billing, 'The Pirate,'*" MPAA Production Code Administration Records, AMPAS.

5. Freed to Esme Ward, July 3, 1947, Folder 1 (1 of 3), Box 19, Arthur Freed Collection, USC; "Main Title Billing," with attached correction, September 2, 1947, *The Pirate* Clippings, Core Collection, Herrick Library, AMPAS.

6. "Analysis Chart," *The Pirate,* October 13, 1947: Joseph I. Breen to Louis B. Mayer, October 14, 1947, MPAA Production Code Administration Records, Herrick Library, AMPAS.

7. Eells, *Life That Late He Led,* 238; Howard Strickling to Freed, September 5, 1947, Folder 1 (1 of 3), Box 19, Arthur Freed Collection, USC; Minnelli to Freed, September 23, 1947, Vincente Minnelli Collection, Folder 118, Box 7, Herrick Library, AMPAS.

8. John Fricke's comments in "A Musical Treasure Chest," *The Pirate,* DVD, 2007; Howard Strickling's report on preview of *The Pirate,* held on October 10, 1947, Folder 2, Box 19, Arthur Freed Collection, USC.

9. Howard Strickling's report on preview of *The Pirate,* held on October 10, 1947, Folder 2, Box 19, Arthur Freed Collection, USC.

10. Ibid.

11. Howard Strickling's report on preview of *The Pirate,* held on November 7, 1947, Folder 2, Box 19, Arthur Freed Collection, USC.

12. Assistant Director's Reports, October 22–23, 27, November 18, 1947, Folder 2, Box 19, Arthur Freed Collection, USC; "Original THE PIRATE — Inc notes from Robert Nathan," December 8, 1947: "THE PIRATE — Retakes," December 16, 1947, Turner/MGM Script Collection, Herrick Library, AMPAS; Fordin, *M-G-M's Greatest Musicals,* 212.

13. Assistant Director's Reports, December 1, 11, 15–19, 1947, Folder 2, Box 19, Arthur Freed Collection, USC.

14. Assistant Director's Reports, December 20, 1947, Folder 2, Box 19, Arthur Freed Collection, USC; Danny Gray to Edith Farrell, April 2, 1948, in "THE PIRATE" "(Music Report and Footage)," April 5, 1948, Turner/MGM Script Collection, Herrick Library, AMPAS.

15. Frank Whitbeck, "'The Pirate,' The Trailer," January 28, 1948, Folder 1 (2 of 3), Box 19, Arthur Freed Collection, USC; "The Pirate (Trailer) Dialogue Cutting Continuity," April 13, 1948: Danny Gray to Edith Farrell, April 9, 1948, Turner/MGM Script Collection, Herrick Library, AMPAS.

16. Programs and Lobby Cards, *The Pirate* Clippings, Microfiche, Core Collection, Herrick Library, AMPAS; *Motion Picture Herald,* June 12, 1948; pages from exhibitors' campaign book for *The Pirate,* Scrapbook 8, Box 9, Gene Kelly Collection, BU.

17. Pages from exhibitors' campaign book for *The Pirate,* Scrapbook 8, Box 9, Gene Kelly Collection, BU; Fordin, *M-G-M's Greatest Musicals,* 213.

18. "'The Pirate' Preview Survey (Motion Picture Research Bureau), March 23, 1948, Loew's 72nd Street Theater, NY, Folder 1 (2 of 3), Box 19, Arthur Freed Collection, USC.

19. Ibid.

20. Ibid.

21. *The Pirate* release dates, www.imdb.com; Fordin, *M-G-M's Greatest Musicals,* 212; Edward Chodorov to Freed, May 25, 1948, Folder 1 (1 of 3), Box 19, Arthur Freed Collection, USC.

22. *The Hollywood Reporter,* March 29, 1948; Ann Helming, "Kelly, Garland Highlight Gay 'Pirate' Musical," *Hollywood Citizen-News,* June 26, 1948; *Cue,* May 22, 1948; Edwin Schallert, "'The Pirate' Gay, Clever Music Play," clipping in Scrapbook 5, Box 8, Gene Kelly Collection, BU.

23. *Variety,* March 31, 1948; *Newsweek,* June 7, 1948; Cecelia Ager, "'The Pirate' Abounds In Ace Showmanship," *P.M. Daily,* May 21, 1948; Ruth Waterbury, "'The Pirate' Colorful Film," *Los Angeles Examiner,* June 26, 1948.

24. Tom Donnelly, "A Veritable Treasure Chest of Beauty," *Washington Daily News,* June 3, 1948; Harrison Carroll, "'The Pirate' Rates Hearty Cheers as Jolly Film," *Los Angeles Herald-Express,* June 26, 1948; "'Pirate,' 'Berlin Express' Win Warm N.Y. Reception," *The Hollywood Reporter,* May 25, 1948; "The Pirate," *Box Office Digest,* April 10, 1948.

25. *Variety,* March 31, 1948; *The Hollywood Reporter,* March 29, 1948; Karl Krug, "Gene Kelly Real Star of 'Pirate,'" *Pittsburgh Sun-Telegraph,* June 11, 1948; Kate Cameron, "Technicolor Musical on Music Hall Screen," *New York Daily News,* undated clipping, Scrapbook 5, Box 8, Gene Kelly Collection, BU; Ernie Schier, "Gene Kelly Performs More Like a Yeoman," *Washington Times Herald,* June 3, 1948; Cecelia Ager, "'The Pirate' Abounds In Ace Showmanship," *P.M. Daily,* May 21, 1948; Rose Pelswick, "'The Pi-

rate': Entertaining Musical Bounces Gaily Along," *New York Journal-American,* undated clipping: Darr Smith, "Film Review," unidentified clipping, Scrapbook 5, Box 8, Gene Kelly Collection, BU.

26. Kaspar Monahan, "Gene, Judy In Frolic At Penn," unidentified clipping, Scrapbook 5, Box 8, Gene Kelly Collection, BU; *Cue,* May 22, 1948; "'Pirate,' 'Berlin Express' Win Warm N.Y. Reception," *The Hollywood Reporter,* May 25, 1948; "Trade Show," unidentified clipping, Scrapbook 5, Box 8, Gene Kelly Collection, BU.

27. Harrison Carroll, "'The Pirate' Rates Hearty Cheers as Jolly Film," *Los Angeles Herald-Express,* June 26, 1948; Rose Pelswick, "'The Pirate': Entertaining Musical Bounces Gaily Along," *New York Journal-American,* undated clipping: Kate Cameron, "Technicolor Musical On Music Hall Screen," *New York Daily News,* undated clipping, Scrapbook 5, Box 8, Gene Kelly Collection, BU; *Time,* June 21, 1948.

28. Sidney Burke, "The Pirate"—songs, dance, good humor," unidentified clipping, Scrapbook 5, Box 8, Gene Kelly Collection, BU.

29. Rose Pelswick, "'The Pirate': Entertaining Musical Bounces Gaily Along," *New York Journal-American,* undated clipping, Scrapbook 5, Box 8, Gene Kelly Collection, BU; T.M.P. "'The Pirate,' With Gene Kelly, Judy Garland and Walter Slezak, at Music Hall," *New York Herald Tribune,* May 21, 1948; Archer Winsten, "'The Pirate' Cavorts at the Music Hall," *New York Post,* May 21, 1948; Cecelia Ager, "'The Pirate' Abounds In Ace Showmanship," *P.M. Daily,* May 21, 1948; Edwin Schallert, "'The Pirate': Gay, Clever Music Play," unidentified clipping, Scrapbook 5, Box 8, Gene Kelly Collection, BU.

30. *The Hollywood Reporter,* March 29, 1948; Oscar Davis, "A Swashbuckler Leads, Oh, Such a Strenuous Life," *Washington Daily News,* June 3, 1948; Karl Krug, "Gene Kelly Real Star of 'Pirate,'" *Pittsburgh Sun-Telegraph,* June 11, 1948; *Cue,* May 22, 1948; Ernie Schier, "Gene Kelly Performs More Like a Yeoman," *Washington Times Herald,* June 3, 1948; Richard L. Coe, "'Pirate' is Rich Swag for Kelly," *Washington Post,* June 4, 1948; "At the Movies," *Kansas City Star,* June 17, 1948; T.M. P., "'The Pirate,' With Gene Kelly, Judy Garland and Walter Slezak, at Music Hall," *New York Herald Tribune,* May 21, 1948.

31. Darr Smith, "Film Review," unidentified clipping, Scrapbook 5, Box 8, Gene Kelly Collection, BU; Tom Donnelly, "A Veritable Treasure Chest of Beauty," and Oscar Davis, "A Swashbuckler Leads, Oh, Such a Strenuous Life," *Washington Daily News,* June 3, 1948; T.M.P., "'The Pirate,' With Gene Kelly, Judy Garland and Walter Slezak, at Music Hall," *New York Herald Tribune,* May 21, 1948; Howard Barnes, "On the Screen," *New York Times,* May 21, 1948.

32. Darr Smith, "Film Review," unidentified clipping, Scrapbook 5, Box 8, Gene Kelly Collection, BU.

33. "Trade Show," unidentified clipping, Scrapbook 5, Box 8, Gene Kelly Collection, BU; Cecelia Ager, "'The Pirate' Abounds In Ace Showmanship," *P.M. Daily,* May 21, 1948.

34. Alton Cook, "'The Pirate' Colorful, Lavish," unidentified clipping: Eileen Creelman, "The New Movies," unidentified clipping, Scrapbook 5,

Box 8, Gene Kelly Collection, BU; Red Kann column in *Motion Picture Daily*, March 29, 1948.

35. *The New Yorker*, May 28, 1948; Agee, *Agee on Film*, 306–307.

36. *Time*, June 21, 1948; Alton Cook, "'The Pirate' Colorful, Lavish," unidentified clipping, Scrapbook 5, Box 8, Gene Kelly Collection, BU; T.M.P., "'The Pirate,' With Gene Kelly, Judy Garland and Walter Slezak, at Music Hall," *New York Herald Tribune*, May 21, 1948; Tom Donnelly, "A Veritable Treasure Chest of Beauty," *Washington Daily News*, June 3, 1948; Howard Barnes, "On the Screen," *New York Times*, May 21, 1948.

37. T.M.P., "'The Pirate,' With Gene Kelly, Judy Garland and Walter Slezak, at Music Hall," *New York Herald Tribune*, May 21, 1948; Archer Winsten, "'The Pirate' Cavorts at the Music Hall," *New York Post*, May 21, 1948.

38. Harvey, *Directed by Vincente Minnelli*, 90; Carter T. Barron to Ralph Wheelwright, June 8, 1948: unsigned, undated report, Folder 1 (1 of 3), Box 19, Arthur Freed Collection, USC; Excerpts of Daily Newspaper Reviews of *The Pirate*, Folder 119, Box 7, Vincente Minnelli Collection, Herrick Library, AMPAS.

39. Fordin, *M-G-M's Greatest Musicals*, 212; Harvey, *Directed By Vincente Minnelli*, 90. Both Fordin and Harvey state that M-G-M reported a net loss of two million dollars, but that number cannot be right because it does not match the revenues and costs reported for the film.

40. Newspaper ad for *The Pirate*, at Loew's Penn, Pittsburgh, Scrapbook 5, Box 8, Gene Kelly Collection, BU; Hess and Dabholkar, *Singin' in the Rain*, 188; Anderson, "Minnelli, Kelly," 38; Minnelli, *I Remember It Well*, 192.

41. Larry Spier to Richard J. Powers, December 11, 1947: Jesse Kaye to Charles Roberts, January 30, 1948: Jesse Kaye to Howard Strickling, March 4, 1948, Folder 1 (1 of 3), Box 19, Arthur Freed Collection, USC; "Operation Guided by One-Man Staff," *The Billboard*, 31.

42. "News From M-G-M Records": Larry Spier to Cole Porter, June 2, 1948, Folder 1 (1 of 3), Box 19, Arthur Freed Collection, USC.

43. Schwartz, *Cole Porter*, 332–333; http://www.thejudyroom.com/soundtracks;http://www.amazon.com/Pirate-Movie-Soundtrack-Rhino-Handmade.

44. Reports filed by Motion Picture Association of America, March 19, 27, 31, April 9, May 14, 26, July 23, 1948, MPAA Production Code Administration Records, Herrick Library, AMPAS.

45. "Gene Kelly Interview," Marilyn Hunt, 1975, 168, 170, Oral History Program, NYPL; Hirschhorn, *Gene Kelly*, 138.

46. *The Pirate* release dates, www.imdb.com.

47. Report filed by Motion Picture Association of America, January 24, 1949, MPAA Production Code Administration Records, Herrick Library, AMPAS.

48. Hess and Dabholkar, *Singin' in the Rain*, 181–182.

CHAPTER SIX: LEGACY OF *THE PIRATE*

1. Kelly quoted in Hirschhorn, *Gene Kelly*, 138; "Gene Kelly Interview," Marilyn Hunt, 1975, 158–159, 161, Oral History Program, NYPL; Kelly quoted in Thomas, *Films of Gene Kelly*, 81.

2. Kelly quoted in Hirschhorn, *Gene Kelly*, 138–139; "Gene Kelly Interview," Marilyn Hunt, 1975, 168, 170, Oral History Program, NYPL; "Reminiscences of Gene Curran Kelly—Oral History, 1958," 14–15, Oral History Research Office, Popular Arts Project, CU; Kelly interview, 1979, in Kelly, "Dialogue on Film," 36; Kelly interview, 1984, Haver, "Pas de Deux," 26.

3. Kelly quoted in Thomas, *Films of Gene Kelly*, 81; "Gene Kelly Interview," Marilyn Hunt, 1975, 170–171, Oral History Program, NYPL; Minnelli, *I Remember It Well*, 187; Minnelli interview with Beth Genné, 1980, in Genné, "Vincente Minnelli and the Film Ballet," 243; Minnelli interview, 1975, Schickel, *Men Who Made the Movies*, 260.

4. "*The Pirate*, Final Musical Breakdown," Folder 1 (2 of 3), Box 19, Arthur Freed Collection, USC; "Reminiscences of Gene Curran Kelly—Oral History, 1958," 11, Oral History Research Office, Popular Arts Project, CU; Minnelli interview (1975), in Schickel, *Men Who Made the Movies*, 250; Fordin, *M-G-M's Greatest Musicals*, 211.

5. "Gene Kelly Interview," Marilyn Hunt, 1975, 167, Oral History Program, NYPL; Thomas, *Films of Gene Kelly*, 79; Siegel, "the Pirate," 29; http://www.imdb.com/title/tt0040694; John Fricke's comments in "A Musical Treasure Chest," *The Pirate*, DVD, 2007; Griffith, *Hundred or More Hidden Things*, 118.

6. Minnelli interview (1975), in Schickel, *Men Who Made the Movies*, 258, 268; Vincente Minnelli interview, 1980, 14, SMU/Ronald L. Davis Oral History Collection, Herrick Library, AMPAS; Minnelli, *I Remember It Well*, 192.

7. "An Oral History with Lela Simone," Rudy Behlmer, 1990, 26, 56, Oral History Program, Herrick Library, AMPAS; Hill, *Brotherhood in Rhythm*, 230.

8. Ericsson, "The Pirate and Summer Holiday," 44–45.

9. Vaughan, "Dance in the Cinema," 12–13.

10. Anderson, "Minnelli, Kelly," 36–37.

11. Johnson, "Films of Vincente Minnelli," Pt. 1, 30.

12. McVay, "Magic of Minnelli," 31.

13. Cutts, "Kelly," Pt. 1, 41.

14. Ibid., 41.

15. Siegel, "The Pirate," 26, 28–31; Minnelli, *I Remember It Well*, 192.

16. Taylor and Jackson, *Hollywood Musical*, 31–32, 61–62, 85–86.

17. Hirschhorn, *Gene Kelly*, 136–137, 139.

18. Ibid., 136, 138.

19. Thomas, *Films of Gene Kelly*, 75, 78–79, 81–82.

20. Minnelli, *I Remember It Well*, 192; Schickel, *Men Who Made the Movies*, 245.

21. Basinger, *Gene Kelly*, 51, 53–55.

22. David Rodowick, "The Pirate," *Program Notes*, Vol. 12, No. 4. (February 7, 1977): 9–16, *The Pirate* Clippings, Microfiche, Core Collection, Herrick Library, AMPAS; Casper, *Vincente Minnelli*, 33–34, 50, 82, 84, 91, 116.

23. Casper, *Vincente Minnelli*, 159–160.

24. Ibid., 84, 127.

25. McVay, "Minnelli and THE PIRATE," 35–36, 38.

26. Rodowick, "Vision, Desire, and the Film-Text," 63, 64, 76–77.

27. Ibid., 57, 59, 79, 81–82.
28. Ibid., 75.
29. Timberg, "Minnellian Nightmare," 71–74, 76, 79–80.
30. Ibid., 86–87, 90n; Casper, *Vincente Minnelli,* 159–160.
31. Delamater, *Dance in the Hollywood Musical,* 149.
32. Telotte, "Self and Society," 182.
33. Rodowick, "Vision, Desire, and the Film-Text," 82–83.
34. Feuer, *The Hollywood Musical,* 40–41.
35. Genné, "Film Musicals," 108–109, 235–239, 243–244, 254; Genné, "Vincente Minnelli and the Film Ballet," 243–245.
36. Schwartz, *Cole Porter,* 229–230.
37. Hemming, *Melody Lingers On,* 171–172.
38. Altman, *American Film Musical,* 77–79, 190, 193.
39. Terry Press, "The Pirate," Los Angeles County Museum of Art, April 25, 1987, *The Pirate* Clippings, Microfiche, Core Collection, Herrick Library, AMPAS.
40. Daney, "The Pirate Isn't Just Décor," 167–168.
41. Harvey, *Directed By Vincente Minnelli,* 90–92.
42. Ibid., 90–91, 93.
43. Ibid., 94.
44. Naremore, *Films of Vincente Minnelli,* 28; Morley and Leon, *Gene Kelly,* 76; Yudkoff, *Gene Kelly,* 182.
45. Clarke, *Get Happy,* 227.
46. Hill, *Brotherhood in Rhythm,* 230–231, 260.
47. Pye, "Being a Clown," 7–9.
48. Ibid., 9–10.
49. Ibid., 4–5, 9, 12–13; Casper, *Vincente Minnelli,* 159–160; Telotte, "Self and Society," 182; Harvey, *Directed By Vincente Minnelli,* 91, 93.
50. Large, "Gene and Judy Go Wild!," www.brightlightsfilm.com; Kael, *5001 Nights,* 461.
51. Farmer, *Spectacular Passions,* 100.
52. Ibid., 100, 103; Dyer, *Heavenly Bodies,* 186.
53. Dyer, *Heavenly Bodies,* 182–185.
54. Tinkcom, *Working Like a Homosexual,* 40; Gerstner, "Queer Modernism," 253–255.
55. Gerstner, "Queer Modernism," 252, 259–260; Tinkcom, *Working Like a Homosexual,* 52, 69–70.
56. Gerstner, "Dancer from the Dance," 59.
57. Ibid., 55–59.
58. Tinkcom, *Working Like a Homosexual,* 67–68; Farmer, *Spectacular Passions,* 85–86; Dyer, *Heavenly Bodies,* 184–185.
59. Callahan, "The Pirate," www.slantmagazine.com.
60. Farmer, *Spectacular Passions,* 102–103, 105.
61. Ibid., 108–109.
62. Hess and Dabholkar, *Singin' in the Rain,* 228–232.
63. http://www.imdb.com/title/tt0040694.
64. For a similar discussion of connections for the classic film musical *Singin' in the Rain,* see Hess and Dabholkar, *Singin' in the Rain,* 232–234.

65. Fordin, *M-G-M's Greatest Musicals,* 223–226; Hirschhorn, *Gene Kelly,* 117, 132; Thomas, *Films of Gene Kelly,* 82; "Gene Kelly Interview," Marilyn Hunt, 1975, 201–202, Oral History Program, NYPL.

66. Frank, *Judy,* 230–233; Minnelli, *I Remember It Well,* 189, 191; Clarke, *Get Happy,* 235–237.

67. Minnelli, *I Remember It Well,* 193–195.

68. Fordin, *M-G-M's Greatest Musicals,* 223–226; Hirschhorn, *Gene Kelly,* 117, 132; Thomas, *Films of Gene Kelly,* 82; Minnelli, *I Remember It Well,* 195; "Gene Kelly Interview," Marilyn Hunt, 1975, 201–202, Oral History Program, NYPL.

69. Hess and Dabholkar, *Singin' in the Rain,* 71–72.

70. http://en.wikipedia.org/wiki/List_of_pirate_films; Helen Geib, "Ten Essential Pirate Movies," http://commentarytrack.com/2007/07/04/ten-essential-pirate-movies/;http://www.stuff.tv/news/past-and-future/movie-classics/25-best-pirate-movies-ever; http://www.imdb.com/search/title.

Appendix A: Discarded Screenplays

1. Joseph L. Mankiewicz, *The Pirate,* temporary complete screen play, August 4–6, 1943, Turner/MGM Script Collection, Margaret Herrick Library, AMPAS.

2. Henry Koster, *The Pirate,* temporary complete screen play, October 28, 1943. to January 5, 1944; Myles Connolly, *The Pirate,* temporary complete screenplay, January 18, 1944, Turner/MGM Script Collection, Margaret Herrick Library, AMPAS.

3. Edwin Blum, *The Pirate,* temporary, incomplete, March 30-May 12, 1944, Turner/MGM Script Collection, Herrick Library, AMPAS.

4. Anita Loos and Joseph Than, *The Pirate,* temporary complete screenplay, n.d., copied June 30, 1946, Turner/MGM Script Collection, Herrick Library, AMPAS; "The Pirate Notes, 11/27/45," and "The Pirate Notes, 12/5/45," Folder 115, Box 7, Vincente Minnelli Collection, Herrick Library, AMPAS.

Appendix B: Behrman's Lines in the Goodrich-Hackett Screenplay and the Film

1. Frances Goodrich and Albert Hackett, *The Pirate,* complete OK screenplay, September 18, 1946, to May 9, 1947, Turner/MGM Script Collection, Herrick Library, AMPAS; S. N. Behrman, *The Pirate.*

Appendix C: Cast and Crew List with Mini-Biographies

1. Cast and crew list, *The Pirate,* www.imdb.com; Assistant Director's Reports, February 17, 27, March 14, July 28, 1947, December 1, 18, 1947, Folder 2, Box 19, Arthur Freed Collection, USC; Harvey, *Directed by Vincente Minnelli,* 88.

2. Minnelli, *I Remember It Well,* 197; *Rufus LeMaire's Affairs,* www.ibdb.com.

3. Fayard Nicholas interview, 1998, www.jitterbuzz.com.

4. Hugh A. Mulligan, "Walter Slezak Gets His Chance in Opera," *New York Citizen-News*, November 27, 1959; Lois Baumoel, "Walter Slezak's Voice Is Familiar: Slimmer Look Is Hard to Recognize," *Boxoffice*, November 27, 1978; Peter B. Flint, "Walter Slezak, 80, a Suicide: Character Actor Had Been Ill," *New York Times*, April 22, 1983.

Bibliography

ARCHIVES

Academy of Motion Picture Arts and Sciences, Margaret Herrick Library, Beverly Hills, California (AMPAS)
  Core Collection
    The Pirate Clippings Microfiche
  Special Collections
    Vincente Minnelli Collection
    MPAA Production Code Administration Records
    Turner/MGM Script Collection
  Oral History Program
    "An Oral History With Lela Simone," by Rudy Behlmer
  SMU/Ronald L. Davis Oral History Collection
    Gene Kelly Interview
    Vincente Minnelli Interview
Boston University, Howard Gottlieb Archival Research Center, Boston, Massachusetts (BU)
  Gene Kelly Collection
Columbia University Libraries, Oral History Research Office, Popular Arts Project, New York, New York (CU)
  "Reminiscences of Gene Curran Kelly: Oral History, 1958"
New York Public Library, New York, New York (NYPL)
  Oral History Program, Dance Division
    "Gene Kelly Interview," by Marilyn Hunt
  Manuscripts and Archives Division
    S. N. Behrman Papers
University of Southern California, Archives of Performing Arts and Warner Bros. Archives, Los Angeles, California (USC)
    Arthur Freed Collection
Wisconsin Center for Film & Theater Research and Wisconsin Historical Society, Madison, Wisconsin (WCFTR-WHS)
    S. N. Behrman Papers
Wisconsin Historical Society, Madison, Wisconsin (WHS)
    Alfred Lunt and Lynn Fontanne Papers

NEWSPAPERS AND MAGAZINES

The Billboard
Boxoffice
Box Office Digest

Cleveland Press
Cue
Daily Variety
Hollywood Citizen-News
The Hollywood Reporter
Kansas City Star
Los Angeles Daily News
Los Angeles Examiner
Los Angeles Herald-Express
Los Angeles Times
Motion Picture Daily
Motion Picture Herald
New York Citizen-News
New York Daily News
New York Herald Tribune
New York Journal-American
New York Post
New York Times
New York Times Magazine
The New Yorker
P. M. Daily
Pittsburgh Sun-Telegraph
Time
Variety
Washington Daily News
Washington Post
Washington Times Herald

DVDs

Anatomy of a Dancer. American Masters, 2002. PBS.
The Pirate. 2007. Turner Entertainment and Warner Home Video.

INTERNET SITES

www.black-face.com
www.brightlightsfilm.com
www.citwf.com
www.commentarytrack.com
www.freewebs.com
www.henrysheehan.com
www.ibdb.com
www.imdb.com
www.jewishencyclopedia.com
www.jitterbuzz.com
www.slantmagazine.com
www.thejudyroom.com
www.wikipedia.org

ARTICLES AND BOOKS

Agee, James. *Agee on Film*. New York: Grosset & Dunlap, 1969.

Ager, Cecilia. "'The Pirate' Abounds In Ace Showmanship." *P.M. Daily*. May 21, 1948.

Altman, Rick. *The American Film Musical*. Bloomington: Indiana University Press, 1987.

Anderson, Lindsay. "Minnelli, Kelly and An American in Paris." *Sequence*. Issue 14 (1952): 36–38.

Barnes, Howard. "On the Screen." *New York Times*. May 21, 1948.

Basinger, Jeanine. *Gene Kelly*. New York: Pyramid, 1976.

Baumoel, Lois. "Walter Slezak's Voice Is Familiar: Slimmer Look Is Hard to Recognize." *Boxoffice*. November 27, 1978.

Behlmer, Rudy. *Behind the Scenes*. Hollywood, CA: Samuel French, 1990.

Behrman, S. N. *People in a Diary: A Memoir by S. N. Behrman*. Boston: Little, Brown and Company, 1972.

———. *The Pirate*, New York: Random House, 1943.

"Boycotted by Wilhelm II." *New York Times*. February 8, 1894.

Brown, Jared. *The Fabulous Lunts: A Biography of Alfred Lunt and Lynn Fontanne*. New York: Atheneum, 1986.

Callahan, Dan. "The Pirate." http://www.slantmagazine.com/film/review/the-pirate. July 18, 2007.

Carey, Gary. *Doug & Mary: A Biography of Douglas Fairbanks & Mary Pickford*. New York: E.P. Dutton, 1977.

Carroll, Harrison. "'The Pirate' Rates Hearty Cheers as Jolly Film." *Los Angeles Herald-Express*. June 26, 1948.

Casper, Joseph Andrew. *Vincente Minnelli and the Film Musical*. South Brunswick, NJ: A. S. Barnes, 1977.

Clarke, Gerald. *Get Happy: The Life of Judy Garland*. New York: Random House, 2000.

Coe, Richard L. "'Pirate' is Rich Swag for Kelly." *Washington Post*. June 4, 1948.

Cutts, John. "Kelly...dancer...actor...director." *Films and Filming*. Vol. 10, No. 11 (August 1964): 38–42.

Daney, Serge. "*The Pirate* Isn't Just Décor." *Vincent Minnelli: The Art of Entertainment*. Ed. Joe McElhaney. Detroit: Wayne State University Press, 2009: 167–168.

Dauth, Brian. Ed., *Joseph L. Mankiewicz Interviews*. Jackson: University Press of Mississippi, 2008.

Davis, Oscar. "A Swashbuckler Leads, Oh, Such a Strenuous Life." *Washington Daily News*. June 3, 1948.

Delamater, Jerome. *Dance in the Hollywood Musical*. Ann Arbor, MI: UMI Research Press, 1981.

Donnelly, Tom. "A Veritable Treasure Chest of Beauty." *Washington Daily News*. June 3, 1948.

Drew, David. "Weill, Kurt (Julian)." *The New Grove Dictionary of Music and Musicians*. Stanley Sadie. Ed. Vol. 20. London: Macmillan, 1980: 300–310.

Dyer, Richard. *Heavenly Bodies: Film Stars and Society.* Houndmills, Basingstoke, Hampshire, UK: Macmillan, 1986.

Edwards, Anne. *Judy Garland: A Biography.* New York: Simon and Schuster, 1975.

Eells, George. *The Life That Late He Led: A Biography of Cole Porter.* New York: G. P. Putnam's Sons, 1967.

Ericsson, Peter. "The Pirate and Summer Holiday." *Sequence.* Vol. 6 (1948-1949): 44–46.

Fantle, David and Tom Johnson. *Reel to Real: 25 Years of Celebrity Interviews From Vaudeville to Movies to TV.* Oregon, WI: Badger Books, 2004.

Farmer, Brett. *Spectacular Passions: Cinema, Fantasy, Gay Male Spectatorships.* Durham, NC: Duke University Press, 2000.

Feuer, Jane. *The Hollywood Musical.* Bloomington: Indiana University Press, 1982.

Flint, Peter B. "Walter Slezak, 80, a Suicide: Character Actor Had Been Ill." *New York Times.* April 22, 1983.

Fordin, Hugh. *M-G-M's Greatest Musicals: The Arthur Freed Unit.* New York: Da Capo Press, 1996.

Frank, Gerald. *Judy.* New York: Harper & Row, 1975.

Frank, Rusty E. *Tap! The Greatest Tap Dance Stars and Their Stories, 1900-1955.* New York: William Morrow, 1990.

Geib, Helen. "Ten Essential Pirate Movies." http://commentarytrack.com/2007/07/04/ten-essential-pirate-movies/.

Genné, Beth Eliot. "The Film Musicals of Vincente Minnelli and the Team of Gene Kelly and Stanley Donen: 1944-1958." Ph. D. Diss., University of Michigan, 1984.

———. "Vincente Minnelli and the Film Ballet." *Vincent Minnelli: The Art of Entertainment.* Ed. Joe McElhaney. Detroit: Wayne State University Press, 2009: 229–251.

Gerstner, David A. "Dancer from the Dance: Gene Kelly, Television, and the Beauty of Movement." *The Velvet Light Trap.* No. 49 (Spring 2002): 48–66.

———. "Queer Modernism: The Cinematic Aesthetic of Vincente Minnelli." *Vincent Minnelli: The Art of Entertainment.* Ed. Joe McElhaney. Detroit: Wayne State University Press, 2009: 252–274.

Goodrich, David L. *The Real Nick and Nora: Frances Goodrich and Albert Hackett, Writers of Stage and Screen Classics.* Carbondale: Southern Illinois University Press, 2001.

Griffith, Mark. *Hundred or More Hidden Things: The Life and Films of Vincent Minnelli.* Cambridge, MA: Da Capo Press, 2010.

Gross, Robert F. *S. N. Behrman: A Research and Production Sourcebook.* Westport, CT: Greenwood Press, 1992.

Harmetz, Aljean. *Round Up the Usual Suspects: The Making of Casablanca,* New York: Hyperion, 1992.

Harvey, Stephen. *Directed By Vincente Minnelli.* New York: Harper & Row, 1989.

Haver, Ron. "Pas de Deux with Saul Chaplin." *American Film.* Vol. 10, No. 5 (March 1985): 23–26, 73.

Helming, Ann. "Kelly, Garland Highlight Gay 'Pirate' Musical." *Hollywood Citizen-News*. June 26, 1948.

Hemming, Roy. *The Melody Lingers On: The Great Songwriters and Their Movie Musicals*. New York: Newmarket Press, 1986.

Herndon, Booton. *Mary Pickford and Douglas Fairbanks: The Most Popular Couple the World Has Ever Known*. New York: W. W. Norton, 1977.

Hess, Earl J. and Pratibha A. Dabholkar. *Singin' in the Rain: The Making of an American Masterpiece*. Lawrence, KS: University Press of Kansas, 2009.

Higham, Charles and Joel Greenberg. *The Celluloid Muse: Hollywood Directors Speak*. Chicago: Henry Regnery, 1969.

Hill, Constance Valis. *Brotherhood in Rhythm: The Jazz Tap Dancing of the Nicholas Brothers*. New York: Oxford University Press, 2000.

Hirschhorn, Clive. *Gene Kelly: A Biography*. 2nd Ed. New York: St. Martin's Press, 1984.

"Hollywood Inside." *Daily Variety*. April 10, 1947.

Johnson, Albert. "The Films of Vincente Minnelli: Part II." *Film Quarterly*. Vol. 12, No. 2 (Winter 1958): 21–35.

Kael, Pauline. *5001 Nights at the Movies: A Guide from A to Z*. New York: Holt, Rinehart & Winston, 1982.

Kelly, Gene. "Dialogue on Film." *American Film*. Vol. 4, No. 4 (February 1979): 33–44.

Krug, Karl. "Gene Kelly Real Star of 'Pirate.'" *Pittsburgh Sun-Telegraph*. June 11, 1948.

Large, Victoria. "Gene and Judy Go Wild!" *Bright Lights Film Journal*. Issue 52 (May 2006): www.brightlightsfilm.com.

Levy, Emanuel. *Vincente Minnelli: Hollywood's Dark Dreamer*. New York: St. Martin's Press, 2009.

Lower, Cheryl Bray and R. Barton Palmer. *Joseph L. Mankiewicz: Critical Essays With an Annotated Bibliography and a Filmography*. Jefferson, NC: McFarland, 2001.

Luft, Lorna. *Me and My Shadows: A Family Memoir*. New York: Simon and Schuster, 1998.

"Lunt Salvages Idea From Play Staged in 1917." *New York Herald Tribune*. November 22, 1942.

Maynard, Richard. *The Black Man on Film: Racial Stereotyping*. Rochelle Park, NJ: Hayden Book Co, 1974.

McBrien, William. *Cole Porter: A Biography*. New York: Alfred A. Knopf, 1998.

McVay, Douglas. "The Magic of Minnelli." *Films and Filming*. Vol. 5 (June 1959): 11, 31, 34.

———. "Minnelli and The Pirate." *The Velvet Light Trap*. Issue 18 (Spring 1978): 35–38.

Minnelli, Vincente. *I Remember It Well*. New York: Samuel French, 1990.

Morley, Sheridan and Ruth Leon. *Gene Kelly: A Celebration*. London: Pavilion Books, 1996.

Mulligan, Hugh A. "Walter Slezak Gets His Chance in Opera." *New York Citizen-News*. November 27, 1959.

Naremore, James. *The Films of Vincente Minnelli*. New York: Cambridge University Press, 1993.

"Operation Guided by One-Man Staff." *The Billboard*. April 15, 1959, 31.

Parish, James Robert and Ronald L. Bowers. *The MGM Stock Company: The Golden Era*. New Rochelle, NY: Arlington House, 1973.

Pasternak, Joe. *Easy the Hard Way*. New York: G. P. Putnam's, 1956.

Peters, Margot. *Design for Living: Alfred Lunt and Lynn Fontanne*. New York: Alfred A. Knopf, 2003.

"The Pirate." *Box Office Digest*. April 10, 1948.

"'Pirate,' 'Berlin Express' Win Warm N. Y. Reception." *The Hollywood Reporter*. May 25, 1948.

Powdermaker, Hortense. *Hollywood: The Dream Factory*. Boston: Little, Brown and Company, 1950.

Previn, Andre. *No Minor Chords: My Days in Hollywood*. New York: Doubleday, 1991.

Pye, Douglas. "Being a Clown: Curious Coupling in *The Pirate*." *Cineaction*. Issue 63 (2004): 4–13.

Ranciere, Jacques. "*Ars gratia artis*: Notes on Minnelli's Poetics." *Vincent Minnelli: The Art of Entertainment*. Ed. Joe McElhaney. Detroit: Wayne State University Press, 2009: 394–404.

Ranney, Omar. "Hanna Play is Gay Escape from War." *Cleveland Press*. September 22, 1942.

Reed, Kenneth T. *S.N. Behrman*. Boston: Twayne Publishers, 1975.

Rodowick, D. N. "Vision, Desire, and the Film-Text." *Camera Obscura*. Issue 6 (Fall 1980): 55–89.

Schatz, Thomas. *The Genius of the System: Hollywood Filmmaking in the Studio Era*. New York: Pantheon Books, 1988.

Schickel, Richard. *The Fairbanks Album*. Boston: Little, Brown and Company, 1975.

———. *His Picture in the Papers: A Speculation on Celebrity in America Based on the Life of Douglas Fairbanks, Sr*. New York: Charterhouse, 1973.

———. *The Men Who Made the Movies: Interviews With Frank Capra, George Cukor, Howard Hawks, Alfred Hitchcock, Vincente Minnelli, King Vidor, Raoul Walsh, and William A. Wellman*. New York: Atheneum, 1975.

Schier, Ernie. "Gene Kelly Performs More Like a Yeoman." *Washington Times Herald*. June 3, 1948.

Schwartz, Charles. *Cole Porter: A Biography*. New York: Da Capo Press, 1992.

Serebrinsky, Ernesto and Oscar Garaycochea. "Vincente Minnelli interviewed in Argentina." *Movie*. Vol. 10 (March 1963): 23–28.

Siegel, Joel. "The Pirate." *Film Heritage*. Vol. 7, No. 1 Fall 1971: 21–32.

Slezak, Walter. *What Time's the Next Swan?* Garden City, New York: Doubleday, 1962.

Stinson, Charles. "Walter Slezak: Character Acting Demands Talent." *Los Angeles Times*. October 19, 1958.

Stokes, Sewell. *Without Veils: The Intimate Biography of Gladys Cooper*. London: Peter Davies, 1953.

Strauss, Theodore. "The Lunts—and a Pirate." *New York Times Magazine*. October 4, 1942.

T. M. P. "'The Pirate,' With Gene Kelly, Judy Garland and Walter Slezak, at Music Hall." *New York Herald Tribune*. May 21, 1948.

Taylor, John Russell and Arthur Jackson. *The Hollywood Musical*. New York: McGraw-Hill, 1971.

Telotte, J. P. "Self and Society: Vincente Minnelli and Musical Formula." *Journal of Popular Film and Television*. Vol. 9, No. 4 (Winter 1982): 181–193.

Thomas, Tony. *The Films of Gene Kelly: Song and Dance Man*. Secaucus, NJ: Citadel Press, 1974.

Timberg, Bernard. "Minnellian Nightmare: Meaning in Color." *Film/Psychology Review*. Vol. 4, Issue 1 (1980): 71–93.

Tinkcom, Matthew. *Working Like a Homosexual: Camp, Capital, Cinema*. Durham, NC: Duke University Press, 2002.

"Twenty-five Best Pirate Movies Ever." http://www.stuff.tv/news/past-and-future/movie-classics/25-best-pirate-movies-ever. September 15, 2011.

Vaughan, David. "Dance in the Cinema." *Sequence*. Vol. 6 (Winter 1948-1949): 6–13.

"Walter Slezak Discloses Plan to Marry Dutch Singer." *Los Angeles Times*. September 30, 1943.

Waterbury, Ruth. "'The Pirate' Colorful Film." *Los Angeles Examiner*. June 26, 1948.

Winsten, Archer. "'The Pirate' Cavorts at the Music Hall." *New York Post*. May 21, 1948.

Yudkoff, Alvin. *Gene Kelly: A Life of Dance and Dreams*. New York: Back Stage Books, 1999.

Zolotow, Maurice. *Stagestruck: The Romance of Alfred Lunt and Lynn Fontanne*. New York: Harcourt, Brace, and World, 1964.

Index

About the Authors

Earl J. Hess is Stewart W. McClelland Chair in History at Lincoln Memorial University. **Pratibha A. Dabholkar** is Retired Associate Professor of Business from the University of Tennessee. The authors are married to each other and live in the southeastern U.S. Although Dr. Hess's principal area of research is the Civil War and Dr. Dabholkar's is technology and service management, both are connoisseurs of the film musical and apply their rigorous academic approach to research and write full histories of classic musicals. Their first book on the comprehensive history of a film musical is *Singin' in the Rain: The Making of an American Masterpiece*. More information about the authors and their work can be found on: www.love-and-learning.info.

Photo by Vasanti Dabholkar